Who Are You God?

HIDDEN TRUTHS IN HIS WORD

OLGA HERMANN

WESTBOW
PRESS®
A DIVISION OF THOMAS NELSON
& ZONDERVAN

WestBow Press books may be ordered through booksellers or by contacting:

WestBow Press
A Division of Thomas Nelson & Zondervan
1663 Liberty Drive
Bloomington, IN 47403
www.westbowpress.com
844-714-3454

ISBN: 979-8-3850-1817-8 (sc)
ISBN: 979-8-3850-1818-5 (hc)
ISBN: 979-8-3850-1819-2 (e)

Library of Congress Control Number: 2024902343

Print information available on the last page.

WestBow Press rev. date: 06/05/2024

Dedication

This book is dedicated to my children: Seth, Gregory, Charlene, Rachel, and their families whose love has taught me about the faithfulness of God. Their unwavering trust still refines the fruits of the Spirit in me, which are love, joy, peace, patience, kindness, goodness, faithfulness, gentleness, and self-control.

Acknowledgement

My heartfelt thanks and blessings go to: All my family, friends, pastors and ministers whose encouragement and prayers helped me grow in understanding our Lord; to those who took part in reviewing and editing, Valerie Jackson, Cecil Ringgenberg, Pete Snell, and especially to Maryal Boumann whose friendship and refining of this book has been invaluable; also to the associates at Westbow Press for their help in the process of this work.

CONTENTS

WHO ARE YOU?

INTRODUCTION

Dear Friends of God and those who are curious:

Several years ago in Israel, I had a visitation from GOD, the Father, Son, and Holy Spirit. It led me to many years of study to learn who He is through His words in the Bible. This book is my perspective of understanding what the prophets and apostles wrote about the most important person in the world.

GOD is so misunderstood and longs to be loved by those He created to love, His people, to whom He says in this deepest love song, "You have ravished my heart with one look of your eyes."[1] As a witness for others to share in His amazing glory and infinite love I've written about my life-changing encounter and His appearances to the people in the Bible written since the first recordings of mankind.

Throughout generations we have all heard or read about our Creator God, with every culture knowing Him in one form or another. God gave us the best knowledge of Himself handed down to the people of Israel in the words of the Torah, and the other writings contained in the Old and New Testaments of the Bible.[2] These writings have stood the test of time for thousands of years and have been translated in languages throughout the world.

The prophets and apostles of Israel were to be the guardians for Yahweh God's words and those of His Son, Yeshua, who was born to be our savior and example in living out those words here on earth. It started with the family of Abraham, Isaac, and Jacob. God gave them a promise that their descendants would be a blessing to the entire world.[3] They were chosen to bring knowledge of our Creator and His instructions to humankind because of His great love for us. Yahweh is our Father!

This book has taken many years to write, with intensive study, biblical Christian life experiences, a multitude of teachers, and much prayer, to put together the amazing attributes of God. Today there are several translations of the Bible, I have used mostly the scriptures of traditional English versions, the New King James, the New International Version, and the Modern English Version for the quotations of this book and the King James for the overall story. You can find these scriptures in the Endnotes.

Because we all see from different perspectives, I encourage everyone to prayerfully study the scriptures for themselves. There is so much to learn about God. The Bible says about Jesus, "Even the world itself could not contain the books that would be written."[4]

Everyone who comes to a greater knowledge of God, will come to know their own destiny and value. We are our Master's painting made in His image; each of us is completely unique to help accomplish His will on earth.[5] We are to be His hands and feet, equipped with the requirements to reestablish Paradise for man and beast.[6]

My hope is that you as a reader who seeks to learn more, will gain a deeper, personal understanding of our LORD as He is God over all. And that you will come to love Him as He passionately loves us and desires each of us to know Him more.

I was searching for the truth and God showed a part of Himself to me. Later I discovered this to be a promise He has made to all mankind: "Ask and it will be given to you; seek and you will find;

knock and it will be opened to you." "You shall seek Me and find Me, when you shall search for Me with all your Heart."[7] God always speaks truth and reveals Himself in different ways when we ask, seek and knock.

My prayer is that this book will be a help to you, as you achieve your amazing future stored up for you by the One who created you. GOD!

Reverend Olga Hermann

Encountering God

TOUCH DOWN

This is the story of my encounter with God in Israel. There I stood, in the lowest room of a massive ancient stone building. Parts of it were more than two thousand years old. The vastness left me feeling small and in awe of the histories of the seventeen known dynasties, built one on top of the other after each invasion that had taken place here in the Holy Land.

The day was September 14, 1996. It was Rosh Hashanah, one of three important feast days that God told Israel to assemble and celebrate.[8] The place was the famous scene of nativity in Bethlehem, where it is said Jesus of Nazareth, the Christ, was born.

Ezra, our Israeli tour guide, did not want us to wait in line while hundreds of people ahead of us visited the site below. So he led our group to follow a procession of Franciscan priests holding ceremonial candles to the other side, which was supposed to be the exit. We walked down a few steps into a stone room where the most historical event, the birth of the Messiah, took place.

There was a small alcove covered with decorative tapestries and hanging lamps. In the center of the floor was the Star of Bethlehem representing the star the wise men followed to find the newborn King. The Bible says, "The star which they had seen in the East went before them, till it came and stood over where the young Child was."[9]

As I watched people descend the stairs, a few of them got down on their hands and knees and crawled into the small space to kiss the star. At first, I was surprised, with millions of germs and the world facing an epidemic of AIDS at the time! Yet they did it. Suddenly I found myself drawn irresistibly, following them on hands and knees into the small space, kissing this most famous Star of Bethlehem.

I moved to the back of the room where two of my tour friends were worshipping God; one of them was on her knees. An argument broke out in front of the site as people were coming in from both the entrance and exit, causing a human traffic jam in this small room located deep in the underground heart of this ancient building. The priest in charge unsuccessfully tried to bring order. In frustration, his voice grew louder, yet wondrously, worship songs could be heard over the noise of confusion.

It was then I looked up in realization of where I was, standing in the birthplace of the most important person in human history, Jesus Christ! Nine months prior, with limited knowledge and faith alone, I had received Him in my heart, was cleansed of my sins, and filled with the Holy Spirit's baptism of fire.

The Bible tells us, "If you confess with your mouth the Lord Jesus and believe in your heart that God has raised Him from the dead, you will be saved."[10] "He will baptize you with the Holy Spirit and fire."[11] Now I stood in the very room where the man who changed the world was born. All I could do was stand in awe and extreme reverence.

As I looked up, the sounds around me began to fade into the distance. It was then, in a vision, I saw beyond the ceiling, and my sight took me further from earth into space. The distance became so great, the universe itself opened, and I could see and feel the limitless expanse. "I saw heaven opened."[12] This continued, as I saw myself standing on the edge of a very small earth looking at the entire universe. In the vision, I saw there was no end, no boundaries, no size, no space, and no time.

I became so aware that the entire universe was alive and throbbing, as if breathing infinitely. Every atom was charged with life, even the very air was pulsating around me like one beating heart.[13]

All the universe was connected, as one entity, one being; everything was one and alive. "The fullness of Him who fills all in all."[14]

And then, at a great distance away, the center of the universe began to fold in on itself, and I saw infinite dimensions unfurling, breaking up into fragments like prisms. From something so vast, an enormous energy emerged from the center in colors and lights of dimensions without number, as it descended toward earth.

Seeing its size, I felt the smallness of my being. As I watched it come closer to earth toward me, I shrank even smaller, and my entire being felt the intense holiness and perfection of this Presence. The Bible says about God, "Holy, holy, holy is the LORD of hosts,"[15] and this is what I felt.

Tears welled up in my eyes, and the words formed in my mind with loud silent shouts. "No, don't come near me. Don't touch me. I'm not worthy." As the apostle John also understood, during his encounter in heaven, he said, "I wept and wept because no one was found who was worthy."[16]

Over and over again, I repeated and begged this energy to stop as it kept falling closer to earth toward me and I became smaller in the process. I was acutely aware of the perfection, purity, and completeness of this Being and that I was a dirty, filthy little grain of sand in comparison. I couldn't bear the thought of defiling this holy Presence by allowing it to come into contact with me. In that moment I understood the prophet Isaiah when he saw the glory of God and said, "Woe is me! I am undone because I am a man of unclean lips."[17]

Finally, He reached me, and I was completely overshadowed. This Presence of pure energy was in me, around me, through me, and the only way to describe Him was pure *love*. This was not a love we have on earth nor could even be imagined. This love was so deep and so vast it is humanly impossible for us as one vessel to fathom or contain it.

I was at His mercy; feeling the pitiful human state I knew I was in, I felt I would die. "Who can endure the day of His coming? And who can stand when He appears?"[18] As I was overwhelmed with grief that such a beautiful, perfect, and holy Presence would defile Himself in this personal contact with me, He then spoke through my entire being with infinite, sweet tenderness and said, **"I love you anyway."**

THE QUEST

This began my quest, the longing of my heart, an unending drive, desire, and thirst that could not be quenched.[19] I was ruined for the ordinary and became a "God Chaser,"[20] "faint with love,"[21] desperately searching for Him,[22] the one whose love surpasses unconditionally anything and everything this world has to offer, who accepts me *just as I am.*

For twenty-five years as an atheist, living in complete darkness without a glimmer of the light of God, I had studied various religions and philosophies in atheism, Hinduism, Buddhism, New Age, humanism, the occult, and others in my attempt to find peace through truth. I traveled throughout numerous countries and visited holy sites in Europe's Christendom, the Middle and Far East, and even to India. I always realized there was more, but like many others, I claimed no higher authority than my own, "having a form of godliness but denying its power."[23]

From this encounter, I knew for certain there is a sovereign, all powerful, omnipresent Master Creator of the Universe, "One God and Father of all, who is over all and through all and in all."[24] I saw the universe as one living, breathing, connected organism; God is at the center as the beating heart of all creation. All that exists without end is Him and in Him. "'I am the Alpha and the Omega, the Beginning and the End,' says the Lord, 'Who is and Who was and Who is to come, the Almighty.'"[25] There is only one way to describe His fullness: He is the Great "I AM."[26]

THREE IN ONE

For the first few years after the encounter, I was unable to fully describe what happened, partly due to limitations in the human language but mostly due to my limited understanding of the supernatural, especially in someone so personal and powerful as I had met.

Growing up as a young girl, I was taught about God. He was the one who made me, Creator of everything, the one who sees *all*, knows *all*, is *all*. I understood His vastness, omnipotence, and omnipresence, yet He was called Father.

In my childish finite mind, I tried to understand the meaning of what a father is. The only one I knew was my human one, so I began to compare the two. In learning that God is my Father, in my thinking, my human father also became God, and the Bible told me he was perfect and could do no wrong. Yet as every teenager soon discovers, their earthly fathers become riddled with faults.

Throughout my life, I had learned many things about Jesus. My strongest belief was Jesus was a great man who taught us a lot, having a better understanding of medicine than most and maybe some magical powers. I felt many overreacted regarding his status as God in the flesh. How did they know for sure?

The Bible tells us about the Father, Son, and Holy Spirit, but what does this mean? God as three in one? Then who was this I had met? Was it the eternal Father, the spirit of Jesus, or the Holy Spirit descending? And then I knew! A scripture revealing the triune nature of our Creator is found in the book of Isaiah. In 1947, one of the greatest archeological finds was discovered in a cave in Israel. They were ancient manuscript parchments known today as the Dead Sea Scrolls, which included the book of Isaiah.

Isaiah, considered to be one of Israel's greatest prophets, lived seven hundred years before the birth of Jesus of Nazareth. He stated, "For unto us a child is born, unto us a son is given; And the government will be upon His shoulder. And His name shall be called Wonderful, Counselor, Mighty God, Everlasting Father, Prince of Peace."[27] This scripture reveals the Son to be born as the Counselor, the Father, the Prince of Peace which describes the oneness of the three.

Yet Jesus also reveals them as separate. He said, "the Advocate, the Holy Spirit, whom the Father will send in My name, will teach you all things and will remind you of everything I have said to you."[28]

Jesus is known as the Prince of Peace as He said, "Peace I leave with you, My peace I give you."[29]

The most astounding scripture I had found to bring the truth of God's trinity into reality was written by the apostle Paul, "The grace of the Lord Jesus Christ, and the love of God, and the communion of the Holy Spirit be with you all."[30] The overpowering love I felt was the love of the Father as He flooded me with that love. The grace of the Son, Jesus Christ, made me acceptable of that love, even though I was profoundly aware of my guilt. The Holy Spirit is the power and presence that enabled this spiritual union with the supreme Godhead, known as "GOD."

I finally and fully understood the exciting revelation of God in three persons, "Blessed Trinity." The Love, the Grace, and the Communion (a.k.a.) The Father, Son, and Holy Spirit. To quench anymore doubts to the status of who Jesus is, our meeting had been in the very place of Christ's birth in Bethlehem.[31] Therefore my mind and intellect completely surrendered to accept the inevitable that Jesus is alive and came down to us as God in the flesh.[32]

Why would this happen to me, you ask? Jesus said, "The wind blows wherever it pleases, you hear its sound, but you cannot tell where it comes from or where it is going, so it is with everyone born of the Spirit."[33] I realized my responsibility is to let everyone reading this book come to know, from my personal human perspective, the beautiful and wonderful truth about our God who came in the flesh as Jesus our Messiah. He wants each of us to know about His passionate love for His creation and for everyone who chooses to be a part of Him.

God is the ultimate mystery, the One who most of us know is there, because we feel the connection, but no one can fully explain. I will do my utmost to share parts of Him through His own words recorded by His prophets and apostles in the ancient scriptures of the Bible. Yeshua told His disciples, "I am the living bread which came down from heaven. If anyone eats of this bread, he will live forever."[34]

CHAPTER TWO

Who Are You God?

WHO ARE YOU?

In the wonderful Book of Life, known to all as the Holy Bible, there are many descriptions of God written by people who had incredible encounters with Him. They wrote poetry, songs, and stories describing the history of fierce battles and God's deliverance. The Spirit of the LORD, the Ruach Ha Chodesh known as the Holy Spirit, used testimonies of simple people with extraordinary revelations of God, as prophets to a small people group called Israel.

The most beautiful song ever written is found in the Song of Solomon. It was penned by King Solomon, a man well acquainted with passionate love. Middle Eastern literature is full of symbolism. Diving into it with open eyes and hearts, we will see more deeply into the character of God, which many scholars believe is described here:

- ❖ "My beloved is radiant and ruddy, outstanding among ten thousand.
- ❖ His head is purest gold.
- ❖ His hair is wavy and black as a raven.
- ❖ His eyes are like doves by the water streams, washed in milk, mounted like jewels.
- ❖ His cheeks are like beds of spice yielding perfume.
- ❖ His lips are like lilies dripping with myrrh.

- ❖ His arms are rods of gold set with topaz.
- ❖ His body is like polished ivory decorated with lapis lazuli.
- ❖ His legs are pillars of marble set on bases of pure gold.
- ❖ His appearance is like Lebanon, choice as its cedars.
- ❖ His mouth is sweetness itself.
- ❖ He is altogether lovely.
- ❖ This is my Beloved, this my friend."[35]

What is His name? Moses had an encounter with the Presence of God who gave him orders to deliver the people of Israel out of slavery in Egypt. Moses asked who it was sending Him so he could tell the people. God described His name and said, YHVH "I AM THAT I AM: Thus shalt thou say unto the children of Israel, I Am hath sent me unto you." These words have been translated to mean: I EXIST, and often pronounced as YAHWEH.[36]

Other prophets throughout recorded history also wrote about their visitations with the magnificence of God. Dare we examine and separate the personas of Him, the one people around the world call GOD and who many Christians' call "The TRINITY"? We will follow the ancient encounters through the written words of the prophets and apostles of Israel.

WHAT ARE YOU?

GOD first spoke to our biblical forefathers Adam, Noah, Abraham, Isaac, Jacob, and Moses. They all tell us about their encounters with Him but have few detailed descriptions. The book of John tells us, "God is a Spirit, and they that worship Him must worship Him in spirit and in truth."[37]

But what does that mean? We will start by researching the scriptures about His GLORY which a Hebrew word calls the "Shekinah." I found a good description from an online site that reads: "Shekinah Glory is a visible manifestation of God on earth, whose presence is portrayed through a natural occurrence. The word Shekinah is a Hebrew name meaning 'dwelling' or 'one who dwells,' referring to the divine presence of God."[38]

THE GLORY OF THE LORD

So, what does the Bible tell us about the "Glory of the LORD"? Moses had several intimate encounters with God. His first meeting with Yahweh was through a burning bush. Moses went to see why it was on fire but didn't burn. Then God called him from the bush and said, "'Moses, Moses!' Moses answered, 'Here am I.'"[39]

God said, "Do not draw near this place. Take your sandals off your feet, for the place where you stand is holy ground. I am the God of your father, the God of Abraham, the God of Isaac, and the God of Jacob."[40] Moses hid his face, because he was afraid to look at God, while he was given instructions to lead Israel's people out of Egypt.

Was this the glory of God that Moses saw in the burning bush? We are left wondering what it really looked like. Was the fire described here, the same glory of God I witnessed in my encounter with Him in Bethlehem?

Later in the story, after the people of Israel were rescued from Egypt, Moses told them they would see the glory of the LORD. They had complained to Moses about the lack of food they had in the desert. Yahweh wanted them to know for themselves that a supernatural God was really with them so "the glory of the LORD appeared in the cloud."[41] From then on God provided food, manna that came from heaven every morning and quail every evening.[42]

When they finally came to Mount Sinai, the LORD gave Moses His Ten Commandments as instructions to the former slaves from Egypt, who had only known orders from human masters. Now they experienced events of terrifying sights and sounds with thunder, lightning, and trumpets from heaven on the fiery mountain.

Laykou delin   Taylor sculp

It was too much for these simple people, so in fear they told Moses to speak to God for them, lest they die.[43] They said, "Surely the LORD our God has shown us His glory and His greatness, and we have heard His voice from the midst of the fire. We have seen this day that God speaks with man, yet he still lives."[44] The Bible described it as a consuming fire on top of the mountain.[45] In the personal vision I had of God's glory, I also felt it was terrifying since there is nothing like it in the natural world.

During the forty years of wandering in the desert that followed, the priests built a tabernacle, a "Tent of Meeting" for the LORD, where Moses would meet with Yahweh. The Bible tells us the cloud (the glory of the LORD), filled the tabernacle covering the meeting place. When the cloud lifted, the entire nation of Israel would break camp and continue their journey. But as long as God's glory remained, they would stay in that camp.[46] It appeared as a cloud by day and as fire by night and everyone saw it.[47]

God instructed Moses to teach the priests how to prepare the animal sacrifices. These included instructions for the merciful and sanitary killing of livestock. "Moses and Aaron went into the tabernacle of meeting and came out and blessed the people. Then the glory of the LORD appeared to all the people, and fire came out from before the LORD and consumed the burnt offering and the fat on the altar. When all the people saw it, they shouted and fell on their faces."[48]

At times, the people complained against Moses and Aaron. In a most important story, God told the Israelites they were finally ready to go into the promised land. They sent twelve scouts ahead, and ten of them reported back that the land was filled with giants.[49] Out of great fear, some of the leaders wanted to stone Moses and Aaron and choose new leaders to lead them back to Egypt, back to slavery. But the glory of the LORD showed up and Yahweh almost destroyed all the people for this act.[50]

Moses got on his knees and fervently interceded for the rebellious people. He told God that the pagan nations would wonder why He couldn't protect His people. Moses did an outstanding job as the advocate for Israel, and the LORD listened to Him. This story is a great example of the awesome power of prayer and intercession, when God listens to a man and holds back His hand of destruction.[51] But because of their unwillingness to go into the promised land when Yahweh told them to, the people of Israel wandered in the desert for forty years, until that generation of adults were dead.

There is the story of one of the leaders named Korah, who riled up two hundred and fifty other leaders against Moses. The glory of the LORD showed up again, but this time in His anger God made an example of them. He told Moses to have Korah and his men separate from the others. Then the ground where the rebellious leaders stood with their families and possessions opened and swallowed them completely, and the earth closed over them. The rest of the rebellious ones were burned alive in God's consuming fire.[52]

With all the miracles Yahweh did through Moses and even showing up Himself, some of them were still not convinced Yahweh meant business, as many are still not today. The book of Samuel says that God does not discriminate, as He chooses who He wants for specific purposes and rank to share His glory.[53]

Another powerful encounter described in the Bible about God's glory is when King Solomon finished building the Temple of God in Jerusalem. He assembled all the elders, heads of tribes and influential families to bring the Ark of the Covenant into the new House of God. The priests brought the Ark into the inner sanctuary of the Temple, to the most Holy Place, under the wings of the cherubim spreading over it. Nothing was in the Ark except the two tablets of the Ten Commandments given to Moses when the LORD made a covenant with the children of Israel.[54]

There were many sacrifices and the priests who were musicians played several instruments along with blasting one hundred and twenty trumpets. "When the priests came out of the Holy Place, the cloud filled the House of the LORD, so that the priests could not continue ministering because of the cloud, for the glory of the LORD filled the House of the Lord."[55] Can we even imagine being there with the presence of God's glory so thick, the priests couldn't minister? This is His Glory! This is our God!

King Solomon said, "But will God indeed dwell on the earth? Behold, heaven and the heaven of heavens cannot contain You. How much less this temple which I have built! Yet regard the prayer of

Your servant and his supplication, O LORD my God, and listen to the cry and the prayer which Your servant is praying before You today, that Your eyes may be open toward this temple night and day, toward the place of which You said, 'My name shall be there,' And may You hear the supplication of Your servant and of Your people Israel, when they pray toward this place. Hear in heaven Your dwelling place, and when You hear, forgive."[56]

"When Solomon finished praying, fire came down from heaven and consumed the burnt offering and the sacrifices, and the glory of the LORD filled the temple. The priests could not enter the temple of the LORD because the glory of the LORD filled it. When all the Israelites saw the fire coming down and the glory of the LORD above the temple, they knelt on the pavement with their faces to the ground, and they worshiped and gave thanks to the LORD, saying, 'He is good, His love endures forever.'"[57]

Yahweh God answered King Solomon and said, "I have heard the prayer and plea you have made before Me. I have consecrated this temple, which you have built, by putting My Name there forever. My eyes and My heart will always be there."[58] But there were conditions to this promise. They needed to keep His commandments, which we all know King Solomon and other kings after him failed to do. The LORD warned him that the temple would become a heap of rubble and a ridicule if they refused to listen, which eventually happened.[59]

But the LORD had promised Israel in the past that He would always be there to restore them, whenever His people returned to Him. And this is where He gave His most sacred promise we are still repeating today. "If My people, which are called by My name, shall humble themselves, and pray, and seek My face, and turn from their wicked ways, then will I hear from heaven, and will forgive their sin, and will heal their land."[60]

Generations later, one of Israel's most faithful prophets, Ezekiel, gave us mysterious details of his encounters with the Shekinah Glory of God. He described, "As the appearance of the rainbow that is in the cloud on a day of rain, so was the appearance of the brightness all around. This was the appearance of the likeness of the glory of the LORD.[61]

Ezekiel recounts his terror at the visitations: "Then the Spirit took me up, and I heard behind me a great thundering voice: 'Blessed be the glory of the LORD in His place. The glory of the LORD stood there, as the glory which I saw by the river of Kebar, and I fell on my face.'"[62]

In another encounter Ezekiel described his spiritual visitations to the holy Temple in Jerusalem: "Then the glory of the LORD went up from the cherub and stood over the threshold of the temple. And the house was filled with the cloud, and the court was full of the brightness of the glory of the LORD."[63] "Then the glory of the LORD departed from off the threshold of the temple and stood over the cherubim. The cherubim lifted up their wings and mounted up from the earth in my sight ... They stood at the door of the east gate of the house of the LORD, and the glory of the God of Israel was above them."[64]

Ezekiel continued, "The glory of the LORD went up from the midst of the city and stood on the mountain which is on the east side of the city."[65] The LORD said, "I will set My glory among the nations, and all the nations shall see My judgment that I have executed, and My hand that I have laid upon them."[66] "And His voice was like a noise of many waters. And the earth shone with His glory."[67]

Through all this the LORD showed Ezekiel many things in the temple and the city of Jerusalem. Then He gave Ezekiel all the architectural schematics for the new temple and the new city as a blueprint for builders to follow.[68] We do not know when or how this will be implemented, but God's word never returns void. This may be why there has always been such a battle over the tiny nation of Israel, since the god of this age tries everything to stop the LORD and His people.[69]

Here are other scriptures describing the amazing and supernatural Glory of the LORD:

❖ The heavens declare the glory of God, and the firmament shows His handiwork.[70]

❖ Lift up your heads, O you gates, and be lifted up, you everlasting doors, that the King of glory may enter. Who is He, this King of glory? The Lord of Hosts, He is the King of glory.[71]

❖ Blessed be His glorious name forever, and may the whole earth be filled with His glory.[72]

❖ For the Lord God is a sun and shield, the Lord will give favor and glory, for no good thing will He withhold from the one who walks uprightly.[73]

❖ Proclaim His glory among the nations, His wonders among all peoples.[74]

❖ The heavens declare His righteousness, and all the peoples see His glory.[75]

❖ So the nations shall fear the name of the Lord, and all the kings of the earth Your glory.[76]

❖ For the Lord shall build up Zion; He shall appear in His glory.[77]

❖ May the glory of the Lord endure forever, may the Lord rejoice in His works.[78]

❖ Be exalted, O God, above the heavens, may Your glory be above all the earth.[79]

❖ The Lord is high above all nations, and His glory above the heavens.[80]

❖ In that day the Lord of Hosts shall become a crown of glory and a diadem of beauty to the remnant of His people.[81]

❖ I am the Lord, that is My name; and My glory I will not give to another, nor My praise to graven images.[82]

❖ Everyone who is called by My name, for I have created him for My glory, I have formed him, and I have made him."[83]

❖ So shall they fear the name of the Lord from the west and His glory from the rising of the sun.[84]

❖ Arise, shine, for your light has come, and the glory of the Lord has risen upon you.[85]

❖ The sun shall no longer be your light by day, nor for brightness shall the moon give light to you, but the Lord shall be an everlasting light to you and your God for your glory.[86]

❖ For I know their works and their thoughts. The time shall come to gather all nations and tongues. And they shall come and see My glory.[87]

❖ I will set a sign among them, and send from them survivors to the nations … to the coastlands afar off who have not heard My fame nor seen My glory. And they shall declare My glory among the nations.[88]

❖ For the earth will be filled with the knowledge of the glory of the Lord, as the waters cover the seas.[89]

❖ His glory covered the heavens, and the earth was full of His praise.[90]

❖ And I will be like a wall of fire all around her, says the Lord, and I will be as glory in her midst."[91]

❖ The Word became flesh and dwelt among us, and we saw His glory, the glory as the only Son of the Father, full of grace and truth.[92]

❖ This, the first of His signs, Jesus did in Cana of Galilee, and He revealed His glory, and His disciples believed in Him.[93]

❖ Lead us not into temptation but deliver us from evil. For Yours is the kingdom and the power and the glory forever.[94]

❖ Whoever therefore is ashamed of Me and of My words in this adulterous and sinful generation, of him will the Son of Man also be ashamed when He comes in the glory of His Father with the holy angels.[95]

❖ An angel of the Lord appeared to them, and the glory of the Lord shone around them, and they were very afraid.[96]

❖ Peter and those who were with him were heavy with sleep. But waking thoroughly, they saw His glory and the two men who stood with Him.[97]

❖ And now, O Father, glorify Me in Your own presence with the glory which I had with You before the world existed.[98]

❖ Father, I desire that they also, whom You have given Me, be with Me where I am, that they may see My glory which You have given Me. For You loved Me before the creation of the world.[99]

❖ Then the sign of the Son of Man will appear in heaven, and then all the tribes of the earth will mourn, and they will see the Son of Man coming on the clouds of heaven with power and great glory.[100]

❖ When the Son of Man comes in His glory, and all the holy angels with Him, then He will sit on the throne of His glory.[101]

❖ Being full of the Holy Spirit, he (Stephen) gazed into heaven and saw the glory of God, and Jesus standing at the right hand of God.[102]

❖ He carried me (John) away in the Spirit to a great and high mountain, and showed me the Holy City, Jerusalem, descending out of heaven from God, having the glory of God.[103]

❖ The city has no need of sun or moon to shine in it, for the glory of God is its light, and its lamp is the Lamb.[104]

CHAPTER THREE

What Do You Look Like?

THE FACE OF GOD

"So, God created man in His own image, in the image of God He created him, male and female He created them."[105] This is fantastic! The Bible says we actually look like God. To get a better idea of who He is, let us see what is said about His looks and we will start with His face.

God's face was first mentioned in the Bible, when Cain the first-born son of Adam and Eve, killed his brother Abel. Cain was banished from God's face, meaning His presence.[106] Then Jacob, whose name was changed to Israel, wrestled with a man for a whole night until he received a blessing. He said of this man, "I saw God face to face, and yet my life was spared."[107] Did Jacob have an encounter with Jesus? With God there are no limits in time and space.

Daniel saw Him and described, "His face as the appearance of lightning."[108] John, in the Book of Revelations, described Him similarly, "His face was like the sun shining in all its brilliance."[109] Matthew described the face of Jesus when He went up to a high mountain, "He was transfigured before them, His face shown like the sun."[110]

As mentioned before, the most wonderful friendship between God and man is told in the story of Moses and his intimate encounters with the Shekinah Glory. Yahweh "spoke to Moses face to face," meaning in person, "as a man speaks to his friend."[111] A heavenly pillar of cloud would come down at the entrance of the place where they would meet, and everyone knew Yahweh was in the cloud.[112]

This fascinating story gives us several clues into the graciousness of God. As their relationship developed, Moses begged his friend if he could see Him. But Yahweh answered Moses that, "No man shall see Me and live."[113] Our mortal bodies cannot withstand the full presence of so great a God.[114] So Yahweh placed Moses in the cleft of a rock and covered him with His hand while His glory passed by.[115]

But fifteen hundred years after Moses' life on earth, in the story of the Mount of Transfiguration, Jesus took His disciples Peter, James, and John to meet with Moses and Elijah who appeared from heaven. Then Moses finally got to see God in the flesh, face to face as he talked with Jesus whose face "shone like the sun."[116] God's faithfulness is unstoppable.

But in Moses day, Yahweh was only seen face to face by the people of Israel as a pillar of cloud by day and a pillar of fire by night.[117] He spoke face to face with Israel, meaning His presence, out of the fire on the mountain.[118] The LORD asks each of us to seek His face, humble ourselves, pray and turn from our wicked ways to be healed.[119] He will not turn His face from us if we turn to Him.[120]

There is joy in seeing God's face, but He hides it from us as King David wrote in a song, "How long will you hide Your face from me."[121] "I will see Your face. I will be satisfied in seeing Your likeness."[122] "My heart said to You, Your face, LORD, I will seek."[123] Which is the true presence of God.

God then explains why He hides His face from us, the reason it is so hard for us to see Him. In anger He hid His face from us for a moment,[124] but He will have compassion for us. He says our sins have separated us from our God and have hidden His face from us.[125]

We can see in the story of Sodom and Gomorrah how dangerous it is to be in a perpetual state of sin. These two cities were destroyed because "the outcry against them has grown great before the face of the LORD."[126] God sees and hears all, watching the affairs of humanity. When we sin, we subject Him to our self-destruction while also ruining the part of the earth, its people and animals, He gave each of us to tend.

Yahweh said to the people of Israel, "I will bring you into the desert of the nations and there face to face I will execute judgment upon you."[127] At the end, the wicked will cry out, "Hide us from the face of Him who sits on the throne and from the wrath of the Lamb."[128] Then in mercy, God answers, "I will no longer hide My face from them, for I will pour out My Spirit on the people of Israel."[129] "They will see His face and His name will be on their foreheads."[130]

Finally, the prophet Isaiah foretold of the coming servant God was sending: "His appearance was so disfigured beyond that of any human being and His form marred beyond human likeness."[131] "He had no beauty of majesty to attract us to Him, nothing in His appearance that we should desire Him."[132] Isaiah was describing Yeshua the Messiah, who would come seven hundred years later and suffer crucifixion and immeasurable pain.

Reading what the prophets wrote about Yahweh, no living person can see His face. Although Adam and Eve met with Him personally in the Garden of Eden until they disobeyed Him. They both ate the forbidden fruit and after being tainted with knowledge of good and evil, God could no longer show Himself to mankind as He is too pure.[133] I also witnessed a feeling of terror that I was going to die in His presence because of His intense holiness. I did not see His form nor His face, but I saw and felt His glory as tremendous energy, lights, and color.

The Bible often states that we must die to our flesh that keeps us in constant desire for earthly decaying pleasures, so we may draw closer to God.[134] This is not something we can do on our own. To see Him and be near Him, we must be hidden in the cleft of the Rock, which is another symbol for Jesus Christ.[135]

HEAD OF CROWNS

The Bible describes God's head adorned in different ways, both as God in the heavens and God here on earth.

- ❖ "His head is purest gold."[136]
- ❖ "A crown of gold on His head."[137]
- ❖ "The helmet of salvation on His head."[138]
- ❖ "Fragrant oil poured on His head."[139]
- ❖ "A crown of thorns put on His head."[140]
- ❖ "The cloth wrapped around Jesus' head."[141]
- ❖ "On His head are many crowns."[142]

By these scriptures we see that God, whose head which symbolizes authority, begins as pure gold, wearing a golden crown of purity as King. He relinquished His crown of gold for a helmet of salvation to save us. Then with His head anointed with oil for burial, He took on another crown, this time with the thorns of suffering. Until the final cloth of death was placed on His head. And in the end, as victor, He wears many crowns to rule the nations as KING of Kings, and LORD of Lords. [143] Amen.

This next story by the Apostle John doesn't say it is Jesus, but by descriptions elsewhere, we are to believe it is Him. John wrote, "I saw still another mighty Angel coming down from heaven, clothed with a cloud, and a rainbow was on His head, His face was like the sun, and His feet like pillars of fire."[144]

The symbol of the rainbow reveals God's multi-faceted covenant with mankind and animals to never destroy the earth through flood again.[145] Today some people use this symbol of God's promise to promote their rebellion against His laws. We each need to be careful of how we use the blessings and promises of God.

Many people don't know what the rainbow means and have gone along with the crowd. But the enemy of our soul, the devil knows, and in his mocking, he has convinced others to mock God also. Do some people really believe that reminding God of His covenant not to flood the earth, He will withhold His wrath on us personally? The Bible tells us, "It is a fearful thing to fall into the hands of the living God."[146]

HAIR BLACK OR WHITE

There are two contrasting mentions of God's hair, the first: "His hair is wavy and black as a raven."[147] The second: "His head and hair were white like wool, as white as snow."[148]

Was God at one time a young man, with black hair, then to be wizened with time to become "the Ancient of Days"?[149] He is the A to Z, the Alpha and Omega, the beginning and the ending,[150] the black and the white. After all, night and day were created by Him and "God saw that it was good"[151]. But the book of Daniel states them to be two separate individuals and the descriptions are about the Father and Son. "One like the Son of Man, coming with the clouds of heaven! He came to the Ancient of Days, and they brought Him near before Him."[152]

In the story of the prophet Elijah when facing execution, he escaped into the desert where God sent ravens to feed Him.[153] In the same way, the symbolic description of His hair as a raven, states that under His headship, the LORD is our provider. Wisdom and purity of the ages are signified by His white hair.

EYES LIKE BLAZING FIRE

"His eyes are like doves by the water steams washed in milk, mounted like jewels."[154] "His eyes like flaming torches."[155] "The Son of God, whose eyes are like blazing fire."[156] The representation of the dove is the Spirit of God, which "descending like a dove and alighted" upon Jesus after He came up from the water during His baptism.[157]

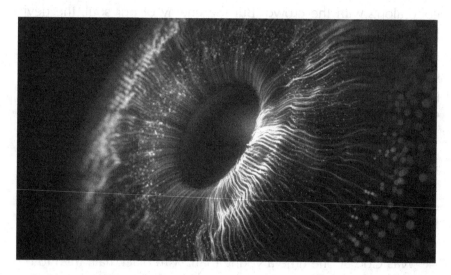

King David sang, "Keep me as the apple of your eye."[158] God's people are the apple of His eye. His eyes watch over those who fear Him, and He guides them.[159] His eyes stay on the righteous and over the nations.[160] His eyes are on the land of Israel continually, and we who love Him are adopted into His beloved Israel.[161] His eyes are reported to be as gentle and soft as doves, yet as consumable as fire in His jealousy for the love of His people.[162]

As much as He watches over His loved ones, the eyes of the LORD are also on the sinful kingdom.[163] The prophet Habakkuk said to Yahweh, "Your eyes are too pure to look on evil. You cannot tolerate wrongdoing."[164] God answered Him that He will deal with the wicked at an appointed time.[165] "His eyes are on the ways of mortals, He sees their every step. There is no deep shadow, no utter darkness where evildoers can hide."[166]

God told the prophet Zechariah that there are seven eyes on a stone He has placed, and they are the seven eyes of Yahweh, which scan the entire earth.[167] In a vision, the apostle John saw a Lamb with seven horns and seven eyes. These are the seven Spirits of God that are sent throughout the earth.[168] The eyes also represent the seven types of churches to whom Jesus sends encouragement and warnings in the book of Revelation.[169] Churches are assigned by the LORD to be the shepherds, keeping watch over cities and nations.

John also saw the day when the Lord returns. He said, "I saw heaven standing open and there before me was a white horse, whose rider is called Faithful and True. With justice He judges and makes war. His eyes are like blazing fire."[170] "He Himself treads the winepress of the fierceness and wrath of Almighty God."[171]

This is the "Great and Terrible Day of the LORD"[172] described in the Book of Joel. For some it will be sheer terror as their wicked lives and works are exposed and destroyed.[173] For others it will be the beginning of a new dawning on the earth for incredible peace, joy, and the restoration of beauty.[174] In which camp will you live? We must each choose before time is up.

EARS TO HEAR US

Does the LORD have ears to hear us? Through the ages, people have been calling out to God, often when in trouble but also to thank Him and praise His existence that we are not alone in our vulnerable state. The Bible tells us about His ears and His hearing just as any good father listens when His children call out to him.[175]

But the LORD stops hearing when His people will not listen as when they wouldn't listen to His messenger, Moses. They decided to go to battle without God's blessing and had to retreat with many losses.[176] Moses told them, "The LORD would not listen to your voice nor give ear to you."[177]

But He does listen to those who mock and threaten His people. When King Hezekiah of Judah was threatened by the King of Assyria, he petitioned God to turn His ear and listen to the words of the invading king who challenged the God of Israel and His people.[178] Yahweh responded to this threat by sending one single angel to kill one hundred and eighty-five thousand Assyrian soldiers because their leader's insults reached God's ears.[179] Do we still dare to mock God or use His name in vain?

The Jewish prophet Daniel was taken to Babylon as a prisoner of war when he was young, and there he became a great leader.[180] In his later years, he discovered Jerusalem was in ruins, so he prayed and asked Yahweh to forgive the nation of Israel and restore the city for the sake of the LORD's own reputation.[181] God had claimed the children of Israel as His people and Daniel believed He would listen to them when asked.[182]

Later Nehemiah, another Jew who was serving Babylon's king, pleaded with the LORD to hear his petition and restore Israel after seventy years in exile. Nehemiah used the term, "Let Your ear be attentive and Your eyes open that You may hear the prayer of Your servant."[183] God responded by giving Nehemiah favor with the new King of Babylon, who sent him to Jerusalem as Governor to restore the city.[184]

King David called on the LORD to cause His ear to hear his cries for justice to the orphans and the oppressed, against wicked men.[185] And David repeatedly asked the LORD to turn His ear toward him to deliver him from danger.[186]

The LORD hears the cries of the fatherless and widows when they cry out to Him and in His compassion and kindness, He will be their avenger.[187] He also hears the poor when they're taken advantage of and left destitute.[188]

The LORD hears our pride as we build ourselves up in positions of self-importance. It was dangerous for Miriam to criticize her brother Moses because of his wife Zipporah. The LORD heard Miriam's words and she was stricken with leprosy for seven days.[189] Like a wise father, there are times the LORD listens to our complaints but then lets us stew in the consequences of our poor attitudes. These rebellious choices have brought about all the world's problems throughout history.

Another bad idea still plaguing us today happened when God's chosen people demanded a human king like the nations around them, to replace the prophet God gave them to represent Him. God, who was leading the nation of Israel through His prophet Samuel, warned them that a human king would demand taxes and turn their children into servants instead of a free people. They still insisted on a man to lead them, so God told Samuel to give them a king, but He wouldn't rescue them from their human imposed laws.[190]

To this day we still have kings ruling over us, in the form of elected officials. They write non-ending streams of political laws keeping us in bondage and ever-increasing taxes to pay for some of their expensive lifestyles and numerous non-essential or even hazardous governmental decisions.

Later Israel's third king, Solomon, entered into an agreement with God and the people, asking God to always hear them when they turn back in repentance, even after they've sinned.[191] When our sins are so wicked and we take part in shedding innocent blood, no matter how much we pray, seek and knock, Isaiah tells us God's words: "When you spread out your hands, I will hide My eyes from you. Even though you make many prayers, I will not hear. Your hands are full of blood."[192]

But finally, there is Jesus, fully God and fully man with all the attributes of mankind, made in God's image.[193] He hears our cries, forgiving our offenses when we repent. And He healed the people as often as they came to Him.[194]

BLAST OF HIS NOSTRILS

God can smell those who reject Him and believe they are too good for Him. He says, "These are smoke in My nostrils."[195] He can smell their contempt and their arrogance toward Him. In His anger, "smoke rose from His nostrils."[196]

Moses and the children of Israel sang that it was Yahweh's very breath that made a highway of dry ground through the Red Sea for Israel to pass through. "By the blast of His nostrils, the waters piled up."[197]

CHEEKS OF SPICES

The Song of Solomon tells us, "His cheeks are like beds of spice yielding perfume."[198] Spices throughout the Bible were costly and precious, only afforded by the rich and sold by specialized spice merchants. His cheeks are desired as beds of spices, costly and full of precious riches.

Micah prophesied about Jesus as the ruler to come who would be born in Bethlehem and stricken. "They will strike the judge of Israel with a rod on the cheek."[199] And He said, "I offered my back to those who beat me, my cheeks to those who pulled out my beard. I did not hide my face from mocking and spitting."[200]

Jesus expects us to follow His example to turn the other cheek when someone strikes us. Even though His cheeks are rich, costly, and pleasing, He offers them freely. And when we choose to scorn His offer and strike Him, He offers the other cheek as well.[201] As many of us, who were stubborn and rebellious, learned about our Savior, Jesus continues to pursue us until we can make the choice to accept Him with wisdom and understanding, or permanently reject Him and lose Him and ourselves forever.

TEETH OF PURITY

The Bible describes the teeth of Shiloh (another name for the Messiah) from the tribe of Judah, "His teeth whiter than milk."[202] This may be a symbol for wisdom and strength in eating the bread of life that means His words in the Bible. The whiteness of milk can also be referred to as purity. God is the Creator of the Universe, the Ancient of Days, and He holds the wisdom of the ages in purity and truth.[203]

SWEETNESS OF HIS MOUTH

"Let Him kiss me with the kisses of His mouth, for your love is more delightful than wine."[204] "His mouth is sweetness itself"[205] meaning the words that come from Him. In the Song of Solomon, His mouth is described seductively as sweeter than wine for the Shulamite woman wanting to be kissed by her king.

Many Jewish scholars believe the Song of Solomon describes God's love for His people Israel. Christians, who believe the followers of Jesus Christ have been adopted spiritually into Israel, feel this story is between Christ and His Bride the Church. In both cases, whether Israel is viewed as a people loved by God or as one solitary lover of God, this book still becomes the greatest love story ever told.

The Song of Solomon describes "His lips are like lilies dripping with myrrh."[206] Myrrh is a bittersweet smelling rare and expensive resin, used in perfumes and ointments. Scriptures often mention it in connection with anointing and healing. "By the word of your lips, I have kept away from the paths of the destroyer."[207] The healing dripping from His lips through His words, will deliver and save us from the effects of sin and death.

There are different facets to that bitter sweetness of myrrh. Jesus said, "Man does not live by bread alone but by every word that proceeds from the mouth of God."[208] King David said, "The Law from Your mouth is more precious to me than thousands of pieces of silver and gold."[209] "The LORD gives wisdom and from His mouth comes knowledge and understanding."[210]

God's mouth is so powerful, it spoke existence into being and breathed life into all creation. He tells us to live by the promises of His word. His love and faithfulness for us are as a consuming fire in His desire for intimacy with us.

But let's make no mistake about Him, there are two sides of God's mouth, "Out of His mouth was a sharp double-edged sword."[211] "Is it not from the mouth of the Most High, that both calamities and good things come?"[212] "Consuming fire came out of His mouth, burning coals blazed out of it."[213]

He tells us, "If you resist and rebel, you will be devoured by the sword. For the mouth of the LORD has spoken."[214] "He will strike the earth with the rod of His mouth, with the breath of His lips He will slay the wicked."[215]

Yet, He always gives us the way out, "Repent therefore! Otherwise, I will soon come to you and will fight against them with the sword of My mouth."[216] He requires each of us to make a choice and we cannot stay indifferent to Him. Even though many churches preach a nice and pacified Jesus, the truth is He left us with a terrifyingly stern warning when we choose to do nothing, "Because you are lukewarm, and neither cold nor hot, I will vomit you out of My mouth."[217]

God also hides from us, and Jesus instructed us to ask, seek and knock.[218] "I will open my mouth in parables, I will utter things hidden since the creation of the world."[219] This prophecy was fulfilled, as Jesus spoke to the people in parables which only some could understand.

The disciple Ananias told Saul who later became Apostle Paul, "The God of our fathers has chosen you to know His will and to see the righteous one and to hear words from His mouth."[220] Paul had direct encounters and conversations with Jesus after His resurrection.

In every instance, circumstance, time frame, spiritual or natural, the sweetness of the LORD's mouth remains the same. As was said of Jesus, "He committed no sin, and no deceit was found in His mouth."[221] "Jesus Christ is the same, yesterday, today, and forever."[222]

BREATH OF GOD

Genesis tells us "The LORD God formed man of the dust of the ground and breathed into his nostrils, the breath of life and the man became a living soul."[223] Job said, "The Spirit of God has made me, and the breath of the Almighty gives me life."[224] If God "withdrew His Spirit and breath, all humanity would perish together, and mankind would return to dust."[225]

Over time, with the disobedience of Adam and Eve and their descendants, the earth had become so corrupted, God sent the flood to cleanse it. "All in whose nostrils was the breath of the spirit of life, all that was on the dry land, died."[226] The Bible says, "With the breath of His lips He shall slay the wicked."[227]

With one breath God can start an ice age, "the breath of God produces ice and the broad waters became frozen."[228] Or with one breath He can start fires, "the breath of the LORD, like a stream of burning sulfur, sets it ablaze."[229] God refreshes the earth with His breath.

God "gives breath to its people and life to those who walk in it."[230] He also restores life to those who were once dead. "This is what the Sovereign LORD said to these bones: 'I will make breath enter you, and you will come to life.'"[231] It is Yahweh who gives everyone breath and life and everything else.[232] It was this same breath of God that Jesus shared with His disciples after His resurrection. "He breathed on them and said, 'Receive the Holy Spirit.'"[233]

HIS BODY SET WITH JEWELLS

There are only a few references to the LORD's body in the Old Testament. The Song of Solomon describes "His hands are rods of gold, set with beryl, His body is carved ivory inlaid with sapphires."[234] We have read about the encounter Moses had with Yahweh where He wasn't allowed to see Him except for His back. We can only wonder, what did Moses see as Yahweh passed by?[235]

In his vision, the prophet Daniel saw a man who some Bible scholars believe to be Jesus. "His body was also like beryl."[236] Some references say "Chrysolite" a gold stone, or yellow-green mineral like the color of olive oil which symbolizes the anointing of the Holy Spirit. The stone is very translucent, a beautiful reflection of God.

The Bible tells us the LORD appeared in bodily form before Jesus' time. He came with two others to tell Abraham that his elderly wife Sarah would bear a son.[237] Then He warned Abraham He was about to destroy the cities of Sodom and Gomorrah.[238] Two generations later, Abraham's grandson, Jacob, wrestled with the LORD all night until he received a blessing and said,[239] "I have seen God face to face."[240]

Could these references to the physical Lord be about Jesus? In my own vision, I saw that time and space don't exist with God as we experience them. He is not contained in the three dimensions that limit us, including the fourth which is Time.[241] Jesus told the Jewish leaders who questioned Him about His reference to history. He said, "Verily, I say unto you, before Abraham was, I AM."[242] Abraham lived almost two thousand years before Christ.

Even in mankind's limited knowledge of physics, in his book Genesis and the Big Bang, Dr. Gerald Schroeder wrote that Einstein's law of relativity shows us that the dimensions of space and the passage of time are not absolute. Their measurement can change in the relationship of the observer and the observed.[243]

In another story about His body, a woman came into the house where Jesus was and poured a bottle of expensive perfume over His head. The disciples complained about the cost and Jesus answered that in pouring the ointment on His body, she did it for His burial.[244]

Later, at the last Passover dinner, "Jesus took bread, blessed, and broke it, then gave it to His disciples and said, 'Take and eat, this is My body.'"[245] The next day He was to become the sacrificial Lamb of God, broken for all the world, through His crucifixion.

After Jesus' earthly body died on the cross, a rich man named Joseph of Arimathea went to Pilate to ask for His body. Joseph and Nicodemus wrapped Jesus with spices and strips of linen according to Jewish custom and placed it in Joseph's own tomb cut out of rock.[246] And he rolled a large stone against the door.[247]

The Romans placed a guard in front of the tomb for fear the disciples would steal the body to claim Jesus rose from the dead, fulfilling His prophecy that He would rise in three days. Jesus had said, "Destroy this temple, and in three days I will raise it up."[248] They discerned the temple Jesus had spoken of was His body.

Whenever we take communion, we are to remember the body of our Lord Jesus Christ as the final Passover Lamb, sacrificed to pay for all sin in those who believe. The apostle Paul instructed us to examine ourselves, so we do not mix our sin with the pure body and blood of the Lord.[249] He said if we eat and drink unworthily, we eat and drink judgment to ourselves, not discerning the Lord's body. For this cause, many are weak and sick among us.[250] This is the best time to search ourselves and repent, not holding on to anything especially unforgiveness.

We are also told when we come together to take communion, we are to wait for each other, as one body.[251] Paul explains, "In Christ we, though many, form one body, and each member belongs to all the others."[252] The body is one unit made up of many parts. "For we were all baptized by one Spirit so as to form one body, whether Jews or Gentiles, slave or free, and we were all given the one Spirit to drink."[253] To this day, Christians as a group are still referred to as "the Body of Christ."[254]

Jesus told us the seed that is sown must die so the plant can grow many seeds.[255] Paul said, "So will it be with the resurrection of the dead. The body that is sown is perishable, it is raised imperishable. It is sown in dishonor; it is raised in glory. It is sown in weakness; it is raised in power."[256] "If there is a natural body, there is also a spiritual body."[257] But first the earthly flesh must die to raise the spirit.

Like the first man Adam, we came from the dust of the earth to become a living being, but Adam's body returned to dust as we all will.[258] The second Adam, Jesus, came from heaven, filled with the life-giving Spirit of God. When His earthly body died, Jesus rose to life in an imperishable, glorified body. For those of us who accept the gift of salvation that Jesus offers, one day we will also receive our new glorified bodies bearing the likeness of Him, the Man from heaven.[259]

Paul described the union between God and man, like Christ's love for His church as He gave Himself up for her to make her holy, washing her in His word.[260] Paul wrote, "A man will leave his father and mother and be united to his wife, and the two will become one flesh. This is a profound mystery, but I am talking about Christ and the church."[261] This is the mystery of Christ and His bride, as one.

The bottom line to all of this as Christ followers, when we genuinely accept Jesus, we become part of Him as the Body of Christ.[262] Although truly, none of us have a full concept of what it means to be part of the Body of the Living God, the resurrected Christ. Our limited human minds cannot completely grasp the depth of this statement, and yet it is His promise. As God continually proves, He is always faithful, so is the promise to all who are called Children of God.[263]

The most amazing part of this promise is that it's made to any one of us who looks to Him.[264] We don't have to deserve this, and it doesn't matter where we've been or what we've done in our past. Our only part now is to CHOOSE Him instead of our selfish lusts and allow ourselves to become one with Him. As a bride to her groom in a union of mind, body, and spirit we say, "Yes LORD, I do." The Holy Spirit will then inhabit us and teach us all things. Jesus is the living Word of God and our example of what to do when we love Him and choose to follow Him.[265] Do you hear Him calling?

UNBROKEN BONES

As the Bride of Christ, we become like the first woman Eve was to her husband Adam. God put him to sleep and took one of his ribs to create Eve.[266] Adam said, she is "bone of my bones and flesh of my flesh."[267] As Christians, we are spiritually taken from the body of Jesus. When His side was ripped open on the cross, water and blood poured out to birth His bride, the Church.[268] "For we are members of His body, of His flesh and of His bones."[269]

King David wrote about the suffering of the Messiah, "I am poured out like water, and all my bones are out of joint."[270] The crucifixion of Jesus happened just as in David's prophecy a thousand years before. None of His bones were broken as Jesus became the final Passover Lamb for humanity[271], just as God had instructed the children of Israel not to break any bones of the sacrificial lamb when they held the first Passover feast in Egypt. Their obedience resulted in freeing them from slavery, completely whole as one people.[272]

After Jesus rose from the dead, He appeared to His disciples and said "Look at my hands and my feet. It is I Myself! Touch me and see; a ghost does not have flesh and bones, as you see I have."[273] Even though His mortal body died, it was resurrected as something new.[274] Jesus was the first fruit of the resurrection. This gives us an example of how we will also be when our renewed bodies become eternally incorruptible.

In Ezekiel's vision of the valley of dry bones, there were a great many bones on the floor of the valley, they were dry but not broken.[275] This is symbolic of God's people when we start out spiritually dead and dry for so long, yet we are not destroyed. In the story, God told Ezekiel to prophesy to the dry bones so that tendons were reattached, and flesh covered the bones with skin.[276] Then finally the breath of God entered them, and they stood up as a mighty army.[277] This prophecy spoke about the people of Israel's return to their God, but it's also a picture of belief in the Jewish Messiah, Yeshua, the Living Word, His Holy Spirit enters us and makes us alive and whole!

LIVING FLESH

We learn in the story of mankind that Adam and Eve were created in God's image.[278] I always wondered if they were spirit beings until they ate from the Tree of Knowledge, because then God clothed them with skin.[279] But the Bible says God put a deep sleep over Adam, the man. "He took one of his ribs and closed up the flesh. The rib which the LORD God had taken from man, made He a woman."[280] So we see Adam and Eve were already made of flesh before they ate the forbidden fruit.

Does this mean God was also already flesh? To try to explain this, we see it was God the Father who was the voice of commanding Creation, and the breath of God the Holy Spirit brought Life into existence. Then it must have been God the Son, the incarnate resurrected and perfected Body of Jesus, in whose image mankind was formed. As I previously wrote, God is not bound by our earthly three-dimensional limits of time, space, and matter.

In the book of Genesis, the original Hebrew text uses the word "Elohim" for GOD. It is the plural for Gods.[281] And Elohim said, "Let US make man in OUR image after OUR likeness,"[282] again a plurality.

The apostle John wrote about Jesus, "In the beginning was the Word. The Word was with God, and the WORD WAS GOD. He was with God in the beginning. All things were made through Him, and apart from Him nothing was made that has come into being."[283]

John then tells us the Son of God is fully human and fully God, "And the Word became flesh and dwelt among us and we beheld His glory." John clarifies that God through Jesus became human flesh and lived with them as "the only begotten of the Father."[284] "As many as received Him, to them He gave the power to become the sons of God, to them that believe on His name. Which were born, not of blood, nor of the will of the flesh, nor of the will of man, but of God.[285]

Jesus told us, "I am the living bread which came down from heaven. If any man eat of this bread, he shall live forever, and the bread that I will give is My flesh, which I will give for the life of the world."[286] The Hebrew word for bread is "Lechem" and can also mean to feed, consume, devour, overcome.

Jesus also said, "He who eats My flesh and drinks My blood abides in Me and I in him."[287] This is done through taking communion, as we often do in church services with grape juice or wine, bread or crackers. Can we spiritually consume the Christ (God's anointed body) so much that we will abide in Him completely or at least as much as we are able?

He promises when we abide in Him, we can ask anything, and it will be granted.[288] Then and only then, can we be in His perfect will, doing only what He wants because we are one with Him. It seems an impossibility, as even the apostle Paul called himself the chief of sinners.[289] Yet we must each strive to become like Christ with every choice we make.

A thousand years before Jesus was born, God had sworn to King David that in the future the Anointed One would sit on his throne. Jesus was one of David's descendants.[290] David foretold about the crucifixion of the Messiah, and that His soul wouldn't be left in the grave nor would His flesh rot.[291]

And still today, the eternal flesh of Jesus, the Bread of Life, the all-consuming, overcoming food when eaten, will never die nor rot away. Through the resurrection of Jesus, we have the same inheritance, and we are promised eternal life but only when we choose to partake spiritually of the Anointed One, Jesus (the Living Word of God). We consume Him by inviting the Holy Spirit to live in us and become "Born Again."[292]

LIFE IS IN THE BLOOD

Blood is one of the most significant words in the Bible. We have read about the flesh, but blood is also inseparable from life. We will explore its amazing purpose. Jesus said, "Whoever eats my flesh and drinks my blood has eternal life and I will raise him up in the last day."[293] Otherwise, there is no life in us. This was a hard saying for the Jews He was talking to, because God's law to Moses forbade them from eating an animal with its life in it, meaning the blood. Before they ate meat, the animal was killed, and its blood completely drained out.[294]

And so, the Messiah also had to die. The principal difference is an animal remains dead; its blood is no longer alive. With the resurrection of Christ, His body and blood became eternal. Therefore, whenever we drink His blood through Communion, in the form of grape juice or wine, we remember the eternal life we now share through His resurrected body and blood.

Before the crucifixion of Jesus, the blood of animals was used in all contracts with God. As High Priest, Moses read the Book of the Law to the people, and they made a covenant with God that they would be obedient to all of them. Moses took the blood of bulls, sprinkled it on the altar and on the people.[295] He said to them, "Behold the blood of the covenant, which the LORD hath made with you concerning all these words."[296] But as we have learned throughout Jewish history, God's people stumbled in all areas of His laws, and even today it's impossible for any of us to keep them completely.

Therefore, in the New Testament, we are given a second chance. Jesus was born as a man to be the Savior of the world, and we were given a new promise.[297] The day before His death, during the Passover supper, Jesus passed a cup of wine to His disciples and said, "This cup is the new covenant in My blood. This do, as often as you drink it, in remembrance of Me".[298]

Jesus has the only blood we are commanded to drink to become part of His eternal blood family. Even today, the Jews use wine or grape juice during Passover and Shabbat celebrations. And Christians take communion, as a representation of the Blood of the Lamb that cleanses sin to overcome eternal death and hell.

Praise God! "In whom we have redemption through His blood, the forgiveness of sins, according to the riches of His GRACE."[299] It's important to keep in mind He had not come to abolish the Law but to fulfill it.[300] When we eat His flesh (His Word) and drink His blood (Eternal Life), we choose to live in Him and He in us. Only in that oneness can we understand and live in obedience to His will and law.

The Law (God's instructions to Moses) states there is no forgiveness except through the shedding of blood.[301] The people of Israel were required to perform many sin and guilt offerings through the sacrifice of animals. The most important was on Yom Kippur, the Day of Atonement. Once a year a goat was killed and its blood sprinkled on the altar to cleanse all of Israel's sins, and a second goat was selected to banish Israel's sins into the desert.[302]

We can see the symbolism with God's first couple after their sin of rebellion. Like the first goat, Eve became the first human to bleed as a part of reproducing mortal flesh.[303] And like the second goat, Adam was banished from the perfect garden of Eden into a cursed and barren earth to toil for food.[304]

Another parallel to the blood atonement and the two goats is through the first human death in the Bible when Cain, the first-born son of Adam and Eve, murdered his brother Abel. He was banished to wander the earth after God told him that He heard his brother's innocent blood crying out from the land.[305]

Then there was Abraham whose name means "Father of Nations", the man Yahweh had chosen to become father of His people and the promise. Abraham had two sons, Isaac and Ishmael. Isaac was to be the sacrificial lamb used by God to test Abraham, but God relented, accepting a rams' blood instead.[306] Ishmael, whose mother was a slave woman, was banished into the wilderness.[307]

And so, we come to the most important parallel, starting again with the first man in the Garden of Eden, Adam, in whom sin and death began through his rebellion. He became the goat with the guilt of mankind's banishment on his head.[308] After being filled with knowledge of both truths and lies from the forbidden fruit he had eaten, Adam was sent out into the wilderness where he, and all of us his descendants, still die to this day.[309]

The second Adam, Jesus, was pure, blameless, and tempted with every temptation in mind, body, and soul. But He overcame ALL disobedience. Jesus was sent to the slaughter as the goat whose blood atones for every sin, as the Lamb of God.[310]

There is so much more to Jesus. He also became the final replacement for both goats. For a moment, He was banished from the presence of the Father as He shouted on the cross, "My God, My God, why hast Thou forsaken Me".[311] So Jesus also became the scapegoat as He took the blame for all of humanity's sins in this world: past, present, and future that were placed on Him as His blood spilled out.[312]

John the Baptist said about Jesus, "Behold the Lamb of God which taketh away the sin of the world".[313] As the sacrificial Lamb, through His immaculate blood shed on the cross, both the curse of eternal banishment from God's presence and the curse of mortal death are finally broken.

How incredible is that! Yes, God allowed His Son's mortal body to die to save the entire world. "For God so loved the world that

He gave His only begotten Son, that whosoever believeth in Him should not perish but have everlasting life."[314] Jesus became the "First Fruit", the first human to receive an immortal body. At the same time, all mankind is given the amazing promise to follow Him into immortality. He said, "I am the resurrection and the life. He that believeth in Me, though he were dead, yet shall he live. "[315]

But there is a catch that requires a spiritual contract. We must BELIEVE in the death, burial and resurrection of Jesus Christ as the Son of God and agree to follow Him and His instructions. Jesus said to His disciples, "If any man will come after Me, let him deny himself, and take up his cross, and follow Me."[316] And "If you love Me, keep my commandments".[317]

The proof of our faith is the ability to repent, give up our sins, and accept forgiveness when we make mistakes. Without forgiveness of the penalty, there is no salvation. Yes, it's that easy. Without believing and accepting the payment of the pure blood of Jesus Christ to cleanse us, none of us can stand before a Holy God while still holding on to our sins. If we haven't let go of our rebellion, our spirit is still under the curse of banishment from God's perfect garden and His holy presence.

The spiritual Garden of Eden is the Kingdom of God. He cannot allow a human spirit or fallen angel tainted with sin to defile heaven. There is a great divide between heaven and hell, faithfulness or rebellion, love or hate. There is no way our sins are allowed into the pure spiritual Garden of Eden living with the pure and holy God in Heaven.[318]

What does this all really mean? Since Adam, mankind has been the goat with sin on our heads wandering around aimlessly in the wilderness, compiling sin upon sins with every new generation equipped with the knowledge of how to do good and evil together. Each one of us not only carries our own sins but the sins of our ancestors, which even scientifically we see the consequences in generational sickness and disease through our DNA. "The wages of sin is death".[319]

So God gave Moses His commandments and statutes. They were instructions to the people of Israel who were supposed to teach the rest of the world how to return to God and live in health and prosperity.[320] The only way a person could be saved from sin (harmful choices) was to follow every part of God's laws. The people of Israel tried, but how can anyone keep a pure and blameless life when hearts, minds and bodies are filled with the sins of their ancestors the moment they are conceived? The blood of sacrificed animals wasn't enough to make them righteous, and it is not enough to make us righteous either![321]

This is where the "Good News of the Gospel" of God enters in. He had compassion on us, knowing it is impossible for man to be completely blameless. God came down in the flesh in the earthly form of His Son, Yeshua. It's as if He was saying "Okay kids, let Father fix the mess." So, He collected all the wrongs we as mankind have ever done and will do, put them on the scapegoat's head of Jesus and allowed His death to offer the only pure blood offering to pay the death penalty for ALL the sins of the world.[322]

We can ask why do we need His blood? Because every ordered society must be ruled by laws. Several of God's laws, when broken, carry penalties of death and the guilty must pay.[323] In our present mortal state, our human body and blood dies and cannot be resurrected. Thankfully God gave us an immortal provision when He supplied the eternal blood of His Son.[324]

The Law states, "The life of the flesh is in the blood … to make an atonement for your souls."[325] Jesus took the cup, gave thanks, and gave it to His disciples and said, "Drink from it, all of you, for this is My blood of the new covenant, which is shed for many for the remission of sins."[326] By shedding His immortal blood for us, our death penalty is paid forever, and we no longer have to face eternal death.[327] "For the wages of sin is death, but the gift of God is eternal life through Jesus Christ our Lord". [328]

We are like little children, who have gone out of our father's house to play in the mud. We get covered in it and can't come back into the house until we are washed clean. Some of us are ready and eager to let our father bathe us and say to Him, "Father, forgive me and cleanse me, I want to come home". But others enjoy their dirty condition, like pigs wallowing in mud day after day, refusing to be clean. Still others believe they can cleanse themselves from the soil of this world and refuse His help.

Unless we believe Jesus came to set up His sinless kingdom here on earth, we won't recognize the seriousness of our dirty state. Without allowing Him to cleanse us with the bath of His blood (new life), we will continue to wander in the wilderness of sin during this physical life and take it with us in the existence to come. It's our choice to enter the Kingdom of God or get shut out completely with all the fallen angels and creatures bound for Hell and eternal death, with no escape.

Jesus told a story of a rich man and a beggar named Lazarus who laid at the rich man's gate to beg for crumbs. Lazarus was starving and deathly ill with no one to take care of him. When he died, his spirit was taken to Heaven and Abraham's bosom.[329] The rich man also died and was taken to Hell, where he pleaded with Father Abraham to be allowed to cross over to Heaven. But Abraham said, "Son, remember that in your lifetime you received your good things, and likewise Lazarus evil things, but now he is comforted, and you are tormented. And besides all this, between us and you there is a great gulf fixed, so that those who want to pass from here to you cannot, nor can those from there pass to us."[330]

Although the rich man had earthly wealth, believed in God, and knew Abraham, he had no love nor compassion for others. We can say we love God, but only our actions will prove it. John wrote, "If someone says, 'I love God', and hates his brother, he is a liar. For he who does not love his brother whom he has seen, how can he love God whom he has not seen?"[331]

Here I would like to add that many times we don't understand riches. We are taught that owning material things in this world makes us rich, but we fail to see supernatural glory, power, and love as true riches. Even Jesus, the true King of kings, said about Himself that the Son of Man has no place to lay His head.

There is a miracle that happens when we repent. The rich man could have been saved before his death, but the hardness of his heart wouldn't go there. The miracle we have been given is that ALL our sins are already paid for and destroyed through the sacrifice of Jesus when He gave up His earthly body in exchange for ours. BUT all of us must make a personal choice to say, "Yes LORD, I do" to His invitation. This powerful declaration and marriage to His covenant allows us to enter the most holy place through the blood of Jesus. The spiritual veil (His flesh) has been ripped open for us to enter the Holy of Holies as our spirits become joined with the Holy Spirit. We become God's holy temple.[332]

The power of blood is so strong! We see an excellent example of that during the ten plagues released on Egypt when Pharaoh stubbornly refused to let the enslaved Israelites go into the desert to worship Yahweh, their God, as He commanded. The people were under severe oppression, held captive under Egyptian slavery. After each of the nine plagues, Pharoah promised to release the Israelites, yet His heart was hardened, and he recanted, until all the first born of Egypt died.[333]

Finally, Moses was commanded by God to tell every Israeli family to select a pure, unblemished male lamb and keep it for five days. Then they were instructed to slaughter their lamb at twilight and put some of the blood on the sides and top of the door frames of their home. They would eat the lamb meat roasted over fire with bitter herbs and bread without yeast. All parts of the lamb not eaten had to be burned. God was very specific, so there would be no contamination.[334]

On that same night, God passed through Egypt and struck down all first-born, both man and animals.[335] But He made a provision for His obedient people to spare the lives of their first-born. God said, "The blood shall be a sign for you on the houses where you are. And when I see the blood, I will pass over you and the plague shall not be on you to destroy you".[336]

This act symbolized the powerful blood of Jesus, the perfect Lamb of God without blemish or defect chosen before the creation of the world. He came to save us from eternal extinction. When the Father sees the blood of the Lamb of God on the houses of our souls, eternal spiritual death passes over us.[337]

In the twelfth chapter of the book of Exodus, God tells Israel to remember this important date of the Passover. He tells us we are to keep it forever. God is not a man that He should lie.[338] He knows we are fickle and have short memories; therefore, He gave the Jews instructions on how to keep these days which they still do today. And for all of us who have given our lives to the God of Israel, these feast days are for us to keep also. This is why they are called Holy-Days (Holidays).[339]

In a bizarre way, Jews and Christians alike still celebrate Passover. However, many western nations mingle the message of extreme sacrifice with chicken eggs to commemorate the story of Esther, who today in the Middle East is worshipped as a goddess of fertility. We have made the story a fun and silly time for children. But I wonder how many people know the symbolism of this important Holy Day to celebrate Queen Esther who saved the Jewish nation at the risk of her own life, and the bloody war that followed.

Passover also celebrates God's amazing deliverance of His people out of the slavery of Egypt at another great cost of human life. Most importantly, the Passover is honored by Christians on Easter to remember the final sacrifice of the Lamb of God through the death and resurrection of Jesus Christ. The eternal saving gift and power of Jesus seem to be free because He paid the ultimate price with His own Blood, but the trade is that every individual must accept His gift. When we do so, we receive His full heavenly pardon and inheritance while also becoming completely indebted to Him. Jesus said, we must deny ourselves and take up our cross (assignment) that was already planned for us.[340] But our desire for self-serving and self-rule have caused many to reject His amazing offer.[341]

The Book of Revelations describes what happens in heaven when the four living creatures and the twenty-four elders fell down before the Lamb.[342] They sang a new song: "You are worthy to take the scroll and to open its seals, because you were slain, and with your blood you purchased for God persons from every tribe and language and people and nation. You have made them to be a kingdom and priests to serve our God, and they will reign on the earth."[343]

There are many of us who say we believe and claim to have given Jesus our lives, but the proof of our faith becomes obvious in an external outpouring. The Fathers greatest commandment is to love the LORD your God with all your heart, mind, soul, and strength.[344] Then Jesus said the second commandment is like it, "You shall love your neighbor as yourself. On these two commandments hang all the Law and the Prophets."[345]

I have met people filled with anger and unforgiveness, refusing to look at themselves with any responsibility. They shift all blame for their problems to others. But Jesus was severe in pointing out, "Whoever hates his brother is a murderer, and you know that no murderer has eternal life abiding in him."[346]

When Jesus spoke to the multitude of people during the Sermon on the Mount, four times he used the word forgive and told the people they must forgive others, otherwise the Father would not forgive their sins. "For if ye forgive men their trespasses, your heavenly Father will also forgive you: But if ye forgive not men their trespasses, neither will your Father forgive your trespasses."[347]

Recently I listened to a woman's story who said she died on the operating table and was immediately taken to Hell where demons tormented her. But just as fast she was brought back to life and her soul returned to her body. She asked God why He allowed her to go to Hell as she was a faithful Christian, attending church on Sundays and serving during the week. The Lord answered her that she had unforgiveness in her heart and that sent her to Hell.

This is a most important lesson for us, if you're harboring offense, anger, or hatred against others, please repent and release it now. Yes, it can be very hard because we often feel we need justice, but holding on the sins of others places us above God, since He has already forgiven them by shedding His blood for them also.

I have found the best way to release anger towards others is to pray God's blessings for them. This is the living example Jesus gave us to: "Love your enemies, bless them that curse you, do good to them that hate you, and pray for them which despitefully use you, and persecute you."[348] No matter how hard it is to start, God will show you His love for them. This doesn't mean we need to trust the offender instantly or continue to be abused, but we need to release their sins in our own hearts and allow God to deal with them.

Our true faith in Him becomes evident by following Jesus' command of love for others, revealed through personal sacrifice.[349] When we love others, we are really loving God, because our neighbor is also made in God's image. When we discipline ourselves to allow His Spirit to use us in mastering the most important commandments of love, the rest of His laws become easier to follow producing abundantly good fruit of peace and joy.[350]

STRENGTH OF HIS ARM

Zeroah is the Hebrew name for arm. Some of its meanings are: Help, force, mighty, power, shoulder, strength, bear, and yield. We will explore these meanings describing our powerful, protective, and fatherly God.[351]

"I will redeem you with an outstretched arm and with mighty acts of judgment. I will take you as My own people, and I will be your God".[352] The realization of this scripture is incredible. Hello! The God of the Universe has invited us to be His people. Even though we may have heard this before, can we dare to really believe it? Is it possible that He wants to know us like family? He is reaching His arm out to each one of us waiting for our decision to welcome His embrace.

"Fear and dread will fall on them, by the greatness of your arm".[353] All the enemies of God's people were afraid because so many who came against them died publicly, no matter how large the armies.[354] He promises to defend all who believe in Him. "The LORD who brought you up from the land of Egypt with great power and an outstretched arm, Him you shall fear, Him you shall worship and to Him you shall offer sacrifice."[355]

In our modern times when we meet or hear about real live heroes, we are awe struck by their strength and have a reverence for them, like our sports or TV heroes. For those of us who know how real God is, we are even more awe struck beyond normal comprehension and place Him above everything else in our lives. That is what it means to love Him with all our heart, soul, mind, and strength.[356]

One of the most difficult books in the Bible to understand is the story of righteous Job who God allowed to be ambushed by Satan.[357] During Job's agonizing losses, sickness, and family deaths, God questioned his many complaints about unfairness. God asked Job, "Have you an arm like God?"[358]

All of us at some point question God's wisdom over our training, especially when going through difficult testing periods. The hardest thing for mankind to do, is to completely trust God. Our human perspective is so limited compared to His. In the end, Job relented that God's wisdom was too great to question, and he was exceedingly blessed with much more than he had lost.[359]

Now I must tell you my own story of the devil's temptations for strength and power. It's hard to believe that my walk with the Lord began with Satan through a series of dreams. In the first dream, Satan came as a businessman and tried to negotiate with me, but I couldn't understand him. A few years later, in another dream, I was given a tour overlooking the pits of Hell where demons of every kind were torturing people, complete with hell's fires and the rotten smell of burning sulfur.

Later still, after I dedicated my life to Jesus but had not yet been baptized, I dreamt Satan met me with a very tempting offer of incredible strength and power, but I sensed his evil intent and cautiously turned him down. In this dream I could not be rid of him, until I called on the help of the Holy Spirit.

A month after the dream, I took a tour to Israel with a Christian group and many of us were baptized in the Jordan River. As soon as I came out of the water, the song being sung by the live band who attended, was "It Is Finished" and I felt I was finally free. My life was completely changed after that, and Satan was no longer allowed to invade my dreams.

It made me think that baptism is like a wedding ceremony. Some people professing belief in Jesus, don't understand this important public spiritual ritual of washing away sin. They are like many couples today, living with their lovers but refusing to make a legal binding covenant in marriage with them, thereby having a superficial commitment. Is this how we should treat our Lord?

I also learned about the extreme authority of power and strength I now wielded, by the Arm of the Lord, as a Christian through prayer. I didn't need Satan's offer that came with strings of bondage attached forever, since God's offer of eternal life and immeasurable love is far greater.

A passage in the Bible about Satan is written by the prophet Isaiah, "How are you fallen from heaven, O Lucifer, son of the morning! How you are cut down to the ground, you who weaken the nations! For you have said in your heart, 'I will ascend into heaven, I will exalt my throne above the stars of God; I will sit also on the mount of the congregation, in the recesses of the north; I will ascend above the heights of the clouds, I will be like the Most High.'"[360]

And this is God's answer to him, "Yet you shall be brought down to Hell, to the sides of the pit. Those who see you shall stare at you and ponder over you: 'Is this the man who made the earth to tremble and shook kingdoms, who made the world as a wilderness and destroyed its cities, who did not open the house of his prisoners?' All the kings of the nations, even all of them, lie in glory, each one in his own tomb; but you are cast out of your grave like an abominable branch and clothed with those who are slain, thrust through with a sword, who go down to the stones of the pit as a corpse trodden underfoot."[361]

Some people believe Satan is the most powerful being, and yes, he is powerful, as he was created to be God's angel of worship and light. And some honor him above God to receive favors for power, riches, and fame. But they should take the warning from God, that they will end up in Hell with Satan, which is the lowest level of degradation. We must remember we are the children of the Creator. Let's not fall into traps for short term gain and end in eternal ruin by worshipping fallen angels, no matter how beautiful they are.[362]

This is also a stern warning to those who proudly worship themselves. Satan's downfall was his arrogance in wanting to place himself above God and His laws, to have his own evil rulership over creation. He is still doing that today in human lives. We can see the results wherever we see sickness and violence.

The Bible gives us this important warning, "Pride goes before destruction, and a haughty spirit before a fall."[363] Yet some people spit in God's face without fear, waving their pride as a badge of honor. They don't realize to reject God is to embrace Satan, while descending into Hell where there is only torturous pain awaiting final death.

My dreams which occurred over the course of several years, finally awakened me to realize that if there was a Hell and a devil, then there must be a GOD and He began to show Himself to me. Like Job, I surrendered fully to the majesty of God, which was the greatest decision of my life.

And as a soldier of the Cross, I have found there is no greater freedom and power than that gained as a follower of Jesus Christ. For those of you, who have given Satan your authority and feel there is no return, please understand, Jesus already paid for you. He will fight for you and deliver you, but only when you repent and turn to Him.

Because Satan and the angels who followed him, were cast out of Heaven for rebelling against the Creator, they are already numbered for judgement. So also, must all people who have broken God's laws during their lives be judged if they refuse to repent and accept Jesus' gift of salvation.[364]

When our spirit leaves our body, all our works have been written in God's great books held for judgement. "And the dead were judged according to their works, by the things which were written in the books." Jesus is the final judge and will sit on His throne of judgement as the books of our lives are opened.[365]

In the last book of the Bible, Jesus warns us that He will come quickly and said, "My reward is with Me, to give every man according as his work."[366] This means our accomplishments during our earthly lives will be judged for good, evil or indifference.

King David described how God helped the people of Israel, "It was not by their sword that they won the land … it was by Your right hand, Your arm, and the light of Your face, for You loved them." [367] God defends and brings victory to those He loves, like a man protecting His family and scattering His enemies. But we must be willing to accept that victory as His provision for us.

Some may wonder why God doesn't always help everyone in the family. The problem often lies in the sins committed, including those passed on from prior generations, that still require justice and judgement in the natural, even the death penalty. The thief on the cross with Jesus repented and he was forgiven of all his crimes against God. Jesus said to him, "Today you will be with Me in Paradise", meaning his soul. But the thief's earthly body was still sentenced to die, and he was crucified agonizingly along with Jesus.[368]

We see sometimes people suffer for a higher purpose as Job did. In a story about a blind man, Jesus' disciples asked Him who had sinned. Jesus answered that neither the blind man nor his parents sinned, but that the works of God would be seen through him.[369] And then Jesus opened the man's eyes and gave him sight! Two thousand years later we are still reading about the miracle Jesus performed as an example of His healing power.

It's impossible for us to accomplish righteousness on our own, and that is why we need Jesus and each other. God's children are part of His royal priesthood, and why wouldn't any person of royalty call on their Father's wisdom and His army to navigate through hostile territory? Life on earth is a battlefield, laced with minefields along the way, compared to the glory of heaven. Will you be one of God's special forces, maybe even a loyal foot soldier? Both are just as valuable to Him and needed to build His Kingdom.

God, whose strength is in His arm, "comes with power and He rules with a mighty arm."[370] Like a King over His kingdom He rules with strength and power. And like a father who knows what's best for us, "He tends his flock like a shepherd, He gathers the lambs in His arms and carries them close to His heart".[371] In these same arms of strength, He gently gathers us, feeding and tending, bringing us to total and complete trust when we allow Him.

"The LORD has made bare His holy arm. The eyes of all the nations and all the ends of the earth shall see the salvation of our God."[372] Whenever God does major things, the whole world sees it. The trouble is, many refuse to acknowledge it's His doing and come up with natural reasons for signs and wonders.

Unless we give God the credit for these works, we'll continue to live in the narrow scope of unbelief, missing all the powerful wonders He performs with "His Holy Arm". We recalled the ten plagues unleashed on Egypt during Moses time that brought complete devastation, and finally caused Pharaoh to let God's people go. He called them "My wonders".[373] How often do we miss God's hand of miracles or judgements today?

"Who hath believed our report? And to whom is the arm of the LORD been revealed?"[374] Just as Pharaoh didn't recognize God's wonders, many of the leaders of Israel didn't recognize the Son of God when He came in human form through Jesus Christ, even though their scriptures foretold His coming.[375]

"He saw that there was no man, and wondered that there was no intercessor, therefore His arm brought salvation".[376] Because no one in mankind was strong enough to stand against sin, God used His own strength to save His people.[377]

"The LORD has sworn by His right hand and by the arm of His strength. Surely, I will no longer give your grain as food for your enemies, and the sons of the foreigner shall not drink your new wine, for which you have labored".[378] When God makes a vow, we can be sure He keeps it. He promises to redeem us, and He also tells us not to give Him any rest until He does.[379]

"The eternal God is thy refuge, and underneath are the everlasting arms, and He shall thrust out the enemy from before thee."[380] Again and again, He tells us He will hold us up forever; therefore, we have no enemies because He will deal with them. This promise is to all who make a choice to come under His protection when we allow Him to be God and King in our lives.

God's arms of strength, protection and shelter are just as fully described when Jesus took a little child in His arms and said, "Let the little children come to Me, and do not forbid them, for of such is the Kingdom of Heaven."[381]

As His believers are used as His physical Body here on earth, we are expected to grow into His likeness, receiving His strength, power, and love. Then we will have His compassion to scoop the young and the weak up in our arms, and the world will know we are His people. They will witness the image and love of Jesus through us. "Therefore, you shall be perfect, just as your Father in heaven is perfect."[382]

THE HAND OF GOD

What is the mighty Hand of God? There is more written about His hand than any other part of Him, so we will explore all the powerful things His hand stands for.

In the story of Moses' first encounter, God told him about Pharoah, "I will stretch out my hand, and smite Egypt with all my wonders which I will do in the midst thereof and after that he will let you go."[383] "But Pharaoh shall not hearken unto you, that I may lay my hand upon Egypt, and bring forth mine armies, and my people the children of Israel, out of the land of Egypt by great judgments. And the Egyptians shall know that I am the LORD."[384]

There are several important points in these verses. First it was God who hardened Pharaoh's heart causing him to be unrelenting until all ten judgments had been poured out on Egypt.[385] Pharaoh was raised to believe he was a god, and his pride caused him to stay stubborn against the God of the slaves. He couldn't admit their God was greater than himself.

But God had a higher purpose for Pharoah. He said, "I have raised you up, that I may show My power in you, and that My name may be declared in all the earth".[386] God made an example using the most powerful man on earth at that time, as He has done countless times before and after.

Through all ten judgements, God in His great mercy gave Egypt time to repent and recognize His status as their Creator and God. His only demand was that His people Israel be allowed to go out into the desert and bring sacrifices to worship Him.[387] Egypt in this case was like a dog biting the hand which feeds it, by not understanding they had become so rich because of God's favor on Israel.

It all began when Joseph, the son of Jacob and Rachel, was sold into slavery by his brothers, to later become the second in command over Egypt. By interpreting Pharoah's dream, God gave Joseph wisdom to prepare for famine so that both Egypt and Israel would survive.[388]

Four hundred years later, the people of Israel had become Egypt's work force as slaves to a new Pharaoh. This Pharaoh refused to let them go probably for fear of destroying Egypt's economy if they didn't come back.[389]

But God's hands worked through the hands of Moses and Aaron his brother, to completely set Israel free. How demoralizing for Pharaoh, competing against the real God. Isn't this like so many of us, when in our rebellious state we think we can outsmart our Creator?

Finally in the end, after breaking every promise to let Israel go, Pharoah released them, but then changed his mind and sent his entire army after God's people to bring them back. But Egypt came to a bitter end.

In Pharaoh's relentless pursuit, God's mercy stopped when He used the rod in Moses' hand, as His hand, to part the Red Sea so Israel could cross over on dry land. As soon as they were safe, God used Moses' hand to restore the waters covering Egypt's army in a watery grave and their bodies washed up on the shores.[390] All the surrounding nations saw the bodies or heard the stories and there was great fear of the God of Israel and His people.[391]

"Your right hand, O Lord, has become glorious in power; Your right hand, O Lord, has dashed the enemy in pieces". "The enemy said, 'I will pursue, I will overtake, I will divide the spoil. My hand shall destroy them.'" "You stretched out Your right hand and the earth swallowed them".[392] And that was the end of Egypt's power in the days of Moses.

Many know Jesus as a good God according to our beliefs in what is good. Others believe He is a king without power. Some even see Him as weak for allowing Himself to be crucified. More often people believe His unwavering mercy won't do anything when we, His people, use the work of our hands to prosper His enemies, even though we are created for His higher purpose. But history teaches us the real struggles of God's chosen people.

After they were freed, the children of Israel began to complain against Moses. They compared the supernatural hand of God to the physical abundance of Egypt that they missed and said, "Oh, that we had died by the hand of the LORD in the land of Egypt, when we sat by the pots of meat and ate bread to the full! For you have brought us out into this wilderness to kill this whole assembly with hunger."[393]

Even after witnessing the terrifying judgements, the plagues of God on Egypt, their main concern was physical comfort and food. The supernatural manna and quail Yahweh provided every morning after their food ran out wasn't enough to stop their complaining.[394] They had already forgotten their slavery and the miracle parting of the Red Sea. They even came away with Egypt's riches, but their memories were as short as their stomachs. Very quickly they rebelled and built a golden calf to replace Yahweh God and worshipped it instead, as the god who saved them from slavery in Egypt.[395]

Soon Yahweh sent Moses down from the mountain with His commandments to teach the acceptable lifestyle of a people chosen by Him. They would learn to be priests and kings, to let the nations know about Him and teach His instructions as a blessing to them, by learning skills to accomplish His purposes on earth.[396]

We often pray and expect God to do all the work, without understanding God is spirit and requires a partnership with us. We must allow Him to use our hands, to build His Kingdom here on Earth as it is in Heaven.[397]

Many of us ask why God allows evil? But we should be asking ourselves, "What is MY role to stop evil?". Do we complain instead of striking the rock with the rod He has given us, meaning the tools in our hands?[398]

Each of us is born with a purpose and talents to accomplish His work. It can be a small order or a large one. Every person has a specific heavenly job to build God's Kingdom. Disobedience, chaos, and evil prevail in families and societies when people refuse to allow God to use our lives to fulfill His purposes. Instead, we often choose to use our talents for personal gain or not use them at all. We can learn a lot of what will happen to us from the stories Jesus told.[399]

We may think that our hand is too small for God to use. But look and see, He used the hand of Aaron, a man born in slavery, to smite the waters with his rod, to turn all the waters in Egypt to blood. [400] All we have to do is say "Yes LORD", and then His hand will perform the miracles through us. Some people wait for God to use them, like He should force us, but His greatest gift to us is "Free Will". God desires loyalty, not slavery.

When we refuse to serve Him, we become like His enemies, cut off from His presence, ultimately leading to our own destruction unless we repent and turn away from rebellion. We must each choose which side we are on. If it's our own, we lose our greater purpose to bring life, love, and peace to those around us, and the short time we have on earth is wasted.

Some believe that everyone belongs to God, and His unlimited mercy will save us all. But we can't possibly be His if we refuse to follow Him. Jesus said, "I AM the Way, the Truth and the Life, no one can come to the Father except through Me", and "If you love Me, keep My commandments".[401]

Can we call someone ours if they aren't committed to us? That's like a man pursuing a woman who doesn't love him, but she tells others she is his so she can receive his benefits. Eventually he will leave her, find another, and have nothing more to do with her.

Since God is Life, without Him we choose death and will be destroyed. "Choose life so that you and your descendants may live".[402] Where His hand can mean destruction for those who hate Him, it means pure love, guidance, and shelter for those who love Him.

We read before about the intimate friendship Moses had with Yahweh and how he longed to see his mysterious friend who had performed such mighty wonders to deliver Israel out of slavery in Egypt. But God told Moses that no human could survive seeing Him. So, Yahweh used His powerful hand and said, "Here is a place by Me, and you shall stand on the rock. So it shall be, while My glory passes by, that I will put you in the cleft of the rock and will cover you with My hand while I pass by. Then I will take away My hand, and you shall see My back, but My face shall not be seen."[403]

God's glory, His splendor, His beauty is so overwhelming and overpowering, that He had to cover Moses in the rock with His hand so the mortal man wouldn't die. In this same way when we are hidden in the Rock, Jesus, we also will live and not die.[404]

Later Moses acknowledged Yahweh's magnitude, and said, "Sovereign LORD, you have begun to show to your servant your greatness and your strong hand. For what god is there in heaven or on earth who can do the deeds and mighty works you do?"[405]

Moses asked the people, "Has any god ever tried to take for himself one nation out of another nation, by testings, by signs and wonders, by war, by a mighty hand and an outstretched arm, or by great and awesome deeds, like all the things the LORD your God did for you in Egypt before your very eyes?"[406] Moses reminded them they had been slaves in Egypt, just as throughout generations, we have all been slaves to sin.[407]

God's promises to His people are even more pronounced as He says what He will do to all our enemies. "You saw with your own eyes the great trials, the signs and wonders, the mighty hand and outstretched arm, with which the LORD your God brought you out. The LORD your God will do the same to all the peoples you now fear."[408]

This alone should make us extremely glad to be on the right side and afraid to be on the wrong side of the LORD, as He is still saying, "See now that I, even I, am He, and there is no god with Me: I kill, and I make alive; I wound, and I heal: neither is there any that can deliver out of My hand ... If I whet my glittering sword, and mine hand take hold on judgment, I will render vengeance to Mine enemies, and will reward them that hate Me."[409]

God is the commander of His armies. "The LORD came from Sinai and rose up from Seir unto them. He shined forth from mount Paran, and He came with ten thousands of saints. From His right hand went a fiery law for them."[410]

God loves His people, "All His saints are in Thy hand, and they sat down at Thy feet, everyone shall receive of Thy words."[411] His Law, the Commandments, are instructions to guide us through this place in time called "LIFE", to live it fully and abundantly. They are an owner's manual for each one of us to live godly lives.

When we follow Him, He will show us how to follow His guidelines, to be perfect as He is perfect.[412] "That all the people of the earth might know the hand of the LORD, that it is mighty, that ye might fear the LORD your God forever."[413] The people of Israel were called to be an example and blessing to the rest of the world, so that all would come to know the God of Abraham, Isaac and Jacob and become a part of His people.[414]

But whenever a generation got too comfortable with God's blessings, they would stray and begin to worship other gods. Whenever they did, the hand of the LORD came against them for their calamity.[415] Unless we stay in His will, covered by His protective mighty hand, all manner of troubles can come our way. Some say this is unfair, but doesn't a good father also know when to discipline His children? Otherwise, they become spoiled instead of great, and hurt the innocent around them.⁴¹⁶

Several generations later, the people of Israel turned away from Yahweh their God and lost their relationship with Him. Their most holy and revered object, which contained the commandments of God, the "Ark of the Covenant", was captured by Israel's enemies.⁴¹⁷ Israel worshipped the Ark and believed it could save them from all their enemies, but they had forgotten to worship their eternal King. Isn't this so much like us? Too often we worship our churches, synagogues, pastors or even the Bible, but we forget to worship and love the LORD Himself who alone is worthy!

The enemies of Israel placed the holy Ark in the temple of their god, Dagon. By the third day, Dagon's statue lay on the ground broken. Even worse for them, a plague came on the people covering many with tumors.⁴¹⁸ With great repentance, they said, "the Ark of the God of Israel must not remain with us, for His hand is harsh toward us and Dagon our god."⁴¹⁹ They recognized that their sickness came from the hand of the God of Israel, and even their greatest god didn't stand a chance against Him.

When they sent the Ark away, the plague got worse: "The hand of the LORD was against the city with a very great destruction, and He struck the men of the city, both small and great, and tumors broke out on them".[420] They sent it to another city, called Ekron, and the same thing happened. The people said, "Send away the Ark of the God of Israel, and let it go back to its own place, so that it does not kill us and our people."[421]

Their pagan priests told them they needed to compensate the God of Israel for the affront against Him in taking the Ark. They said, "You shall give glory to the God of Israel. Perhaps He will lighten His hand from you, from your gods, and from your land."[422] So they sent the Ark back to Israel along with golden images of tumors and rats that had ravaged their land as trespass offerings so they would be healed.[423]

When the Ark returned to the outskirts of Israel, to a town called Beth Shemesh (House of the Sun), the Israelites who lived there had little reverence for Yahweh and were possibly sun worshippers. Their hearts were just as impure as the nations around them, and they also couldn't stand under the holiness of God's hand. They looked inside the Ark, and God struck those Israeli men with the same plague of tumors. Over fifty thousand in that region died.[424]

Because they were part of Israel, they presumed they were His chosen and clean enough to look on the holiest of objects, the laws of God which condemned them. Like many of us today, we may seek God's power and benefits while breaking His most important commandments. How often do we believe we are good enough to save ourselves until we find ourselves in deep water, where we are confronted by the holiness of God's hand which metes out justice to everyone alike? Could this be one of the reasons so many in modern times have cancers?

Living as a child of God is not an easy thing. We have a Father who is raising His children in His image. The training to spiritual adulthood can be intense, especially for those of us who insist on choosing an easier path or prefer blatant rebellion. Our fight is then directly with Him.

Many of us can easily remember the disappointments, anger, and punishments our earthly parents displayed when we chose to disobey them. Although our spiritual Father God is not in the least bit surprised at our behavior, He will not let us get away with anything that may hurt us or others. And in a very real sense He spanks us for our own good.[425]

One of the biggest mysteries for us, is that God doesn't hold the same level of importance on our physical lives as we do. Even though He longs to see us prosper in every way, He regards our spirits and character, the matters of the heart, as the most important. It's easier for Him to deal with our flesh, allowing sickness and even death, and view this as temporary to achieve a greater goal in perfecting our souls for eternity. The life of Job is a perfect example!

Just like today, in modern Israel and in many Christian societies, ancient Israel flourished in the land God promised them. That is, until they again rebelled against God's instructions. The LORD caused King David to sin for the nation.[426] David was given a choice to be punished by the hand of God or by men, and David chose to be judged by the hand of the LORD for His mercies are great, and not to fall into the hand of man."[427] David knew God could be trusted to be more merciful than men. Yet seventy thousand people died in a plague when God stretched out His hand of justice through an angel.[428]

Now let's look at the God of promises and the fulfillment of His great purposes through His mighty hand to those who love Him. David said of Him, "Both riches and honor come from You, and You reign overall. In Your hand is power and might. In Your hand it is to make great and to give strength to all."[429]

Over time, Israel amassed so much wealth and David wisely acknowledged that it was through God's hand, and that everything belongs to Him. "O LORD our God, all this abundance that we have prepared to build You a house for Your holy name is from Your hand and is all Your own."[430]

After King David served as Israel's king, his son Solomon became king. God chose Solomon to build His Temple according to the written plans the hand of God had given David.[431] Everything God promised to the nation of Israel was fulfilled as quoted by Solomon, "That all peoples of the earth may know Your name and fear You, as do Your people Israel".[432] To fear God means to honor, respect, and revere Him as we should all do.

Now we can look at other descriptions of God's hand. After three years of drought, the prophet Elijah prayed for rain, until his servant saw a cloud as small as a man's hand, and the rains came down. This was the LORD's wonderful provision, but God only moved His hand when Elijah pressed in prayer seven times to release the rain.[433] Then another miracle happened, "the hand of the LORD was on Elijah", and he was able to run on foot ahead of King Ahab who was in a chariot.[434]

In another event, when the prophet Elisha needed to prophesy concerning war, He asked for a musician to play, and the hand of the LORD came upon him, and he was able to prophesy accurately.[435]

The prophet Micaiah had a vision of God and said, "I saw the LORD sitting upon His throne, and all the host of heaven standing on His right hand and His left."[436]

In one of Israel's many battles, they were completely outnumbered by their enemies. King Jehoshaphat led the people in prayer and worship, saying "LORD, the God of our ancestors, are You not the God who is in heaven? You rule over all the kingdoms of the nations. Power and might are in Your hand, and no one can withstand You."[437] Because the king gave God all the glory, the people began to sing in worship to the LORD and a miracle was done; their enemies turned and killed each other.[438]

When we allow God to be King in our lives and governments, the enemy cannot win against us. We will always have the victory because our LORD controls the nations with His mighty hand. We only lose when we get scared or proud, and run into the battle without Him.

God will keep us on His path, as He did for the tribe of Judah who believed in Him. "The hand of God was on the people to give them unity of mind to carry out what the king and his officials had ordered, following the word of the LORD."[439]

Now we can look at God's favor through His hand. Ezra, a skilled scribe in the Law of Moses, came to Jerusalem from his exile in Babylon. The King of Babylon granted Ezra everything he requested because the hand of the LORD his God was upon him.[440] His assignment was to restore the Law of the LORD in Israel.[441]

Amazingly, the current king of the enemy nation, Babylon, which seventy years earlier had plundered Israel and made slaves out of all their leadership and their children, was now supplying everything to rebuild the Temple in Jerusalem that had been destroyed. The seventy years of Israel's banishment had come to an end.[442]

Our next story is one of the best displays of God's Hand, again through the story of Job. Let's see what we can learn from him. God bragged to Satan about His faithful servant Job, who He considered to be the most righteous man in all the earth.[443] Satan replied, "Stretch out Your hand and touch all that he has, and he will surely curse You to Your face!"[444] Then the LORD said, "Behold, all that he has is in your power, only do not lay a hand on his person".[445]

Satan was allowed to torment Job but not to kill him, and God removed His hand from protecting Job, who lost everything including his health. It was Satan who destroyed all Job had. He killed Job's children and servants, his livestock and wealth were stolen, and finally caused boils all over his body.[446] Job's wife couldn't stand it anymore and said to him, "Do you still hold fast to your integrity? Curse God and die".[447]

Knowingly, Job didn't even mention Satan. He knew where his salvation was from and said to God, "You know that I am not wicked, and there is no one who can deliver from Your hand?"[448] "Who among all these does not know that the hand of the LORD has done this. In whose hand is the life of every living thing, and the breath of all mankind?"[449] "Withdraw Your hand far from me and let not the dread of You make me afraid."[450]

At the end of his horrific trial, Job described the awesomeness of the hand of God to his doubting friends. "By His Spirit He adorned the heavens, His hand pierced the fleeing serpent. Indeed, these are the mere edges of His ways, and how small a whisper we hear of Him! But the thunder of His power who can understand?"[451] "He puts his hand on the flint, He overturns the mountains at the roots."[452]

Chapters 38 and 39 of the Book of Job are the most profound, where God describes Himself and His astonishing works. I suggest every person read them to catch a glimpse of the indefinable majesty of Yahweh.[453]

At the end of this story, Job passed the test. Even through his numerous complaints, which most of us would have done, he did not curse God. Through all the generations after him, we have the example of Job's extreme faithfulness that can be upheld in time of great loss and suffering. God rewarded Job abundantly, giving him twice as much as he had before. The story highlights that his rewards included having a new family of seven sons and three daughters, who were the most beautiful women in all the land.[454]

The Book of Psalms summarizes many other beautiful and powerful attributes of God's Hand. Here are some of them:

❖ You, God, see the trouble of the afflicted, You consider their grief and take it in hand.[455]
❖ You will fill me with joy in Your presence, with eternal pleasures at Your right hand.[456]
❖ Show me the wonders of Your great love, You who save by Your right hand.[457]
❖ You make Your saving help my shield, and Your right hand sustains me.[458]
❖ Your hand will lay hold on all Your enemies.[459]
❖ Into your hands I commit my spirit, deliver me, Lord, my faithful God.[460]
❖ My times are in Your hands.[461]
❖ For day and night Your hand was heavy on me.[462]
❖ Though he may stumble, he will not fall, for the Lord upholds him with His hand.[463]
❖ Your arrows have pierced me, and Your hand has come down on me.[464]

❖ Remove your scourge from me. I am overcome by the blow of Your hand.[465]

❖ Your right hand is full of righteousness.[466]

❖ In His hand are the deep places of the earth.[467]

❖ We are the people of His pasture, and the sheep of His hand.[468]

❖ When You open Your hand, they are satisfied with good things.[469]

❖ The Lord's right hand has done mighty things.[470]

❖ May Your hand be ready to help me, for I have chosen your precepts.[471]

❖ Even there Your hand will guide me, Your right hand will hold me fast.[472]

❖ Reach down Your hand from on high, deliver me and rescue me.[473]

❖ You open Your hand and satisfy the desires of every living thing.[474]

The Book of Proverbs makes a startling revelation about leaders chosen to represent us and why it's so important to pray for them. "The king's heart is in the hand of the LORD, Like the rivers of water, He turns it wherever He wishes".[475] I've heard many times that prayer moves the hand of God. Wouldn't it make sense then, that when we pray for our leaders as God directs us, His plans will be fulfilled no matter how dark they may seem? As the LORD repeatedly said, He is the one who hardened Pharaoh's heart.[476]

As stated before, God wants us to prosper in all that we do. King Solomon said, "Nothing is better for a man than that he should eat and drink, that his soul should enjoy good in his labor. This also was from the hand of God".[477]

The Song of Solomon is the most romantic book in the Bible and takes us into a love song of intimacy, which many view as the soul's loving relationship with a loving God. In this song, God's hand is viewed as tender yet ever so passionate: "His left hand is under my head, and His right hand embraces me".[478] If we are to really consider this verse for what it says, it means nothing can snatch us away from

Him. He has us completely covered, like an intimate lover who will never let go unless we ourselves pull away.[479]

"My beloved put His hand by the latch of the door, and my heart yearned for Him".[480] This beautiful verse resounds the later words of Jesus: "Behold I stand at the door and knock, if any man hear My voice and open the door, I will come in to him and will sup with him and he with Me".[481]

Just as the lover of our soul yearns to come into an intimate relationship with us, Spirit to spirit, our spirits are made to surrender to Him and let His Spirit enter. Oh, it's so easy, we often struggle so hard in this battle to stay in control. Yet when we finally give in to our LORD's passion, we are completely undone by the waves of love that roar over us. King David wrote, "Deep calls to deep: In the roar of Your waterfalls, all Your waves and breakers have swept over me. By day the LORD directs His love, at night His song is with me."[482]

If only we wouldn't hurt Him. He offers us everything, His entire Kingdom, pouring out His love, His life, all that He is to us, but so often, humankind rejects Him. Then we see another side of the Creator of the Universe, an angry and jilted God. In these next few books, we'll see His hand used quite differently. He lets us know how He reacts as a lover spurned, scorned, and betrayed by the ones He loves the most.

His people Israel left Him and turned to the demon gods of the nations around them, refusing to recognize Him for all He had given them just as many Christian nations are doing today. He is still saying, "I will turn My hand against you, and thoroughly purge away your dross, and take away all your alloy (false worth)".[483]

"Therefore, the LORD's anger burns against His people. His hand is raised and He strikes them down. The mountains shake, and the dead bodies are like refuse in the streets. Yet for all this, His anger is not turned away, His hand is still upraised."[484] The people fought against each other.[485] "Everyone is a hypocrite and an evildoer, and every mouth speaketh folly".[486] "Without Me they shall bow down under the prisoners, and they shall fall under the slain." Five times in the Book of Isaiah it is written, "For all this His anger is not turned away, but His hand is stretched out still."[487]

Because God is merciful yet sovereign, His anger and His hand are only against those who come against Him just long enough to give them an opportunity to turn their hearts to Him. "And it shall come to pass in that day, that the LORD shall set his hand again the second time to recover the remnant of His people, which shall be left."[488]

"This is the purpose that is purposed upon the whole earth, and this is the hand that is stretched out upon all the nations." He had already planned it all along. "His hand is stretched out, and who will turn it back?"[489] Even Egypt will fear because of the shaking of the hand of the LORD of hosts.[490] As He stretched out His hand over the sea, kingdoms shook. Is He doing it again?[491]

And finally, after subduing all those who hate Him, it is written, "The song of the ruthless ones shall be brought low. In this mountain the LORD of Hosts shall prepare for all people a lavish feast. He will destroy the covering which is over all peoples, even the veil that is spread over all nations. He will swallow up death for all time, and the LORD God will wipe away tears from all faces, and the reproach of His people He shall take away from all the earth, for the LORD has spoken it. It shall be said in that day: Look, this is our God for whom we have waited that He might save us. We will be glad and rejoice in His salvation. For in this mountain the hand of the LORD shall rest."[492]

The amazing thing about God is that like any good father, He has to discipline His children, but afterwards He gives them comfort and peace again. "Speak comfort to Jerusalem, and cry out to her, that her warfare is ended, that her iniquity is pardoned. For she has received from the LORD's hand double for all her sins."[493]

To the nations who love Him, God still promises, "Fear not, for I am with you. Be not dismayed, for I am your God. I will strengthen you, yes, I will help you, I will uphold you with My righteous right hand".[494]

He continues, "I will open rivers in high places, and fountains in the midst of the valleys. I will make the wilderness a pool of water, and the dry land springs of water. I will plant in the wilderness the cedar, the shittah tree, and the myrtle, and the oil tree. I will set in the desert the fir tree, and the pine, and the box tree together. That they may see, and know, and consider, and understand together, that the hand of the LORD hath done this, and the Holy One of Israel hath created it."[495] In His words God describes the trees as the many cultures of our world receiving His blessing.

Then God tells us He will save His people by sending the one true Light into the world. "Behold! My Servant whom I uphold, My Elect One in whom My soul delights! I have put My Spirit upon Him, He will bring forth justice to the Gentiles".[496] "I will hold Your hand, I will keep You and give You as a covenant to the people, as a light to the Gentiles."[497]

God reveals to us His salvation will come through the suffering of this Servant. The LORD's purpose will prosper in His hand through His seed in Yeshua which means, "God saves".[498] He was and is the living example for us to follow.

God's promises are so sure, He swears to save us. "Behold, I will lift My hand in an oath to the nations and set up My standard for the peoples. They shall bring your sons in their arms, and your daughters shall be carried on their shoulders." "The LORD's hand is not shortened, that it cannot save, neither His ear heavy, that it cannot hear."[499]

He made a promise to Jerusalem, "Thou shalt also be a crown of glory in the hand of the LORD, and a royal diadem in the hand of thy God."[500] He swears by His right hand, "Surely I will no longer give your grain as food for your enemies. And the sons of the foreigner shall not drink your new wine, for which you have labored."[501]

Isaiah acknowledged that we are all the work of God's hand when he said, "You are our Father, we are the clay, and You our potter."[502] Here is God's most important answer, "For all those things My hand has made, and all those things exist, but on this one will I look: On him who is poor and of a contrite spirit, and who trembles at My word."[503]

Is God really saying that without our understanding that He created us, and not realizing our desperate need of Him and rejecting His command to follow His instructions, He also won't see us and won't move His hand to help us? He will not force us to turn to Him, He will look to those of us who look to Him. The prophet Isaiah said it very well, "The hand of the LORD shall be known toward His servants, and His indignation to His enemies".[504]

The prophet Jeremiah described his encounter with God, and that the LORD's hand placed His words in Jeremiah's mouth.[505] He felt the indignation the LORD felt and empathized with Him.[506] The LORD sent Jeremiah to a potter's house as an illustration to Israel to tell them, "Can I not do with you as this potter? Look, as the clay is in the potter's hand, so are you in My hand",[507] meaning Israel is His creation, so He will shape her as He had planned.

But God's judgement was heavy on the people calling themselves priests and prophets who were involved in terrible sins and who lied about Him, saying they heard Him speak through dreams and visions. God said, "I did not send these prophets, yet they have run with their message. I did not speak to them, yet they have prophesied. But if they had stood in my council, they would have proclaimed my words to my people and would have turned them from their evil ways and from their evil deeds."[508]

Does this sound familiar, through some of today's religious experts who preach sin as acceptable or don't preach about the pitfalls of sin at all, or worse yet when they practice sin in secret? "Am I only a God nearby," declares the LORD, "and not a God far away?"[509] God's heart cry is for us to recognize His nearness as our maker and at the same time as God of the universe. Because of the lies of their religious leaders, Jerusalem had become so wicked that God sent Jeremiah to pronounce judgement on them.

We can hear Yahweh's despondent cry as He reminds Jeremiah how He made a covenant with their fathers when He took them by the hand and led them out of slavery. He said, "My covenant which they broke, though I was a husband to them".[510] The LORD is a husband who protects, provides for, and loves in a binding covenant relationship.

The LORD tells us what happens when He lets mankind have their own way without His guidance. They become deranged as we see today. The great city "Babylon hath been a golden cup in the LORD's hand, that made all the earth drunken: the nations have drunken of her wine; therefore the nations are mad."[511]

But He will repay the systems of the ungodly for the sins against His people. He said to Babylon, "Behold, I am against thee, O destroying mountain, which destroyest all the earth. I will stretch out Mine hand upon thee, and roll thee down from the rocks, and will make thee a burnt mountain."[512]

Even to those who look good, God is "standing like an enemy, He has bent His bow. With His right hand, like an adversary, He has slain all who were pleasing to His eye."[513] Dare we come against the one who gives life and causes death, even to nations?

Out of all the people in the Bible, the prophet Ezekiel had some of the strangest encounters with the living God. He described it as the "hand of the Lord". Ezekiel said, "When I looked, there was a hand stretched out to me; and a scroll of a book was in it."[514]

In another experience Ezekiel said, "the Spirit lifted me up and took me away". Here his heart was heavy, and he was angry about the warnings he had to tell the people, "But the hand of the Lord was strong" on him.[515] God's warnings to Israel came through Ezekiel as it did the prophets before him, "I will stretch out My hand upon them and make the land desolate … And they shall know that I am the Lord."[516]

One day Ezekiel sat in his house with other leaders and the hand of the Lord God fell on him. Ezekiel said, "He stretched out the form of a hand, and took me by a lock of my hair; and the Spirit lifted me up between earth and heaven, and brought me in visions of God to Jerusalem, to the door of the north gate of the inner court, where the seat of the image of jealousy was, which provokes to jealousy."[517]

Can you imagine being carried by your hair into another place by God's hand? Then Ezekiel was shown all the perversion and idol worship Jerusalem's priests and leaders were committing through the worship of demon gods.[518]

God told Ezekiel how His hand was against the prophets who preach futility and lies, and He would allow them to speak to their own detriment.[519] God explained that a nations sin would cause Him to stretch His hand against the land through famines killing man and beast.[520] When the people sin against God, their power, authority and favor is diminished and their enemies will take control over the land.

With the same hand God uses to swear an oath, as a legal binding contract like one makes in a courtroom or swears allegiance, God had sworn an oath to His people lifting His hand. His promise was to bring them out of the land of Egypt into a land flowing with milk and honey, which was the best of all lands.[521]

But oh no! God tells Ezekiel that He withdraws His pledge because Israel didn't keep their part of the agreement, instead choosing disobedience and sin. God said He has a reputation to protect His name, that it should not be profaned in the sight of the Gentiles.[522] So He must discipline His people.

The LORD had made another oath when Israel was still in the wilderness, that He would scatter them among the nations. Because when the people saw the high hills and fertile trees where He led them, they began to offer sacrifices to thank their demonic idols instead of the God whose hand delivered them from slavery into the beautiful new land.[523]

Despite all the prophets God sent to warn them, the people of Israel were exiled to Assyria and Babylon. From Assyria, ten of the tribes were scattered throughout the nations with their descendants still unknown to this day. But the tribes of Judah and Benjamin came back from Babylon to reestablish the land. Then over two thousand years ago the Romans conquered Israel and forced them out until recently.

The LORD said, "I stretched out My hand against you, diminished your allotment, and gave you up to the will of those who hate you".[524] Even the daughters of the Philistines were ashamed of Israel's immoral behavior. The LORD told them, "As I live, surely with a mighty hand, with an outstretched arm, and with fury poured out, I will rule over you".[525]

We can see a similarity in the United States, a nation's laws built and united on the Bible's statutes with Jesus as our unifier as evidenced by the words, "In God We Trust". Yet, in recent years we had become the largest exporter of pornography and a vast number of other forms of immorality, even inflicted on our children, teaching the world to worship human flesh instead of God our Creator.

God's covenant with Israel included hard training as it does to everyone who gives Him allegiance as a son or daughter. God's words are timeless. He said, "As I judged your ancestors in the wilderness of the land of Egypt, so I will judge you".[526] "I will take note of you as you pass under my rod, and I will bring you into the bond of the covenant. I will purge you of those who revolt and rebel against me".[527]

Even now, each of us will pass through His inspection to measure our true allegiance. It's important that we search ourselves, to discover our real motives, because God reads our hearts and weighs our works. There are some of us who accept Him outwardly yet refuse Him inwardly. Can a person not know if their beloved truly loves them, more so our God?

If we're not sure, then we can ask Him to search the secrets of our hearts as King David did, admitting that he couldn't read his own real motives and errors.[528] Then there was Jeremiah who said, "The heart is deceitful above all things, and desperately wicked. Who can know it?"[529] If we are truly willing, all we have to do is ask for His forgiveness and accept His cleansing. God is faithful and waiting to help us change our hearts of stone to hearts of flesh and our works from toxic to life-giving.[530]

Many of us have heard the story of Ezekiel and the dry bones. It's about restoring a nation from death to life. Ezekiel said, "The hand of the LORD came upon me and brought me out in the Spirit of the LORD and set me down in the midst of the valley, and it was full of bones".[531]

God told Ezekiel to speak to the dry bones, "Surely I will take the stick of Joseph, which is in the hand of Ephraim, and the tribes of Israel, his companions, and I will join them with the stick of Judah, and make them one stick, and they will be one in My hand."[532] It's interesting to see that the two houses of Israel, will one day become one, but only under God's hand.

It began when Jacob, the son of Isaac and grandson of Abraham, came back to the land God had promised them. Jacob had an encounter with God, who changed his name to Israel.[533] He took his two wives Leah and Rachel, their two maidservants and his thirteen children and divided their households into two companies.[534]

At Israel's death bed, Joseph's son Ephraim, was given the leadership of one camp and received the blessing of many nations.[535] Joseph was the first-born son of Rachel. Leah's fourth son, Judah, had been given leadership of the other camp.[536] God bypassed Leah's three oldest sons whose sins were too grievous. First-born son's rights would carry the rulership and responsibility for the entire tribe, passed from one generation to another as we have seen throughout history with kings. They would become two separate governments, known as the Kingdom of Israel and Kingdom of Judah.

Some believe the story of the two sticks in the LORD's hand are about the full restoration of the children of Israel, by unifying the tribes of Judah and Joseph through the Jews and Christians. Whether this is the meaning, the LORD said all of Israel would be one in His hand. The apostle Paul may have referred to this reunion when he said, "Blindness in part has happened to Israel until the fullness of the Gentiles has come in. And so all Israel will be saved".[537]

The Kingdom of Israel, led through Joseph's descendants, was composed of ten of the tribes that were exiled to Assyria, and history doesn't report them returning to the land of Israel. Although the descendants of Judah, son of Leah, the Jews, returned from Babylon.

The LORD told Ezekiel to tell them, "I will take the Israelites out of the nations where they have gone. I will gather them from all around and bring them back into their own land. I will make them one nation in the land, on the mountains of Israel. There will be one king over all of them and they will never again be two nations or be divided into two kingdoms."[538] "My servant David will be king over them, and they will all have one shepherd. They will follow my laws and be careful to keep my decrees."[539]

God continues these incredible promises, "I will make a covenant of peace with them, it will be an everlasting covenant. I will establish them and increase their numbers, and I will put My sanctuary among them forever. My dwelling place will be with them; I will be their God, and they will be My people. Then the nations will know that I the LORD make Israel holy, when My sanctuary is among them forever."[540]

Going back to the story of the dry bones, it's important to know that the bones didn't come to life until God united them in His hand. God's prophecy to Ezekiel was to a future ruler from Judah's line, God's servant who will rule the entire Kingdom. "The scepter shall not depart from Judah, nor a lawgiver from between his feet, until Shiloh come, and unto him shall the gathering of the people be."[541]

Amazingly the prophecy began to take place as the Jews, the Kingdom of Judah, with the tribe of Benjamin and a portion of Levites, returned to the land of Israel after two-thousand years in 1947.[542] Yet, the whereabouts of the Kingdom of Israel (the House of Ephraim, son of Joseph and the ten tribes) has not been fully known since they were scattered throughout the nations which God said would happen.

But the LORD also tells us the two kingdoms of Israel's family, headed by the tribes of Judah and Ephraim, will become united as one people, and one kingdom with one King.[543] And then, oh what a beautiful promise for eternity, Ezekiel was shown the New City and the New Temple and life in the future under God's government.[544]

Although Israel today has a very small land mass, it's hard to say if God will enlarge the physical territory and adopt Israel's neighbors as part of this new Kingdom to accommodate this huge increase of population, or if this prophecy is a spiritual and interdimensional representation. And there may be another interpretation as the LORD tells us, "I create new heavens and a new earth and the former shall not be remembered, nor come into mind."[545]

In his vision of the future, Ezekiel described a man whose appearance was like the appearance of bronze. He had a line of flax and a measuring rod in His hand, and he stood in the gateway of the city.[546] The man showed him all the measurements of the temple.[547] No wonder, when He was born into the world, Jesus, the Master Builder became a carpenter by trade using His powerful creative hands.

Just as God made a promise to Ezekiel for the future of Israel, His promises can never die and He will be faithful to complete them, regardless of how often His people fall short. The LORD said, "You shall inherit it equally with one another, for I raised My hand in an oath to give it to your fathers, and this land shall fall to you as your inheritance."[548]

The Prophet Daniel adds more insight about God, when he said, "No one can restrain His hand or say to Him, 'What have You done'?"[549] God does what He wants because He knows best.

During Daniel's time, God showed His hand publicly, when His fingers appeared and wrote a judgment on the wall of the palace in Babylon, against the most powerful king of that time.[550] Later a hand touched Daniel which made his knees tremble when he had an encounter with heavenly beings.[551]

The hand that seems so invisible to most of us, was so real to the prophets of old. As when God told Amos, "Though they dig into hell, from there My hand shall take them. Though they climb up to heaven, from there I will bring them down".[552] No one can run from the hand of God.

Incredibly, the prophet Habakkuk had a powerful description of the LORD's hand and saw, "His brightness was like the light. He had rays flashing from His hand, and there His power was hidden".[553]

Yet Zechariah described a man with wounds in these same powerful hands. Someone will ask, "What are these wounds in thine hands? Then he shall answer, those with which I was wounded in the house of My friends".[554] This is a perfect prophecy of Jesus hands nailed to the cross centuries later in His own homeland, Israel.

Some wonder why Father God allowed His Son to be wounded when He said, "'Awake, O sword, against My Shepherd, against the Man who is My Companion', says the LORD of hosts. 'Strike the Shepherd, and the sheep will be scattered, then I will turn My hand against the little ones.'"[555]

This seems like a cruel set up, and God warns us that two thirds of the people will be cut off and die. But the third that is left He will have tested and refined as pure gold and silver. They will call on His Name and He will call them His people and they will say, "the LORD is my God".[556]

I would like to pause here to address a most important point that's often asked about God. Many people don't understand how a loving God can allow so many of His creation to be lost forever. Many of us don't really believe it and churches rarely preach on it. Others have made up their own faith that there are many paths to God, and if we're a "Good Person" in our own opinion, we will go to heaven.

Then there is a popular Christian teaching that if a person believes Jesus is real, they are saved and automatically go to heaven regardless of how much they keep on willfully sinning. But the Bible says even demons believe in Jesus and yet are still bound for eternal destruction.[557] This teaching also doesn't explain why we need to be refined by fire as gold and silver, which are melted down under extreme heat to take out impurities.[558] So, what's the catch? The answers to these questions come from the lips of Jesus Christ, as we search the New Covenant.

HANDS OF JESUS

In the last book of the Old Testament, the prophet Malachi said God would send a messenger who would prepare the way for Him.[559] This messenger was John the Baptist who told his disciples that he came to baptize by water, but one would come after him who would baptize with the Holy Spirit and fire.[560] This is the refiner's fire the prophet Malachi mentioned.[561]

John continued, "His winnowing fan is in His hand, and He will thoroughly clean out His threshing floor, and gather His wheat into the barn, but He will burn up the chaff with unquenchable fire."[562] John was describing people who will be saved and those who won't by the LORD's own hand. The most important word in salvation was the first word recorded by Jesus which was: "REPENT, for the Kingdom of Heaven is at hand."[563] He is still saying it today.

As human beings, we are all prone to focusing mostly on our own needs, especially when it comes to our mortality through sickness in us or our loved ones. Jesus came to set us free after we became captives of the curse of death that began with Adam. Jesus, the Son of God as the second Adam, came down to earth to restore the Kingdom of God and many healing miracles were done through His hands. Here are just a few of them:

Peter's mother-in-law was sick; Jesus touched her hand and the fever left.[564]

Jesus walked on the waters of the sea toward the boat his disciples were in, and Peter got out to meet Him, but he became afraid and began to sink. Jesus stretched out His hand and caught Peter, then said to him, "O you of little faith, why did you doubt?"[565]

A leper asked Jesus if he was willing to heal him. Jesus stretched out His hand, touched him and said, "I am willing, be cleansed."[566]

A man, deaf and mute, was brought to Jesus. His friends begged Jesus to put His hand on him. Jesus put His fingers in the man's ears, He spit and touched his tongue, and the man was healed.[567]

There was a blind man Jesus took by the hand and led him out of the town. He then spit on the man's eyes, put His hands on him, and the man's eyes were healed.[568]

A father brought his mute son to Jesus, the boy also had violent seizures. The father repented of unbelief, and Jesus cast out a deaf and dumb spirit, leaving the boy lifeless. But Jesus lifted him up by the hand and the boy was healed. Jesus told His disciples this kind of demon could only be cast out through prayer and fasting, but do we also notice a key here was the repentance by the father.[569]

The hand of Jesus even raises the dead. A synagogue ruler with tremendous faith came to Jesus and told him his daughter had just died. He asked Jesus to come and lay His hand on her, believing she would live.[570] Jesus followed him home and went to the dead girl, took her by the hand, and she rose up.[571]

These are only a few recorded healing miracles Jesus did with His powerful hands. Others were performed just by His words. As I mentioned before, the apostle John wrote about Jesus that there were so many amazing works, the world couldn't contain enough books to document them.[572]

RIGHT OR LEFT?

The next few scriptures describe sitting at the LORD's right hand or left hand. Let's explore what this means. Jesus said to the mother of two of His disciples, that the decision of who would sit at His right or left hand, was up to Father God.[573] "The LORD said to the Lord, 'Sit at My right hand, until I make Your enemies Your footstool.'"[574]

There is a most glorious and the most terrifying future event to come: "When the Son of Man comes in His glory, and all the holy angels with Him, then He will sit on the throne of His glory. All the nations will be gathered before Him, and He will separate them one from another, as a shepherd divides his sheep from the goats. And He will set the sheep on His right hand, but the goats on the left."[575]

"Then the King will say to those on His right hand, 'Come, you blessed of My Father, inherit the kingdom prepared for you from the foundation of the world.'" "Then He will say to those on His left hand, 'Depart from Me, you cursed, into the everlasting fire prepared for the devil and his angels'".[576]

It surprises me that in political circles today, those who profess to believe God are called "the Right" and those against Him are called "the Left". The LORD won't need to do much sorting as individuals are already choosing sides for themselves to be for or against Him. Oh foolish man! How little you understand the choices we make today stand for eternity.

When Jesus stood on trial before the ruling priests, the High Priest said to Him, "I put You under oath by the living God, tell us if You are the Christ, the Son of God!" Jesus answered, "It is as you said. Nevertheless, I say to you, hereafter you will see the Son of Man sitting at the right hand of the power and coming on the clouds of heaven."[577] The priests felt this was the highest affront blaspheming God, so they sent Jesus to the Romans who twisted a crown of thorns for His head and put a reed for a scepter in His right hand of authority to mock Him.[578]

The last to have seen Jesus in His earthly form were His disciples who watched as He was received up to heaven to sit at the right hand of God. What a glorious sight![579]

The right hand symbolizes the closest and greatest place of honor. Before the wedding vows are said, the bride stands on the left side of a man, but once they are pronounced married, they both turn around and she now stands at the right hand of her husband. So it is with God the Father: His Son Jesus is at His right hand.[580] Those called to be the bride of Christ will be at the right hand of Jesus.

After His resurrection, His closest disciple Peter told the people in Jerusalem that Yahweh God had exalted Jesus to His right hand, "to be Prince and Savior and give repentance to Israel for the forgiveness of sins."[581]

The disciple Stephen, while being stoned to death by the Pharisees for perceived blasphemy said, "Look, I see the heavens opened and the Son of Man standing on the right hand of God!"[582] God the Father is the one who raised Jesus from the dead and "we have such a high priest, who is set on the right hand of the throne of the Majesty in the heavens."[583]

After Jesus had offered His life as the only sacrifice worthy and able to conquer sin and death forever, He took His place and sat down at the right hand of God.[584] We can now look to Jesus as the author and finisher of our faith. He knew the joy that would follow after He endured the public torture and death at the cross and earned His rightful place at the right hand of the throne of God.[585]

The Bible tells us we now have a clear conscience because of Jesus Christ, "who is gone into heaven and is on the right hand of God, angels and authorities and powers being made subject unto Him."[586]

In his vision, the apostle John saw the throne in heaven with four living creatures and twenty-four elders bowing before our great God.[587] The Lamb who was slain, symbolic of Jesus Christ, was the only one in all of creation worthy to take the scroll of judgments out of God's hand to unseal it and release what is to come.[588]

How do we discern these strange and wonderful, yet terrifying scriptures of God's hands? First, we are shown the comparisons of sitting on the right or left of God. The Father is the final judge who decides where we will spend eternity.[589] Those on His right will be accepted, and those on His left will be destroyed.

Jesus sits at the right hand of the Father and His sheep, those who follow Him, will be on the right side of Jesus. The goats, those who selfishly continue to build their own kingdom, will go on His left. On the right hand are the blessed who inherit the Kingdom of God, on the left is hell with the devil and his demons.[590]

So how can we make sure that God places us on His right hand? Jesus gave His disciples the answer when they asked this same question. He said, "You know that the rulers of the Gentiles lord it over them, and their high officials exercise authority over them. Not so with you. Instead, whoever wants to become great among you must be your servant, and whoever wants to be first must be your slave. Just as the Son of Man did not come to be served, but to serve, and to give His life as a ransom for many."[591]

Here are two living examples of being on the right hand of God and the left. The first is of the disciples telling people the good news of Jesus. "The Lord's hand was with them, and a great number of people believed and turned to the Lord."[592] The second is a story of a sorcerer trying to turn an official away from faith in Jesus.[593] Paul said to him, "Now the hand of the Lord is against you. You are going to be blind for a time, not even able to see the light of the sun." "Immediately mist and darkness came over him, and he groped about, seeking someone to lead him by the hand."[594]

When we've made the choice to trust Jesus, His promises are sure and He tells us, "I give unto them eternal life; and they shall never perish, neither shall any man pluck them out of my hand. My Father, which gave them me, is greater than all, and no man is able to pluck them out of my Father's hand."[595] This is wonderful! He holds all who believe and trust in Him, in His hand.

POWER OF THE RIGHT

What is the power of His right hand? The Book of Revelation reveals great insight about the spiritual nature of God's character and awesomeness of who He is.

The apostle John described an encounter he had with heaven. He saw the Son of Man, Jesus, holding seven stars in His right hand.

The terror of the Lord was so strong that when John saw Him, he fell at His feet like he was dead. But Jesus laid His right hand on John and told him not to be afraid saying, "I am the First and the Last." "The seven stars are the angels of the seven churches, and the seven candlesticks are the seven churches." Then Jesus instructed John to write His words of promises and warnings to each church.[596]

Recently I've heard people teaching about heavenly visitations where visitors say they are allowed to spend time with the Father and Son. But Yahweh God told Moses, "You cannot see My face, for no man shall see Me, and live."[597] However there have been recorded heavenly encounters with the Son during death experiences, where the flesh has died, and the spirit is allowed to visit until returned to the body. Yet I don't recall any of them seeing the face of the Father. But I don't want to discount anything God does, since the apostle Paul wrote that he had visits to heaven and heard inexpressible things that he wasn't allowed to speak about.[598]

In the Book of Revelations, John describes the terror of "Him that sat on the throne that liveth forever and ever". Even the four living creatures and the twenty-four elders can only worship Him saying, "Holy, Holy, Holy".[599] Moses, Daniel, Isaiah, John and all the people of Israel couldn't endure God's holiness on their own.[600] In my personal encounters with God, I was not able to see Him and felt as if I would die even at the close encounter of His presence. This is not because He wishes harm to us, but only because our corrupted human flesh cannot survive the perfection of His absolute holiness.

John continued that he saw a scroll in the right hand of Him who sat on the throne, with writing on the inside and back, sealed with seven seals. "In the midst of the throne and the four living creatures and elders, stood a Lamb as though it had been slain. He came and took the scroll out of the right hand of Him who sat on the throne." The Lamb was the only one found in all of heaven worthy to open the seals of judgement.[601] John was to be a witness to all the events of the judgements written on the scrolls, to warn the nations even to this day.

Later John wrote, "I looked, and behold a white cloud, and on the cloud sat One like the Son of Man, having on His head a golden crown, and in His hand a sharp sickle." An angel came out of the temple, shouting to Him who sat on the cloud, "Thrust in Your sickle and reap, for the time has come for You to reap, for the harvest of the earth is ripe". [602]

This tells about the end time harvest where some of us are destined for eternal life, others for hell where there is weeping and eternal destruction.[603]. We each have a choice. Where do we want to spend eternity? The price is extremely high either way: one offers his life to God during our time here on earth, and the other to himself and to Satan.

When the books are opened on Judgement Day, where do we think we will spend eternity?[604] Being a "Good Person" in our own self-centered estimation doesn't come close to God's design and expectations for us. Only surrendering our authority to our King is sufficient to be a part of His people and His loyal army.

I must add this additional warning from John's revelation. He tells us about the worship of the end time beast. Whoever receives his mark on their right hand or forehead will share in the punishment of the evildoers as they are marked as belonging to the beast. It will be challenging for all, as no one can buy or sell without the mark.[605]

But then we must remember the promises to those who keep the commandments of God and faith in Jesus:[606] "Blessed are the dead who die in the Lord from now on. Yes, says the Spirit, that they may rest from their labors, and their works follow them."[607]

MIGHTY FINGER OF GOD

Most of us have seen pictures of the powerful rendition painted by Michelangelo on the ceiling of the Vatican in Rome. In it, God the Creator is surrounded by the Hosts of Heaven, bringing life to Adam through the touch of His finger. God's power is as close as His fingertips. With it, He brings life and with it He brings death, in judgments as He did during the time of Moses with the ten plagues that came down in Egypt.[608]

After the people of Israel were finally set free to leave Egypt, they needed a new system of government to live by. So, Yahweh wrote a simple system "by the finger of God" on two tablets of stone, still known to us as His irrevocable "Ten Commandments".[609]

King David wrote in the Book of Psalms that God created everything with His fingers: "When I consider Your heavens, the work of Your fingers, the moon and the stars which You have ordained."[610]

This same finger reached down and wrote a personal judgement against Babylon's King Belshazzar to whom God had given rulership over the entire known world. In his arrogance, this king dared to humiliate Yahweh by using the holy ceremonial articles of gold and silver his father, the previous king, had confiscated from Yahweh's temple in Jerusalem. Belshazzar wanted to impress a drunken party of one thousand lords, wives, and concubines to eat and drink from the holy cups and plates. He even brought out Israel's golden lampstand, the Temple menorah, and then used them to worship idols of gold and silver.[611]

Yahweh responded by physically writing on the wall with His own finger, for everyone to see. The prophet Daniel was brought in to interpret the words for the terrified king which were, "MENE: God has numbered the days of your reign and brought it to an end. TEKEL: You have been weighed on the scales and found wanting. PERES: Your kingdom is divided and given to the Medes and Persians."[612]

Yes, God always rules the affairs of mankind and even allows the ungodly to rule over His people and bring them to repentance. That very night King Belshazzar was killed, and the Medes and Persians took control of his kingdom[613] This is an excellent reminder to all of us, whether we are believers or not, God's laws are still in effect.

Years later we see the Messiah, God who came down in the flesh, use His fingers to finish a job of creation. Jesus put His fingers in a deaf man's ears and commanded them to open. He then used His spit to touch the man's tongue which was loosened, because the man also had a speech impediment.[614] Soon after that, Jesus touched a blind man's eyes to make them see. He explains that He casts out demons using the finger of God.[615]

In another story, Jesus used His finger of authority to write in the sand after a group of men, seeking to test Him, brought out a woman caught in adultery with the intent to stone her to death. Jesus made His famous one-line speech, "He that is without sin among you, let him first cast a stone at her." All her accusers left having the good sense to know that every one of them had broken God's laws. Perhaps Jesus was recording their sins, or He may have been entering the woman's name in the Book of Life. Then the judge of all creation told her there was no one left to accuse her, and He wouldn't either. He said, "Go and sin no more".[616]

Jesus said to the people remaining, "I AM the light of the world", and those who follow Him "shall have the light of life".[617] Yeshua is that light, the golden lampstand, the only way we can be saved since without Him, we cannot see our way out of the darkness.

SHOULDERS OF STRENGTH

When we were little children, some of us were fortunate to have a father who put us on his broad shoulders to see over a crowd, or just to make us feel like we were on top of the world. For just that moment in time, we felt the strength, power, and authority of being so honored and one with our father. So it is with our heavenly Father God as He lifts us up on His shoulders of immortality.

How will He lift us up? The prophet Isaiah tells us, "Unto us a child is born, unto us a Son is given, and the government will be upon His shoulder. Of the increase of His government and peace there will be no end".[618] This is a promise written eight hundred years before the birth of Jesus, about the One who was to come through the genealogy of the throne of David who would judge with perfect justice, forevermore. He alone has the keys of authority to shut and to open.[619]

How does this apply to us? As we accept Yeshua, the Son of God (the earthly image of our Father), we are adopted as God's children, sealed in His blood that was offered at the cross, and redeemed us from sin. As a child of God, we are given the Father's strength, power, and authority. When He walks, leads, and carries us on His shoulders, we move as one with Him to establish His government on earth as it is in Heaven. Again, this is a personal choice for each of us and demands long-term discipline on our part.

The apostle Paul gives us a warning not to appoint an inexperienced person in leadership for the church. This is also sound advice in business, politics, or family life. He said, "Not a novice, lest being puffed up with pride he fall into the same condemnation as the devil".[620] This is a serious problem in all leadership today, because so many in modern times, have drifted away from God's wisdom, puffing themselves up in self-importance, assuming God's place as the expert in all.

The Bible contains instructions how we are to govern by carrying out His will here on earth. This world would be absolutely amazing if each of us allowed our heavenly Father to carry us by accepting Jesus as our King and following His laws of instructions!

An example and a compassionate reference to God's broad shoulders is in the story where Jesus tells of a man who'll leave his ninety-nine sheep to go after the one who is lost. Then when he finds it, he places it on his shoulders. Not only are His shoulders a place of authority but also of safety and rescue. Jesus was talking about Himself, and when we are His, He will stop at nothing to rescue us and carry us home when we've lost our way, which each of us either already have or will face at one time or another.[621]

SHADOW OF HIS WINGS

There are so many stories, pictures, poems, songs, and even dreams of angels with wings. Most of us believe them to be true. But do we know the Bible describes God having wings?

One of the great men of Israel, Boaz, told the foreign woman Ruth who worked in his fields, that because of her hard work, moral lifestyle, and loyalty to the mother of her dead husband, she had found shelter under the wings of the God of Israel and she would receive a full reward.[622] Boaz later married Ruth and they became the grandparents of King David, and the forebearers of Yeshua of Nazareth, the promised Messiah Jesus Christ.[623]

The Bible also mentions the shadow of God's wings, offering us guidance and protection when we put our trust in Him. A mother eagle begins to dismantle her nest to encourage her young to fly off when they're old enough. But she keeps an eye on them, spreading out her wings to catch them while they are still weak, as the LORD does with His people.[624]

Even knowing his many wrong doings, faults and weaknesses, King David understood the shadow of God's wings as a place of mercy, rescue, and peace. He said, "How precious is Your lovingkindness, O God! Therefore, the children of men put their trust under the shadow of Your wings".[625] "Be merciful to me, O God, be merciful to me! For my soul trusts in You. And in the shadow of Your wings, I will make my refuge until these calamities have passed by".[626] "I will abide in Your tabernacle forever, I will trust in the shelter of Your wings."[627]

"He shall cover you with His feathers, and under His wings you shall take refuge. His truth shall be your shield and buckler."[628] This verse is a most wonderful promise to us when we find ourselves overwhelmed with trouble that we can't sustain on our own. It promises that we are hidden in Him and protected by His words. His truth is that ALL our fear means nothing, and false accusations are only lies.

We get in trouble and become weak when we accept lies as truth about ourselves. F E A R is "False Evidence Appearing Real". But when we sincerely believe God and His promises, we can remain in His truth and live under the full protection, provision, and power of His wings.

How sincere is God? Well, Jesus sat on a hill looking over the city of Jerusalem, and sorrowfully said, "O Jerusalem, Jerusalem ... How often I wanted to gather your children together, as a hen gathers her chicks under her wings, but you were not willing!"[629]

Like a perfect loving father, God wants each of us to come under His wings of complete protection and well-being. But because we don't trust Him enough, most of us keep trying to fix things ourselves. Like little chicks out of their mother's protection, we become bait to an assortment of predators in the natural and spiritual world. They pretend to offer what only God the Father, His Son, and Holy Spirit can give, yet instead they plunder us in the process. Be careful little children!

Throughout the written history of Israel, many have come against the land and the people God has claimed as His own. How futile are the plans of mortal men? Those who opposed God in the past are all dead and their short-lived empires returned to dust. Yet in arrogance, those of a new generation continue to try, empowered by the LORD's arch enemies. As with generations before us, God still laughs at the pitiful power-grabbing plans of foolish mortal men.[630]

The prophet Malachi explained God's intense faithfulness when we come under His wings with reverence and respect. "To you that fear My name shall the Sun of righteousness arise with healing in His wings, and ye shall go forth, and grow up as calves of the stall."[631] Healthy, safe, and well taken care of.

Lastly, oh, how pleasurable to hear the passionate declarations of these words of love expressed by Yahweh for His people Israel. "When I passed by you again and looked upon you, indeed your time was the time of love, so I spread My wing over you and covered your nakedness. Yes, I swore an oath to you and entered into a covenant with you, and you became Mine," says the LORD God.[632]

This is the absolute perfect marriage covenant and union between the Creator and His creation. A true husband who cannot lie, nor break His promises.[633] Can anyone be more in love than that? He fills His people with His unending presence. When we choose Him, we are His Temple, HE IS OUR GOD![634]

Knowing this truth, why wouldn't everyone want to come under the wings of this amazing love-struck God? No one needs to be left out. Entering a love relationship is always a choice, as He will not force Himself on anyone. We each have a choice to say, "I DO".

Come make your decision today and say "Yes" to Him. When you surrender to God's love, His Spirit will overshadow you and live in you, saturating every part of your mind, body, and soul. You will be filled with the Spirit of God Himself and your life will be transformed in the process called "Born Again,"[635] forever living in the shelter of God's spiritual wings. Yes, Yes, LORD!

We are given an earthly taste of this Holy Spirit union in the love between a man and a woman. This human relationship is so intimate in mind, body, and soul that God gave us instructions to keep it pure and defend it as holy. Many find it in marriage, but miss out on the union with God, which can lead people who do not know this intimacy with the Holy Spirit, prone to the frailty of human passion only. Without God, our earthly, selfish desires often limit the sacrificial surrender required of each person in a perfect union.

Without fully knowing God's law of love, humans can go so far astray that some look for this holy union in all the wrong places and are then easily led to infidelity and immorality. We should consider the separation from God as the main cause of sexual impurity and addictions.

In adultery and betrayal, people look for someone else to fill the void for spiritual intimacy which only God can satisfy. Some men longing for the Spirit of God seek intimacy with other men to draw closer to Father God. Likewise, women needing the intimacy of the love of the mother's heart look for it in the comfort of other women. God's heart is both male and female. King David wrote, "When my father and my mother forsake me, then the Lord will take care of me." [636]

Or they look for that necessary spiritual infilling with multiple sexual partners, drugs, or alcohol. But as that old Rolling Stones song says, "I Can't Get No Satisfaction". When the union with the Holy Spirit is missing, our human spirits are lacking and desperately longing to be under the wings of God, as He is our spiritual father, mother, and spouse to cover and fill us.[637]

The saddest thing is that instead of fulfilling us, sexual immorality can lead to a death sentence, including disease. I was recently told that some (supposed) Bible scholars are teaching Sodom and

Gomorrah's sin was their lack of hospitality. But the book of Jude tells us plainly their destruction was for sexual perversion, "As Sodom and Gomorrah, and the cities around them ... having given themselves over to sexual immorality and gone after strange flesh, are set forth as an example, suffering the vengeance of eternal fire".[638]

The men in those cities were so sexually and violently obsessed that all of them, of every age, gathered to rape the two angels whom God had sent as two witnesses against them, to determine their guilt. This sealed their fate, and both cities were completely destroyed as a warning to all people throughout history.[639] Do we dare presume God won't do the same as our children are being taught that sexual deviance is acceptable, even in many schools?

But there is a way out for each of us suffering addictions and unhealthy attractions. Again, we can read the promises of Psalm 91 to remember, "He shall cover you with His feathers, and under His wings you shall take refuge. His truth shall be your shield and buckler."[640] It will not be easy, because it takes trust and commitment, but when we surrender ourselves and accept the Holy Spirit of God, we are then hidden under His wings of refuge against the devil's seduction which tempts our every weakness.

It's important to know and remember the promise of what Jesus did for us. Isaiah tells us, "He was wounded for our transgressions, He was bruised for our iniquities. The chastisement for our peace was upon Him, and by His stripes we are healed."[641] It means the crucifixion of Jesus covered our crimes against the Father. He took on our weaknesses and replaced our spiritual punishment with peace, and with every stripe of the whip that He bore for us, we are healed.

Please receive these most wonderful gifts our Savior gives to every one of us covered under His wings. All you have to do to start, is to confess your sins asking Him to forgive you, then give your life to Jesus Christ as Lord and invite the Shadow of God, the Holy Spirit in. If you really mean it, you will be a new creation,[642] born of the Spirit, "and the peace of God, which passeth all understanding, shall keep your hearts and minds through Christ Jesus."[643]

There was a time I was asked to lead an intercessory team in prayer for a worship conference. For two days I spent most of the time in prayer. Then when the worship began, I felt a shadow in me, that was independent of myself. I realized at that time, this was the shadow of the Holy Spirit, the shadow of His Wings.[644]

If we really believe this three-dimensional world is all there is, we are blind. This is only a shadow of things to come. True reality is that we are spirit beings, in temporary bodies of clay. We have a choice to do this life alone or in union with the Spirit of God.

LEGS AS MARBLE PILLARS

The reference to God's legs is in the Song of Solomon, where they are described as "Pillars of marble set upon sockets of fine gold."[645] Even today, we see ruins of buildings still standing because of the strength, durability, and resistance of marble to corrosion. And we all know the value of gold as an incorruptible element which can change shape but always keeps its same properties without rust or tarnish.

In the New Testament we read about Jesus, as the representation of God in human form, hanging on the cross with a criminal on either side. The soldiers were instructed to break their legs to hasten the prisoner's deaths by suffocation. But when they came to Jesus, they saw His mortal body was already dead, so they did not break His legs. Centuries before Jesus was born, King David prophesied about the crucifixion, "all my bones are out of joint" but none of Jesus' bones were broken.[646]

PLACE OF HIS FEET

The first clue we are given about God's feet is in the book of Genesis, "In the Beginning". It describes the first humans, Adam and Eve, hearing the sound of the LORD God walking in the Garden.[647]

Moses was invited to bring seventy elders of the people of Israel to Yahweh's holy Mount Sinai. After much preparation, they saw the God of Israel and ate in His presence. But there is no description given about Him except Moses tells us, "They saw the God of Israel:

and there was under His feet as it were a paved work of a sapphire stone, and as it were the body of heaven in His clearness."[648]

Centuries later, the prophet Daniel also recorded his visitation from the LORD where he saw God in the form of a man and said, "His arms and His feet like in color to polished brass."[649]

Later still, after Jesus had ascended to Heaven, the apostle John saw Him in a vision. John described Him as "One like the Son of Man, clothed with a garment down to the feet and girded about the chest with a golden band." "His feet like fine brass."[650] Like Daniel five hundred years before, John tells us his encounter with the Lord nearly killed him: "When I saw him, I fell at his feet as dead."[651]

God revealed Himself to the prophet Samuel, as "He bowed the Heavens also, and came down, and darkness was under His feet" [652] trampling on every hidden evil. He will always have victory over His enemies.

The book of Nahum reflects the justice of the LORD. "The LORD is slow to anger, and great in power, and will not at all acquit the wicked. The LORD hath His way in the whirlwind and in the storm, and the clouds are the dust of His feet."[653] "Before Him went pestilence, and burning coals went forth at His feet."[654] His power is so great, without His favor we are completely helpless. But to stay under His protection we must be faithful to Him.

In the book of Psalms, the writer asks God to "Lift up Thy feet" to the destruction the enemy has caused.[655] The expression of placing one's feet is used in the Bible to show where a person occupies that place. God said about His Temple, "This is the place of My throne and the place of the soles of My feet, where I will dwell in the midst of the children of Israel forever.[656]

For God's people, He promises the same authority and rulership on earth as He said, "The glory of Lebanon shall come to you, to beautify the place of My sanctuary. And I will make the place of My feet glorious. The sons of those who afflicted you shall come bowing to you, and all those who despised you shall fall prostrate at the soles of your feet. And they shall call you The City of the LORD, Zion of the Holy One of Israel".[657]

Often encounters with the Lord would cause people to worship at His feet. Those who recognized His godly authority feared Jesus and fell at His feet as Jairus, the ruler of a synagogue did, for mercy to heal his daughter.[658] Then a non-Jewish woman, whose young daughter had an unclean spirit heard about Jesus, and she also came to Him and fell at His feet. Jesus healed her daughter because of the woman's true faith in Him.[659]

One of the greatest stories of worship and redemption happened to a man possessed by a legion of demons. But he still had enough of his own strength to fall down before Jesus. After Jesus cast the many demons out of the man into a herd of pigs, the amazed people found him sitting at the feet of Jesus, completely sane.[660]

Then there is the story of the ten lepers who were healed after meeting Jesus, and only one came back glorifying God; he fell on his face at Jesus feet giving Him thanks.[661]

Often great multitudes came to Him bringing the lame, blind, mute, maimed, and many others who were sick, laying them down at Jesus' feet, and He healed them.[662]

When a beloved young man named Lazarus died, his sister, Mary fell down at Jesus' feet and said, "Lord, if You had been here, my brother would not have died."[663] She knew His authority and power to heal, then threw herself at His mercy. Jesus called Lazarus to come out of the tomb, even though he had been dead for four days. Lazarus came out, alive and well! [664]

The Bible also uses the term to "sit at His feet" as a picture of learning about God's laws and ways. Mary sat at the feet of Jesus to listen to His teaching, which He described as the best thing for Mary to do.[665]

In the ancient Middle East, foot washing was an important practice since most people walked on dry, dusty roads. Offering guests water to wash their feet was a normal custom of hospitality. So it was when Abraham greeted the three men who came to his tent, and he acknowledged one of them as Lord. "My Lord, if I have found favor in Your sight, do not pass by Your servant. Please let a little water be brought to wash Your feet and rest yourselves under the tree".[666]

Two thousand years later, one of the most heartfelt stories of the Lord's feet is the story of the woman washing Jesus' feet with her tears and wiping them with her hair. She kissed and anointed them with fragrant expensive oil. It was an act of perfect love and humility.[667] Jesus explained to the Pharisee, His host, "Her sins, which are many, are forgiven; for she loved much: but to whom little is forgiven, the same loveth little. And He said unto her, thy sins are forgiven."[668] Do you know, your sins and my sins, no matter how many, are completely forgiven when we love Jesus and repent through our actions?

Then at the last supper, one of Jesus' final acts on earth was to wash His disciple's feet. He said, "If I then, your Lord and Master, have washed your feet, ye also ought to wash one another's feet."[669] Again the example of God in the flesh, asking us to humble ourselves as He did, serving and loving one another.

In the natural, God's Holy Spirit descended on His Son, Yeshua, to be the light of the world.[670] Instead of accepting God's light, the religious leaders had Jesus convicted and executed by a slow death on the Roman cross, hung with nails through His hands and feet. They were the hands and feet of God in human flesh.

One of King David's songs centuries before foretold this would happen to the Messiah. David prophesied, "You lay Me in the dust of death. Dogs surround Me, a pack of villains encircles Me, they pierce My hands and My feet. All My bones are on display, people stare and gloat over Me."[671]

But death couldn't kill Him, and the grave couldn't hold Him. When two of the women went to Jesus' tomb to prepare His body with the necessary herbs and spices for burial, they met an Angel who told them "He is risen". His body was gone! As they ran back to tell His disciples, Jesus met them, and they held Him by His feet and worshiped Him. Then Jesus said to them, "Be not afraid: go tell my brethren, I am going into Galilee, and there shall they see me."[672]

The apostle Paul tells us, the Father "Hath put all things under his feet, and gave Him to be the head over all things to the church, which is His body, the fullness of Him that filleth all in all." "He left nothing that is not put under Him."[673]

The prophecy of Zechariah five hundred years before Jesus, explains what will happen at His second coming. "I will pour on the house of David and on the inhabitants of Jerusalem the Spirit of grace and supplication, then they will look on Me whom they pierced. Yes, they will mourn for Him as one mourns for his only son and grieve for Him as one grieves for a firstborn." "In that day His feet will stand on the Mount of Olives, which faces Jerusalem on the east. The Mount of Olives shall be split in two."[674]

Finally, Isaiah tells us, "How beautiful upon the mountains are the feet of Him who brings good news, who proclaims peace, who brings glad tidings of good things, who proclaims salvation, who says to Zion, 'Your God Reigns!'"[675]

CHAPTER FOUR

The Character of God

VOICE OF THE LORD

"In the beginning God created the heaven and the earth. And the earth was without form, and void, and darkness was upon the face of the deep. And the Spirit of God moved upon the face of the waters. And God said, 'Let there be light' and there was light. And God saw the light, that it was good: and God divided the light from the darkness. And God called the light Day, and the darkness he called Night."[676]

This is the beginning of the Bible when God's voice boomed across the great void of darkness and sparked all Creation with the sound of the voice of the LORD.

A few years ago, I spoke with an expert in sound-recording. He said that sound causes vibration which in turn produces light. Vibration is how sound travels through tiny wires and is captured by signal to produce images we see on television or computers.

Because God is the author of Life, when He spoke, His voice created a living vibration of light which we are each a part of. It's too amazing for us to grasp that we are all living images created by God's thoughts, His plans, and His voice. King David wrote, "Your eyes saw my substance, being yet unformed. And in Your book, they all were written, the days fashioned for me, when as yet there were none of them."[677]

The first time the LORD's voice is recorded speaking to mankind was after He finished creation and He gave the man, Adam, the command of what to eat and what not to eat. God told Adam, "Of every tree of the garden you may freely eat, but of the tree of the knowledge of good and evil you shall not eat, for in the day that you eat of it you shall surely die."[678]

Then later after Eve was fashioned from Adam's rib, they both disobeyed God and ate from the forbidden fruit.[679] God called on Adam, "Where are you?"[680] Like most disobedient children, they knew they were in trouble. Adam replied, "I heard Your voice in the garden, and I was afraid because I was naked, and I hid myself."[681]

The rest of the story is extremely sad as the world's first parents were cast out of Eden to toil the land as we still do today.[682] It can make us wonder how beautiful and perfect Earth would have been if temptation and sin hadn't entered in.

Through the generations of Adam and Eve's children, others would hear the voice of the LORD. And finally, God spoke to a man named Abraham to give him a new promise for humanity after a great cost of testing. God said to him, "In your seed all the nations of the earth shall be blessed, because you have obeyed My voice."[683]

Later still, God told Abraham's son Isaac that the blessing would be continued through his lineage.[684] Then God passed that blessing to Isaac's son, Jacob, and his descendants, who became the nation of Israel.[685]

A few generations later, there is the famous story of Moses and the talking bush. "There appeared to him in the wilderness of Mount Sinai an Angel of the LORD in a flame of fire in a bush … The voice of the LORD came unto him, saying, 'I am the God of thy fathers, the God of Abraham, and the God of Isaac, and the God of Jacob.'"[686]

Yahweh God directed Moses to go to Egypt and tell Pharoah to "Let My people go that they may hold a feast to Me in the wilderness".[687] Pharoah questioned Moses, "Who is the LORD, that I should obey His voice to let Israel go? I do not know the LORD, nor will I let Israel go."[688] But God forced Pharoah's hand by sending ten plagues until God's people were released permanently.[689]

After the Israelites left Egypt, Moses led them through the desert to Mount Sinai, where they met the God of Israel. "There was thunder and lightning, with a thick cloud over the mountain, and a very loud trumpet blast. Everyone in the camp trembled. Then Moses led the people out of the camp to meet with God, and they stood at the foot of the mountain. Mount Sinai was covered with smoke because the LORD descended on it in fire. The smoke billowed up from it like smoke from a furnace, and the whole mountain trembled violently."[690]

"As the sound of the trumpet grew louder and louder, Moses spoke, and the voice of God answered him. The LORD descended to the top of Mount Sinai and called Moses to the top of the mountain. Moses went up and the LORD said to him, 'Go down and warn the people so they do not force their way through to see the LORD and many of them perish.'"[691] We should each be warned, that even the priests had to cleanse themselves at the risk of death as we should all do.

Earlier while wandering through the desert, Moses had told the people Yahweh's words: "If you diligently heed the voice of the LORD your God and do what is right in His sight, give ear to His commandments and keep all His statutes, I will put none of the diseases on you which I have brought on the Egyptians. For I am the LORD who heals you".[692] This is an incredible message from our LORD. He promises healing if we obey His voice and keep the instructions given to Moses that are still written in our Bibles today.

COMMANDMENTS OF GOD

What are those instructions? Ten of them were written by Yahweh's own finger on Mount Sinai and given to Moses to bring to the people.[693] This was the first day of Pentecost. The Ten Commandments written on two stone tablets were God's marriage contract. The people of Israel were chosen to be the stewards of His prenuptial agreement with the human race.

The contract terms were:

1. I am the Lord your God, who brought you out of Egypt, out of the land of slavery. You shall have no other gods before me.[694]
2. You shall not make for yourself an image in the form of anything in heaven above or on the earth beneath or in the waters below. You shall not bow down to them or worship them; for I, the

Lord your God, am a jealous God, punishing the children for the sin of the parents to the third and fourth generation of those who hate me, but showing love to a thousand generations of those who love me and keep my commandments."[695]

3. You shall not misuse the name of the LORD your God, for the LORD will not hold anyone guiltless who misuses his name."[696]

4. Remember the Sabbath day by keeping it holy. Six days you shall labor and do all your work, but the seventh day is a sabbath to the LORD your God. On it you shall not do any work, neither you, nor your son or daughter, nor your male or female servant, nor your animals, nor any foreigner residing in your towns. For in six days the LORD made the heavens and the earth, the sea, and all that is in them, but He rested on the seventh day. Therefore the LORD blessed the Sabbath day and made it holy.[697]

5. Honor your father and your mother, so that you may live long in the land the LORD your God is giving you.[698]

6. You shall not murder.[699]

7. You shall not commit adultery.[700]

8. You shall not steal.[701]

9. You shall not give false testimony against your neighbor.[702]

10. You shall not covet your neighbor's house. You shall not covet your neighbor's wife, or his male or female servant, his ox or donkey, or anything that belongs to your neighbor.[703]

Later Moses was given a total of six hundred and thirteen laws listed in more detail in the Book of Leviticus.[704] Several were to explain how to keep the basic ten for our health and safety. It's important to keep God's laws to maintain right order, but we must also acknowledge that some of them we may not always have control over in today's modern society.

More importantly, we must remember that all life is a learning process, and we all fall short at times. We need to be gracious with one another while doing our best to achieve God's holiness. Jesus came to pay the price of our mistakes when we miss the mark (sin) of keeping His perfect laws.

In a smaller example of missing the mark of His holiness, Christian teachers often claim we are free from God's dietary laws of abstaining from eating pork and shellfish. Yet these animals are scavengers and science has proven pigs are a toxic meat. Shellfish feed at the bottom of rivers, lakes, and ocean floors. God calls these foods unclean, meaning they are unhealthy for human consumption.[705] The people of the Middle East don't eat these foods, and have the lowest rate of cancers. We would be wise to listen to God and abstain, since many people professing to believe the Bible also get cancer and other diseases that God said we shouldn't have.[706]

In larger examples, we see the devastation of relationships in the aftermath of sexual sins God told us to avoid. In these modern times, included in these sins are sex outside of marriage without a father's blessing,[707] multiple sexual partners, pornography, fornication, adultery, homosexuality, child molestation, incest and other behaviors deviating from healthy biblical norms.[708]

Whenever we stray from God's laws of righteousness, we end in worse sin. Until we finally submit to killing our weakest, by aborting our children, and euthanizing our elders and disabled. We even agree to launching selfish wars on weaker nations for financial strength. We use our human selfish logic to justify these as merciful and accepted by God. But what part of shedding innocent blood do we not understand that the LORD hates?[709] How do we dare beg Him to heal us, after we have rolled in the stench of death like a dog? There is no salvation without repentance, which means we need to stop our sins and ask forgiveness.[710]

As a child of God, we are each called to be watchmen to the people around us. Yes, God does call us to be our brother's keeper.[711] Ezekiel tells us what happens to everyone who turns a blind eye and claims it's none of their business. "If the watchman sees the sword coming and does not blow the trumpet, and the people are not warned, and the sword comes and takes any person from among them, he is taken away in his iniquity, but his blood I will require at the watchman's hand."[712]

Is it better for us to obey God's voice or test Him? Jesus said, "It is written, you shall not tempt the LORD your God."[713] Yahweh made this promise to us: "Now therefore, if you will indeed obey My voice and keep My covenant, then you shall be a special treasure to Me above all people, for all the earth is Mine".[714] Isn't this what all of us want? We each have a choice to obey or not, but please don't blame God.

Israel wandered in the desert for forty years before they entered the Promised Land, and the people built a tent for Yahweh where Moses would go in and speak with Him. The LORD also instructed them to build an Ark of Testimony where the two stone tablets of His commandments were to be kept along with Aaron's rod which proved his leadership as priest.[715] Moses would go into the Tent of Meeting and "he heard the voice of One speaking to him from above the mercy seat that was on the Ark of the Testimony, from between the two cherubim."[716]

It took forty years for Israel to finally reach their destination because of the disobedience of a generation. God said, "Not one of those who saw my glory and the signs I performed in Egypt and in the wilderness but who disobeyed me and tested me ten times, not one of them will ever see the land I promised on oath to their ancestors. No one who has treated me with contempt will ever see it."[717] God kept His word and all the older generation died in the wilderness, except Caleb, who with Joshua, had made the good report that they could win against the giants who lived there.[718]

The armies of Israel made the ultimate mistake when they refused to heed God's timing to enter the Promised Land because they believed a report of fear. Later they changed their mind and wanted to go in, but Moses told them God wouldn't be with them. They went anyway and lost the battle.[719] How often do we miss God's timing, then strike out on our own only to get defeated? Worst of all, how often do we blame God for our defeat when we won't listen to Him?

Israel was without excuse since each person heard God's voice. Moses said, "The LORD spoke to you out of the fire. You heard the sound of words but saw no form, there was only a voice. He declared to you His covenant, the Ten Commandments, which He commanded you to follow and then wrote them on two stone tablets."[720]

Moses warned them that in the future their descendants would forget God and be scattered throughout the nations. "But if from there you seek the LORD your God, you will find Him if you seek Him with all your heart and with all your soul. When you are in distress and all these things have happened to you, then in later days you will return to the LORD your God and obey. For the LORD your God is a merciful God, He will not abandon or destroy you or forget the covenant with your ancestors, which He confirmed to them by oath."[721]

Moses also reminded the descendants of Israel how special they were. He asked, "Did any people ever hear the voice of God speaking out of the midst of the fire, as you have heard, and live?"[722] "Out of Heaven He let you hear His voice, that He might instruct you. On Earth He showed you His great fire, and you heard His words out of the midst of the fire".[723]

The people were terrified of God after hearing His voice thundering from the fire on the mountain.[724] So, they asked Moses to go in their place and they would obey everything the voice of the LORD spoke to him.[725]

Since that time, throughout Israel's history, it has been the same song and dance. The voice of the LORD sent prophets to remind Israel to listen, obey, and be blessed, or suffer the consequences of turmoil like the pagan nations suffer, as they worship demon gods.

Throughout every generation, God's people have been given the choice to dance to the voice of the LORD or sit it out. We each still have that choice today. Moses' words still warn us, "As the nations which the LORD destroys before you, so you shall perish, because you would not be obedient to the voice of the LORD your God".[726]

As hard as it is to obey the LORD, and not our own inclinations, God offers us incredible rewards and power when we do so. He is still saying, "If you fully obey the LORD your God and carefully follow all his commands I give you today, the LORD your God will set you high above all the nations on earth."[727]

We have seen how God blessed the return of Israel since the year 1947, when they became a nation again after two thousand years. Today, still as the land of milk and honey, Israel has incredible fertile soil producing quick growth in farming and other industries. We also see how God has blessed the United States for our stand with Israel and keeping His words, until now. But today we are hanging in the balance with war and rumors of war all around us.

BLESSINGS OF OBEDIENCE

Here are God's promises given in the book of Deuteronomy recorded by Moses. "All these blessings will come on you and accompany you if you obey the LORD your God:"[728]

❖ You will be blessed in the city and blessed in the country. [729]
❖ The fruit of your womb will be blessed, and the crops of your land and the young of your livestock, the calves of your herds and the lambs of your flocks.[730]
❖ Your basket and your kneading trough will be blessed.[731]
❖ You will be blessed when you come in and blessed when you go out. [732]
❖ The LORD will grant that the enemies who rise up against you will be defeated before you. They will come at you from one direction but flee from you in seven. [733]
❖ The LORD will send a blessing on your barns and on everything you put your hand to. The LORD your God will bless you in the land He is giving you. [734]
❖ The LORD will establish you as His holy people, as he promised you on oath, if you keep the commands of the LORD your God and walk in obedience to him. [735]
❖ Then all the peoples on earth will see that you are called by the name of the LORD, and they will fear you. [736]
❖ The LORD will grant you abundant prosperity—in the fruit of your womb, the young of your livestock and the crops of your ground, in the land He swore to your ancestors to give you. [737]
❖ The LORD will open the heavens, the storehouse of His bounty, to send rain on your land in season and to bless all the work of your hands. You will lend to many nations but will borrow from none. [738]
❖ The LORD will make you the head, not the tail. If you pay attention to the commands of the Lord your God that I give you this day and carefully follow them, you will always be at the top, never at the bottom. [739]

❖ Do not turn aside from any of the commands I give you today, to the right or to the left, following other gods and serving them.[740]

CURSES OF DISOBEDIENCE

Then here are the "curses" of disobeying the LORD's voice given to Moses, which outnumber the blessings. We should all pay close attention. As I already mentioned, often God's people think they can keep on breaking God's laws because they're already forgiven. That may be the case if they repent, but we still face the consequences. We see this as Israel and the Christian nations also suffer when we allow sin to prosper.

Do these curses sound familiar? "If you do not obey the LORD your God and do not carefully follow all His commands and decrees, I am giving you today, all these curses will come on you and overtake you:"[741]

❖ You will be cursed in the city and cursed in the country.[742]
❖ Your basket and your kneading trough will be cursed.[743]
❖ The fruit of your womb will be cursed, and the crops of your land, and the calves of your herds and the lambs of your flocks.[744]
❖ You will be cursed when you come in and cursed when you go out.[745]
❖ The LORD will send on you curses, confusion and rebuke in everything you put your hand to, until you are destroyed and come to sudden ruin because of the evil you have done in forsaking him.[746]
❖ The LORD will plague you with diseases until He has destroyed you from the land you are entering to possess. The LORD will strike you with wasting disease, with fever and inflammation, with scorching heat and drought, with blight and mildew, which will plague you until you perish.[747]
❖ The sky over your head will be bronze, the ground beneath you iron. The LORD will turn the rain of your country into dust and powder, it will come down from the skies until you are destroyed.[748]

- The LORD will cause you to be defeated before your enemies. You will come at them from one direction but flee from them in seven, and you will become a thing of horror to all the kingdoms on earth.[749]
- Your carcasses will be food for all the birds and the wild animals, and there will be no one to frighten them away.[750]
- The LORD will afflict you with the boils of Egypt and with tumors, festering sores and the itch, from which you cannot be cured.[751]
- The LORD will afflict you with madness, blindness, and confusion of mind. At midday you will grope about like a blind person in the dark. You will be unsuccessful in everything you do, day after day you will be oppressed and robbed, with no one to rescue you. [752]
- You shall betroth a wife, but another man shall lie with her. You shall build a house, but you shall not dwell in it. You shall plant a vineyard but shall not gather its grapes.[753]
- Your ox will be slaughtered before your eyes, but you will eat none of it. Your donkey will be forcibly taken from you and will not be returned. Your sheep will be given to your enemies, and no one will rescue them.[754]
- Your sons and daughters will be given to another nation, and you will wear out your eyes watching for them day after day, powerless to lift a hand.[755]
- A people that you do not know will eat what your land and labor produce, and you will have nothing but cruel oppression all your days.[756]
- The sights you see will drive you mad.[757]
- The LORD will afflict your knees and legs with painful boils that cannot be cured, spreading from the soles of your feet to the top of your head.[758]
- The LORD will drive you and the king you set over you to a nation unknown to you or your ancestors. There you will worship other gods, gods of wood and stone. You will become a thing of horror, a byword and an object of ridicule among all the peoples where the LORD will drive you.[759]

❖ You will sow much seed in the field but you will harvest little, because locusts will devour it. You will plant vineyards and cultivate them but you will not drink the wine or gather the grapes, because worms will eat them.[760]

❖ You will have olive trees throughout your country but you will not use the oil, because the olives will drop off. [761]

❖ You will have sons and daughters but you will not keep them, because they will go into captivity. [762]

❖ Swarms of locusts will take over all your trees and the crops of your land. [763]

❖ The foreigners who reside among you will rise above you higher and higher, but you will sink lower and lower. They will lend to you, but you will not lend to them. They will be the head, but you will be the tail.[764]

❖ All these curses will come on you. They will pursue you and overtake you until you are destroyed, because you did not obey the LORD your God and observe the commands and decrees He gave you.[765]

❖ They will be a sign and a wonder to you and your descendants forever. Because you did not serve the LORD your God joyfully and gladly in the time of prosperity, therefore in hunger and thirst, in nakedness and dire poverty, you will serve the enemies the LORD sends against you. He will put an iron yoke on your neck until he has destroyed you.[766]

❖ The LORD will bring a nation against you from far away, from the ends of the earth, like an eagle swooping down, a nation whose language you will not understand, a fierce-looking nation without respect for the old or pity for the young.[767]

❖ They will devour the young of your livestock and the crops of your land until you are destroyed. They will leave you no grain, new wine or olive oil, nor any calves of your herds or lambs of your flocks until you are ruined.[768]

❖ They will lay siege to all the cities throughout your land until the high fortified walls in which you trust fall down. They will besiege all the cities throughout the land the LORD your God is giving you.[769]

❖ If you do not carefully follow all the words of this law, which are written in this book, and do not revere this glorious and awesome name, the LORD your God, the LORD will send fearful plagues on you and your descendants, harsh and prolonged disasters, and severe and lingering illnesses. [770]

❖ He will bring on you all the diseases of Egypt that you dreaded, and they will cling to you. The LORD will also bring on you every kind of sickness and disaster not recorded in this Book of the Law, until you are destroyed.[771]

❖ You who were as numerous as the stars in the sky will be left but few in number, because you did not obey the LORD your God. Just as it pleased the LORD to make you prosper and increase in number, so it will please Him to ruin and destroy you. You will be uprooted from the land you are entering to possess.[772]

❖ Then the LORD will scatter you among all nations, from one end of the earth to the other. There you will worship other gods, gods of wood and stone, which neither you nor your ancestors have known. [773]

❖ Among those nations you will find no repose, no resting place for the sole of your foot. There the LORD will give you an anxious mind, eyes weary with longing, and a despairing heart. You will live in constant suspense, filled with dread both night and day, never sure of your life.[774]

❖ In the morning you will say, "If only it were evening!" and in the evening, "If only it were morning!" Because of the terror that will fill your hearts and the sights that your eyes will see. [775]

❖ The LORD will send you back in ships to Egypt on a journey I said you should never make again. There you will offer yourselves for sale to your enemies as male and female slaves, but no one will buy you. [776]

Oh my! These are terrible curses for every generation of every people group, and we never seem to learn that God's voice never returns void, meaning He will do what He says He will do. It's important that we don't lose the FEAR of the LORD. As the Bible tells us,

"The fear of the LORD is the beginning of knowledge, but fools despise wisdom and instruction."[777] Yet as always throughout the Bible, God does not leave His people to perish completely. Although it usually takes generations to fall away and generations to take us back to God.

Moses continued with this final prophecy and also hope: "When all these blessings and curses I have set before you come on you and you take them to heart wherever the LORD your God disperses you among the nations, and when you and your children return to the LORD your God and obey him with all your heart and with all your soul according to everything I command you today, then the LORD your God will restore your fortunes and have compassion on you and gather you again from all the nations where he scattered you."[778]

Yes, the LORD is faithful, kind, and merciful, but as we move away from Him, He moves away from us, and with Him goes His blessings of provision and protection. It's not difficult to understand. Wouldn't we also stop helping those who mock us by treating us as though we aren't important or that we don't even exist? And wouldn't we favor and protect those who are loyal and love us instead?

HOW TO OBEY HIS VOICE

By now you must be thinking to yourself that keeping all of God's laws is a very tall order and no one can possibly follow them all perfectly. You are correct! There was only one human who kept all Yahweh God's laws in the Torah, and that was the Lord Yeshua, who was the Torah, the Word of God made alive. The LAW is Yahweh's voice. And the LAW became flesh.[779]

The apostle Paul explained how we are saved from the penalties of breaking God's laws. He said, "As it is written, cursed is everyone who does not continue to do everything written in the Book of the Law." No matter how small the crime in breaking them, there are curses in doing so. Yet it's humanly impossible to keep them all perfectly. So "Christ redeemed us from the curse of the law by becoming a curse for us." [780]

He said, "The blessings promised to Abraham would also come to the Gentiles through Christ Jesus, so that by faith we might receive the promise of the Spirit."[781] By faith means that each of us must believe and accept that the crucifixion of Christ paid the penalties of the curses we have earned. And His resurrection proved He conquered the curses for us to be released. We are then redeemed and receive adoption as sons (children) of God. [782]

Paul continues, "The Law was our tutor to bring us to Christ, that we might be justified by faith. But now that faith has come, we are no longer under a tutor. You are all sons of God by faith in Christ Jesus."[783] We need God's law to know how to obtain righteousness and to turn back when we begin to move away and get in trouble.

Are God's laws dead, should we ignore them? Absolutely not! Even within the Church there is confusion. We must still know and practice His laws to live peaceable and healthy lives. But even if we kept them all in the natural, yet our hearts aren't right in the spiritual, we would still not receive eternal salvation because the most important law is faith proven through love. Yet God's laws are still vital for a well-structured society for both man and animal.

A few years ago, I spoke with a Jewish woman who was raised with all points of the Law given to Moses and the laws written in the Tanach by Rabbis. I told her I felt some of God's laws were not relevant anymore. As an example, I used the laws of washing and bathing in the scriptures of Leviticus and the Tanach. But she enlightened me by saying the laws about washing taught them hygiene. And I realized these laws are the reason we wash our hands before meals as well as bathe. God is very specific about our cleanliness leading to good health.

Some nations which don't know God's guidebook, the Torah, often have poor hygiene and many diseases that come from a lack of proper sanitation. The Jews were chosen and given the job to teach God's law throughout the world in the dispersions where they were sent. This is what Paul meant when he said, "What advantage then does the Jew have? Or what profit is there in circumcision? Much in every way! Chiefly because the oracles of God were entrusted to them."[784]

There are also passages which tell us to burn the fat and organs of animals as a sacrifice to God and not to eat them.[785] This law is to keep us healthy as many people suffer from obesity. It's especially forbidden to eat the flesh of pigs, because their purpose is gleaning rotted waste and those dietary toxins are stored in their fat. Bacon anyone?

There is even a law about digging a hole and burying our bodily refuse outside the camp and taking a shower after certain discharges.[786] I have traveled through some countries which had a shortage of toilets, and everyone had to watch where they stepped on public sidewalks. This is now happening in Western cities where unlimited immigration has taken place too quickly without helping newcomers learn our biblical ways. Some adults as children have not been taught God's words and advice even of basic cleanliness and sanitation.

So, what is the answer? We must learn God's laws, study them, teach them to our children and those in our sphere of influence by our example of living them out. We must also choose righteous leaders to represent us, those who also love God and keep His laws as best as they can. More importantly, we must accept the gift of Jesus' sacrifice for the forgiveness of sin through repentance whenever we miss the mark (sin), so we may be healed and blessed.

Jesus is our role model to follow in keeping all points of the Law which He did, but God also knew that with our tainted DNA, no other human alive can keep them all, all the time. And it is written when you break one, it's as serious as breaking them all.[787] This is why Jesus died in our place and paid for all our crimes against the Father.

Knowing the laws of God helps us understand when we fall short, which leads to godly sorrow, repentance, and finally salvation.[788] The teaching that Jesus forgives our every sin without repentance is wrong. Yes, He loves the world and sinners, but cannot save us until we turn from our wicked ways in our hearts. Otherwise, we would be just like the wicked around us and sin is left to reign and destroy us, and all we come near.

On the last night of His life Jesus prayed to the Father. He said that He had saved all those the Father had given Him except for one, which was Judas Iscariot.[789] Judas' sin was like Satan's when he placed himself above God by betraying the Son of God. Although Judas had extreme sorrow in the end, his repentance was more like remorse, and wasn't accepted.

It's like a person who is extremely sorry when they're caught in a crime, but not sorry for committing it unless there is a negative outcome that affects them personally. Judas realized his betrayal led to shedding innocent blood, a severe crime against God's law. For the thirty pieces of silver Judas received for betraying Jesus, he lost everything else, and in the end hanged himself.[790]

There is a key given that will help us understand how to have a right heart with God and keep His commands. Moses tells us, "That you may love the LORD your God, that you may obey His voice, and that you may cling to Him, for He is your life and the length of your days".[791] The KEY to staying faithful is to love the LORD your God. Do we love Him enough to keep His commandments as much as possible?[792]

There is a beautiful story of a boy named Samuel, whose mother offered him to the service of God's temple before he was even conceived. Hannah was barren, which according to God's law is a curse, so she offered her first born son to God's service if He would allow her to have other children.[793] God answered! Samuel became a great prophet and leader over Israel before the people had kings ruling over them.

As a boy, Samuel heard the voice of God calling him to pronounce judgement over Israel's current High Priest Eli who had two wicked sons.[794] Eli raised Samuel to become High Priest over Israel and Samuel delivered every word God gave him, good or bad. He became a powerful prophet and judge in keeping the heart of Israel pure.[795]

Through all the generations of prophets, their continual instruction was to obey the voice of the LORD. Samuel said, "Has the LORD as great delight in burnt offerings and sacrifices as in obeying the voice of the LORD? To obey is better than sacrifice".[796] Samuel learned that hard lesson in his youth, when He had to issue the harsh judgement against the House of Eli because of their corruption.

King David gave a powerful description of the voice of God to be feared: "The LORD thundered from Heaven, and the Most High uttered His voice".[797] How often do we take Him for granted or worse yet, complain against the consequences of our sins, instead of listening to His words to change? David also tells us, "The LORD rewarded me according to my righteousness, according to the cleanness of my hands."[798] Eventually King David failed God through sexual sin and murder, which cost the lives of four of his sons.[799]

One of the saddest stories is about David's son Solomon, Israel's third king who was given everything. His father David fought many battles, acquired much wealth from the pagan nations around them, and he united all of Israel. Solomon used his father's conquests to build the greatest kingdom on earth and his main duty was to build the House of God.[800]

Once Yahweh's Temple was completed, Solomon had a visitation from God, and he heard the LORDs voice directly. God said, "I have heard the prayer and plea you have made before Me. I have consecrated this temple, which you have built, by putting My name there forever. My eyes and My heart will always be there. As for you, if you walk before Me faithfully with integrity of heart and uprightness, as David your father did, and do all I command and observe My decrees and laws, I will establish your royal throne over Israel forever, as I promised David your father when I said, 'You shall never fail to have a successor on the throne of Israel.'"[801]

Then Yahweh gave Solomon a warning that if he or his sons turned away from following His commandments and served other gods by worshiping them, they would be cut off from Israel and the land which God had given them, and He would reject the temple consecrated to His name. Israel would become a byword and ridiculed among the nations, and eventually the temple would be destroyed. People would laugh and ask why the God of Israel had done that to them. The answer would be because they forsook the LORD their God to worship other gods and that the LORD who saved their ancestors from the slavery of Egypt brought all that disaster on them.[802]

It didn't take very long for Solomon to fail God, even though Solomon had been given the privilege of meeting God personally and building the greatest earthly Temple for Yahweh to inhabit. God also favored Solomon with the richest kingdom on earth and made him the wisest man alive. Solomon still failed pitifully, and he died an old fool. "Why did he fail," we may ask? I believe we should each ask ourselves, "Who do we love"? Jesus said, "He who has My commandments and keeps them, it is he who loves Me. And he who loves Me will be loved by My Father."[803] Solomon loved his women more than God. How sad for him.

God warned Israel not to intermarry with foreign women, because they would pollute the land with foreign gods and that is just what happened. Solomon had an addiction for women, regardless of their faith. He married three hundred wives and had seven hundred concubines. To make them happy he built temples for his wives' pagan gods.[804] The people's worship of those idols brought Israel into demonic slavery, infighting, and eventual invasion.

Generations later, the land of Israel was full of demon gods, and Israel's prophet Elijah had an intense but successful battle against the prophets of Baal and Asherah. Then Elijah had all four hundred and fifty of Baal's occultic prophets executed.[805] Queen Jezebel ordered his death, but Elijah ran away to find God.[806] Finally, after chasing the wind, earthquake and a fire, Elijah heard a still small voice. He received encouragement and instruction from the LORD to find the prophet Elisha to be his replacement as High Priest for the God of Israel.[807]

What happens when a once godly nation ignores the voice of the LORD and refuses to keep His instructions? One story tells us the people of the northern Kingdom of Israel were invaded and carried off to Assyria, "because they did not obey the voice of the LORD their God but transgressed His covenant and all that Moses the servant of the LORD had commanded".[808] All their wealth was plundered along with the people as they became slaves to a foreign nation again.

In another story, the armies of Assyria surrounded the Kingdom of Judah. But King Hezekiah prayed to the God of Israel, and the prophet Isaiah encouraged him and said God had given a message to their enemy. The message to the King of Assyria from God, was, "Whom have you reproached and blasphemed? Against whom have you raised your voice, and lifted up your eyes on high? Against the Holy One of Israel."[809]

King Hezekiah was faithful to the God of Israel, so God sent one angel to destroy the Assyrian army of one hundred and eighty-five thousand men which had invaded the Kingdom of Judah.[810] The King of Assyria returned to his own country and was then killed by his own sons.[811] King Hezekiah had turned to God and God spared the Kingdom of Judah. Yes, God's voice was heard then, as He is still speaking today when we turn to Him.

WHAT IS HIS VOICE

The book of the Bible that best describes God speaking is the book of Job. Job's friend Elihu proclaimed Yahweh's majesty and reminds us Yahweh is a real being. He said, "Hear attentively the thunder of His voice and the sound that goes out of His mouth. He lets it loose under the whole heaven and His lightning unto the ends of the earth. After it a voice roars, He thunders with His majestic voice, and He does not restrain them when His voice is heard. He does great things that we cannot comprehend."[812]

For me personally, the book of Job was the hardest part of the Bible to read. In it, Satan challenged God to test Job. He said Job was only faithful because God blessed and protected him. So, God removed His favor from Job and let Satan devastate him and his family to the point that Job lost everything, his family, wealth, reputation, and health.[813] And probably like millions of people before me, I couldn't understand the cruelty of God for allowing Job's misery.

Later still, as I also faced personal disasters testing my own faith in our LORD, I jumped to the same conclusions as Job did in my anger against my Savior. I asked Him why He allowed these things to happen, and I said to Him, "I've done everything you wanted me to do, and you treat me like this".

In my pain I demanded an immediate answer from the Bible. I threw it down, opened it and placed my finger at whatever scripture the page fell open to. And do you know; Jesus gave me the answer that shut me up and stopped my complaining? The passage where my finger landed was on Jesus words: "Whoever does not bear his cross and come after Me cannot be My disciple."[814] At that moment I realized, yes, my trials were a heavy burden for me, but they were nothing compared to the horrendous torture, pain, and betrayal our

Lord Jesus endured at His crucifixion to pay for my salvation for eternity.

Job knew God as all powerful and that He had allowed Satan to attack him. Having nothing left and covered in boils, Job sat in the ash pit consumed with self-pity and self-righteousness.[815] How many of us would do the same or worse?

Finally, God challenged Job out of the whirlwind. He said, "Prepare yourself now like a man; I will question you, and you will answer Me. Will you indeed annul My judgment? Will you condemn Me, that you may be righteous? Have you an arm like God? Or can you thunder with a voice like Him? Adorn yourself now with majesty and excellence and array yourself with glory and beauty. Let loose the rage of your wrath, look on everyone who is proud and bring him low, and tread down the wicked in their place. Hide them in the dust together and imprison them in the hidden place of the grave."[816]

Everyone who wants to know God in a greater way should read the Book of Job, as God explains Himself and His incredible power so majestically in Chapters 38 and 39. God also gave a message to the prophet Jeremiah for us to realize about ourselves when we sink deep into self-absorption and pride. He said, "O house of Israel, can I not do with you as this potter? Look, as the clay is in the potter's hand, so are you in My hand."[817] The LORD wants to mold us into His image, not the other way around as we often try to mold God into our image.

King David was another one who really understood the majestic power of God's voice. He described, "The LORD also thundered in the heavens, and the Most High gave His voice, hailstones and coals of fire."[818] "The voice of the LORD is over the waters; the God of glory thunders; the LORD is over many waters. The voice of the LORD sounds with strength; the voice of the LORD with majesty. The voice of the LORD breaks the cedars of Lebanon. The voice of the LORD flashes like flames of fire. The voice of the LORD shakes the wilderness. The voice of the LORD makes the deer to give birth and strips the forests bare; and in His temple everyone says, 'Glory!'"[819]

There were several times David cried out to God in despair, especially when the nation of Israel was deeply in trouble surrounded by enemies. But David always returned to acknowledge the sovereignty and power of Yahweh and worshiped His majesty as he wrote, "The nations raged, the kingdoms were moved, He uttered His voice, the earth melted".[820]

The book of Proverbs compares the voice of the LORD to the spirit of wisdom. "Out in the open wisdom calls aloud, she raises her voice in the public square."[821] "Does not wisdom call out? Does not understanding raise her voice? Beside the gate leading into the city, at the entrance, she cries aloud: 'To you, O people, I call out; I raise my voice to all mankind. You who are simple, gain prudence; you who are foolish, set your hearts on it.'"[822] King David wrote, "The fear of the LORD is the beginning of wisdom. A good understanding have all they who do His commandments."[823]

My favorite description of our LORD's voice is in the Song of Solomon: "The voice of my beloved! Behold, He comes leaping upon the mountains, skipping upon the hills".[824] "Let me see Your face, let me hear Your voice, for Your voice is sweet, and Your face is lovely."[825] "I sleep, but my heart is awake. It is the voice of my beloved! He knocks, saying, 'Open for Me, My sister, My love, My dove, My perfect one'"[826]. Whenever I read these verses, my spirit rises in anticipation of His Spirit. Do you feel His presence?

Then there was the prophet Isaiah who also had personal and powerful encounters with God. He recognized his unclean humanity and asked for mercy on his mouth: "Woe is me, for I am undone! Because I am a man of unclean lips, and I dwell in the midst of a people of unclean lips. For my eyes have seen the King, the LORD of hosts."[827] Then an angel came and put a hot coal to Isaiah's lips to purge his mouth from sin as he was sent to speak for God.[828] Our mouth can often cause a lot of harm, and sometimes feels as if it has a mind of its own!

Isaiah heard the voice of the LORD, saying: "Whom shall I send, and who will go for us?" Isaiah answered, "Here am I! Send me."[829] So God sent him to tell the people they will not be able to see or hear to have understanding until the land of Israel was barren and only a tenth of them would be left.[830]

Today in our modern Christian nations, are we at the same point of judgement? Few prophets are sounding the alarm to turn us away from our bad behaviors. Instead, in anticipation of Jesus return, several are preaching a strong authoritative offensive to rule and reign. But the cry of repentance is still rarely heard. "Which side of the tipping scales are we?"

The judgement came because the people broke the covenant with God by refusing to keep His laws. Is that a reminder of where we are now? We have shed innocent blood by killing our babies, our elderly, and the disabled by legally calling it "compassion". We are bringing up our children by calling every sexual immorality and deviance "Good".

Isaiah's first warning from God was that He would no longer answer their prayers: God said, "When you spread out your hands, I will hide My eyes from you. Even though you make many prayers, I will not hear. Your hands are full of blood."[831] But in His infinite mercy, God always gives His people a chance to redeem themselves. "'Come now, and let us reason together,' says the Lord, 'Though your sins are like scarlet, they shall be as white as snow'".[832]

Isaiah makes an important point when he tells us to listen to the teachings of God. He explains God is like a farmer when He harvests his grain. He only threshes it to shake out the seed or crushes the wheat until it's fine flour for bread, not to destroy them.[833] We should all understand this to learn quickly, so that whenever we find ourselves in difficult situations, we won't complain and wallow in self-pity.

The Lord shall have vengeance on His enemies, and on the people who try to destroy Israel. "The Lord shall cause His glorious voice to be heard, and shall shew the lighting down of His arm, with the indignation of His anger, and with the flame of a devouring fire, with scattering, and tempest, and hailstones."[834]

We may be in a similar period as when Isaiah had a special warning to the women of Israel for their complacency. He warned that hard times were coming and to trade their finery for the sackcloth of poverty.[835] His meaning was to put practical living first. Is this the same warning to the Church today? Was this to punish them? NO! It was to turn their hearts back to what was important, in doing the work for which God had created them.

Isaiah said the land would turn to wilderness. "Till the Spirit is poured on us from on high, and the desert becomes a fertile field. The LORD's justice will dwell in the desert, his righteousness live in the fertile field. The fruit of that righteousness will be peace. My people will live in peaceful dwelling places, in secure homes, in undisturbed places of rest. Though hail flattens the forest, and the city is leveled completely, how blessed you will be, sowing your seed by every stream, and letting your cattle and donkeys range free."[836] Isaiah's meaning calls us to focus on the work of the LORD, to labor in the human harvest of souls even through hard times, we will be fruitful.

Isaiah foretold the purpose of the coming Messiah. "He shall bring forth judgment unto truth. He shall not fail nor be discouraged, 'til He has set judgment in the earth: and the isles shall wait for His Law."[837] Isaiah also tells us the LORD's intended plans for the world; he heard the voice of the LORD saying, "Heaven is My throne, and Earth is My footstool".[838] God tells us Zion will birth a male child. His land will give birth to her children (His people). He will not shut up the womb of the earth.[839] "Shall I bring to the time of birth, and not cause delivery,"[840] says the LORD?

"It shall be that I will gather all nations and tongues and they shall come and see My glory".[841] Those who survive the judgements, the LORD will send to declare His glory to the Gentile nations to teach them about Him. Finally, they will bring His people back from the nations where they've been scattered as a clean and holy offering to the LORD.[842]

"For as the new heavens and the new earth, which I will make, shall remain before me, saith the LORD, so shall your seed and your name remain. And it shall come to pass, that from one new moon to another, and from one sabbath to another, shall all flesh come to worship before me, saith the LORD."[843] This is the final goal. We may wonder why God needs humanity to worship Him. Worship is our love song communicating our relationship with Him, like a happily married woman in love, praising her husband.

Next, we come to the prophet Jeremiah, who is known as the weeping prophet. He warned the House of Judah to turn from their sins of serving other gods through idol worship, which always led to selfish power, hardness of hearts, and perversion.

Jeremiah wept continually and identified himself with the people in their sins. He saw the destruction of Jerusalem coming and said, "We lie down in our shame, and our confusion covereth us: for we have sinned against the LORD our God, we and our fathers, from our youth even unto this day, and have not obeyed the voice of the LORD our God."[844] He reminded the people of God's words: "Obey my voice, and I will be your God, and ye shall be my people: and walk ye in all the ways that I have commanded you, that it may be well unto you.'"[845]

Jeremiah also reminds us about the difference between our true God and idols. He described the God of Israel as no other. "He has made the earth by His power. He has established the world by His wisdom and has stretched out the heavens by His discretion. When He utters His voice, there is a multitude of waters in the heavens and He causes the vapors to ascend from the remote parts of the earth. He makes lightning with rain and brings out the wind from His storehouses."[846]

The LORD spoke His warnings to Jeremiah. These are still relevant for us today as every generation has to make a choice whether to serve God or ourselves. He told Israel they were the clay on the Masters potter's wheel[847] and said, "If it does evil in My sight so that it does not obey My voice, then I will relent concerning the good with which I said I would benefit it."[848] Who do we take God for, that we should blaspheme Him with one side of our mouth and praise Him with the other? Do we presume to believe He will bless us in this lifetime, and then welcome us into Heaven?

Jeremiah, as the prophet of that generation, was the voice of God to remind His people how long their rebellion against His words had been happening. "I spoke to you in your prosperity, but you said, 'I will not hear.' This has been your manner from your youth, that you did not obey My voice."[849] "I will take from them the voice of mirth and the voice of gladness, the voice of the bridegroom and the voice of the bride, the sound of the millstones and the light of the lamp."[850] Jeremiah's writings are still warning us to amend our ways and deeds, and obey the voice of the LORD, "that He may relent concerning the doom that He has pronounced against you."[851]

Just like all the generations before Jeremiah's time and even up to the present, God promised again and again He will bring them back to Himself, "Out of them shall proceed thanksgiving and the voice of those who make merry, I will multiply them, and they shall not diminish."[852] It is a wonderful time for the generations living under God's blessings, but a very difficult time for those who do not.

This pattern has been happening since Adam and Eve, whom God formed on the sixth day of creation; they were blessed until they disobeyed. All the generations after them would live in these cycles from order to disorder to order. Perhaps that is what's needed to produce a good harvest of souls for God's Kingdom in humanity's spiritual evolution.

There is an actual scientific law for this strange phenomenon in physics, called "Entropy" which is the measure of disorder. Dr. Gerald Schroeder, in his book, Genesis and the Big Bang, explains that when anything is left unattended, whether it's alive or not, moves toward increasing entropy which is increasing disorder.[853] This could be the reason God was specific in proclaiming creation began in the evening of darkness and void. Then the morning came, from darkness to light, from chaos to order, each cycle evolving into something greater during the six days of creation.

Scientists have discovered that much of space is still unknown with Black Holes and Dark Matter, named that because they cannot be seen or measured accurately. God's works in existence are greater than our human imagination can even conceive. There are many things God has not given us answers for yet including these cycles of darkness to light.

It was a time of chaotic darkness in the prophet Jeremiah's day as He had to prophesy God's voice to the king and rulers of Jerusalem, telling them that they would be conquered. Instead of listening to Jeremiah, they had him arrested. He prophesied, "A voice was heard in Ramah, lamentation and bitter weeping, Rachel weeping for her children, refusing to be comforted for her children, because they are no more."[854]

Jeremiah said to the King of Judah, "Please, obey the voice of the LORD which I speak to you. So it shall be well with you, and your soul shall live."[855] "Now the LORD has brought it and has done just as He said. Because you people have sinned against the LORD, and not obeyed His voice, therefore this thing has come upon you."[856]

Just as today, we often blame our political leaders for our troubles, but we must also look at ourselves and our churches. The real issue is our rebellion against God who removes His favor like a father dealing with disobedient children.

California, the once Golden State, is a good example of disorder as we see the results in our once beautiful cities, plagued by the worst poverty ever seen in the United States, a Christian nation, through homeless squalor and crime. How the mighty have fallen.

Yet most of us turn a blind eye and a deaf ear to the plight of the poor as city leaders build shiny new buildings to replace the old homes where our poor used to live, without having offered alternative housing to them. To quench our shame, we tell ourselves the homeless are on drugs and have done this to themselves. But as a people we are without excuse, as the truth is, we have left the 'LORD of love and compassion' and have been ruled by our own callous hearts in a chaos none of our civic or spiritual leaders know how to fix.

Like other true prophets before him, Jeremiah was often mocked and abused, then finally thrown down a pit of mud to silence the voice of warnings from the LORD. [857] How often does our modern world silence those who dare speak against sin by throwing them into the mire of public opinion, and many agree to their chastisement? Let us not be on the side against God.

Interestingly, according to the Law of Entropy, the outcome of disobedience causing the cycle of disorder is normal and necessary to develop into a greater beginning, a morning of order. Can we hope and dream that out of this chaotic nightmare we are witnessing through a godless society, our new morning is arising? The prophet Isaiah said, "Arise, shine; For your light has come! And the glory of the LORD is risen upon you."[858]

Thankfully, the LORD promised the House of Judah's deliverance and return from Babylon after their capture, even though we know it took seventy years and a new generation. "Refrain your voice from weeping, and your eyes from tears; for your work shall be rewarded. And they shall come back from the land of the enemy," says the LORD."[859] So we know God is true to His word and even now, our nation is in the throngs of revival with more of our youth turning to Jesus.

Jeremiah ends his writings proclaiming the glory of our amazing God. "When He utters His voice, there is a multitude of waters in the heavens, He causes the vapors to ascend from the ends of the earth; He makes lightnings for the rain, He brings the wind out of His treasuries."[860]

The prophet Ezekiel begins by telling us more about God's voice in his vision of the heavenly living creatures. He said, "When they went, I heard the noise of their wings, like the noise of many waters, like the voice of the Almighty, a tumult like the noise of an army. A voice came from above the firmament that was over their heads."[861] "Like the appearance of a rainbow in a cloud on a rainy day, so was the appearance of the brightness all around it. This was the appearance of the likeness of the glory of the LORD. So, when I saw it, I fell on my face, and I heard a voice of One speaking."[862]

Like John's revelations, Ezekiel wrote details on heaven's beings, but also gave us the same warnings as Jeremiah. Speaking as the voice of God, Ezekiel wrote, "Therefore I also will act in fury. My eye will not spare, nor will I have pity. And though they cry in My ears with a loud voice, I will not hear them."[863] In Ezekiel's time, the priests had defiled God's holy temple. In visions, the LORD showed him the evil and perverse acts these priests were doing.[864]

How terrible it is when we won't listen to our beloved God. All our enemies are strengthened by our weaknesses and betrayal when we move away from our LORD's protection. The enemy plunders us personally, as a community, and even as a nation.

The LORD spoke through Jeremiah to tell Jerusalem that they were about to fall. He said, "Your own conduct and actions have brought this upon you". "How bitter it is, how it pierces to the heart! Oh, My anguish, My anguish! I writhe in pain, Oh, the agony of My heart! My heart pounds within me."[865] Here we can feel the heart of God through His prophet agonizing over the downfall of His people in these words. Jeremiah was describing God's breaking heart.

"The whole land lies in ruins, in an instant My tents are destroyed, My shelter in a moment."[866] Hebrew meanings for tents are coverings, homes, and tabernacles as a temple. Gods says His home is Israel, He lives in His people. But once we become destroyed for straying after sin, He becomes displaced, and His homes are in ruins in our lives. God undergoes frustration and pain in betrayal and abandonment caused by our love for sin more than our love for Him. Our horrible choices and disobedience lead to our own destruction, and to His breaking heart.

Because God has given us free will, like a father for His child, He hopes we will imitate His standards of righteousness and justice instead of lawlessness and murder. He told the people through Moses, "I have set before you, life and death, blessings and cursing, therefore choose life, that both you and your descendants may live."[867] When we choose against God's code of ethics, He feels the distress as any parent would, whose child rebels against them and treats them with contempt.

God gave a message through the prophet Ezekiel to the Prince of Tyre: "Thus saith the Lord God, because thine heart is lifted up, and thou hast said, 'I am a god, I sit in the seat of God, in the midst of the seas. Yet thou art a man, and not God, though thou set thine heart as the heart of God".[868]

Some ascribe this passage as God speaking to Satan, whose goal has always been to take God's place as ruler of the universe, to set himself in the center of the throne of God. Often people follow Satan by also trying to achieve supreme godhead above God, claiming He doesn't exist or not giving Him authority over their lives. Then they work to stop others from worshiping Him and even influence children to doubt. Jesus warns, "Whoever causes one of these little ones who believe in Me to sin, it would be better for him if a millstone were hung around his neck, and he were drowned in the depth of the sea".[869]

God becomes passionately angry against the enemies of His loved ones. "I trampled them in my anger and trod them down in my wrath, their blood spattered my garments, and I stained all my clothing. It was for Me the day of vengeance, the year for Me to redeem had come."[870] We must each search ourselves to make sure we are not His enemy, because He has no provision for those who hate Him.

Most disturbing to Him is our decisions to choose the death of our innocent and most vulnerable. God talks about His people killing their own children as they sacrificed them on altars of fire to demon gods. He said that He did not command them, "Nor did it come into My heart".[871]

As with all the other prophets, after judgements for removing the evil doers, God always ended with prophecies of hope for the people of Israel that His covenant promises would save forever. The LORD showed Ezekiel the future Temple of God.[872] "Afterward he brought me to the gate, the gate that faces toward the east. Behold, the glory of the God of Israel came from the way of the east, and His voice was like a noise of many waters, and the earth shined with His glory."[873]

God also speaks directly to kings and those who make a difference in history. Nebuchadnezzar, a pagan king, bragged about the great city of Babylon he felt he himself had built.[874] "While he was still speaking, a voice from Heaven said to him "The kingdom has departed from thee."[875] Why? Because he dared take sole credit for building the greatest government on earth at that time, instead of giving the honor to God who had chosen him to lead it, so a judgement was pronounced against him. He would be insane for several years, including eating grass like an animal. When his sanity returned, Nebuchadnezzar gave all glory to God.[876]

Daniel was another prophet who had incredible visions and encounters with God. He wrote, "I heard a man's voice between the banks of the Ulai, which called and said, 'Gabriel, make this man to understand the vision.'"[877] His visions were explained to him about future kingdoms and the end of time for mankind's rule.[878]

It was seventy years after Babylon took Jerusalem captive that God raised up the prophet Daniel to give the word of the LORD for their return. Daniel reminds us that Israel was invaded because they didn't obey the voice of the LORD. So, the curses of the Law, God had given to Moses, were poured out on them because of their sins against God."[879]

Daniel described a man he saw in a vision and used the same description of the Man's appearance and His voice, as John did in Revelations: "The voice of His words like the voice of a multitude"; "His voice as the sound of many waters."[880] Could it be, the LORD's voice as a multitude is speaking to all of creation at the same time?

There are other prophets who described God's voice. Joel tells us, "The LORD shall utter his voice before his army, for His camp is very great, for He is strong that executeth His word: for the day of the LORD is great and very terrible; and who can abide it?"[881]

Amos said, "The LORD will roar from Zion, and utter His voice from Jerusalem. The habitations of the shepherds shall mourn, and the top of Carmel shall wither."[882]

Micah said, "Listen! The LORD is calling to the city and to fear Your name is wisdom "Heed the rod and the One who appointed it."[883]

Haggai described God's sorrow because of the way the people prioritized: "Because of My house, which remains a ruin, while each of you is busy with your own house. Therefore, because of you the heavens have withheld their dew and the earth its crops. I called for a drought on the fields and the mountains, on the grain, the new wine, the olive oil, and everything else the ground produces, on people and livestock, and on all the labor of your hands."[884]

Then the priests and the people listened and obeyed the voice of the LORD their God, through the words of Haggai the prophet who the LORD had sent to them, and the people feared God's presence. So, they began to restore God's temple, and God said He was with them.[885]

The prophet Zechariah said that "Those who are far away will come and help to build the temple of the LORD, and you will know that the LORD Almighty has sent me to you. This will happen if you diligently obey the LORD your God."[886]

Often people feel it's strange when someone says they hear God. But even in modern times, we are supposed to hear Him. In my personal life, there were three distinct times I was in life threatening situations, when I heard a voice speak to me clearly. I believe it was the Lord because all three times, the voice gave me just a few words that saved my life. As a little girl, I was almost hit by a car, the voice said "Jump" and I jumped out of the way, with the car missing me by inches.

A second time, I was standing with my little brother when he shot an arrow with a metal head straight up in the air (they were still legal as toys then). Not knowing what else to do, I covered my eyes with my hands fearing where the arrow would land. A voice said, "Move" and I moved both feet forward just a couple of inches and the arrow came straight down behind my heels where I had stood, missing my young soft skull.

The third time, as an adult, I was swimming at the beach and got caught in a strong current. The harder I swam to get back to shore, the more the tide dragged me farther out to sea. Completely exhausted, I was about to go under water for the final time, but the voice said, "Get on your back". Believing it was the Holy Spirit I was able to stop panicking, and time the approach of the waves over my face while controlling my breathing, swimming backstrokes to shore.

Through these experiences, I'm convinced that when we belong to Jesus, He will not let anything happen to us without intervening, until our time here on earth is up. But we must obey when He tells us to do something. Everyone can hear His voice when we believe because the Spirit of God comes to live in us. I believe the Holy Spirit was the voice I heard so clearly that saved my life those times, as well as the quiet voice I hear who guides me daily.

GODS VOICE IN THE NEW TESTAMENT

In the New Testament, Matthew quoted the prophecy from Isaiah that Jesus fulfilled: "Here is My servant, whom I uphold, My chosen one in whom I delight. I will put My Spirit on Him, and He will bring justice to the nations. He will not shout or cry out or raise His voice in the streets. A bruised reed He will not break, and a smoldering wick He will not snuff out. In faithfulness He will bring forth justice; He will not falter or be discouraged till He establishes justice on earth. In His teaching the islands will put their hope."[887] This passage is repeated in the New Testament about Jesus.[888]

Have you heard of the 'red letter version' of the Bible? Those are the words highlighted in red ink that are considered as being spoken by Jesus. I highly recommend everyone read the red letters so they will personally know what Jesus said. There are too many of them to quote in this book. Every single one of His words produces wisdom and life. Jesus truly is the Living Word.[889]

Next we will focus on the passages that mention the voice of the Father and the Son. The first time the voice of Father God was heard in the New Testament was when Jesus was baptized by John the Baptist. Mark wrote, "Immediately, coming up from the water, He saw the heavens parting and the Spirit descending upon Him like a dove. Then a voice came from heaven, 'You are My beloved Son, in whom I am well pleased.'"[890]

Later, the voice of Father God spoke out again about His love for His Son. Jesus took Peter, James, and John to a high mountain where they met Moses and Elijah, who had lived their earthly lives centuries before. The Bible makes it a point to tell us their bodies were never found to let us know they were transported directly to heaven.[891] On the mountain, "a bright cloud overshadowed them, and suddenly a voice came out of the cloud, saying, 'This is My beloved Son, in whom I am well pleased. Hear Him!'"[892]

Peter described this prophetic voice of the Father about the Son as coming from the "Excellent Glory".[893] And we are to heed the knowledge of Jesus "as a light that shines in a dark place, until the day dawns and the Morning Star rises in your hearts".[894]

John the Baptist told us he was not the Christ but was sent ahead to prepare the way. John said, "The bride belongs to the bridegroom. The friend who attends the bridegroom waits and listens for Him and is full of joy when he hears the Bridegroom's voice."[895]

Jesus tells us the voice of God will be heard through His Son. He said, "Verily, I say unto you, the hour is coming, and now is, when the dead shall hear the voice of the Son of God, and they that hear shall live."[896] Yes, the Gospel of Jesus, our Messiah, turns us from death of sin to resurrected life with Him. Jesus continued, "The hour is coming, in which all that are in the graves shall hear His voice."[897] "Believe Me that I am in the Father and the Father in Me."[898] The voice of the Father and Son are the same, as they are one.

Then Jesus tells us, "I am the Good Shepherd. The good shepherd giveth His life for the sheep."[899] "To Him the doorkeeper opens, and the sheep hear His voice, and He calls His own sheep by name and leads them out. And when He brings out His own sheep, He goes before them, and the sheep follow Him, for they know His voice. Yet they will by no means follow a stranger, but will flee from him, for they do not know the voice of strangers."[900]

"And other sheep I have, which are not of this fold: them also I must bring, and they shall hear My voice; and there shall be one-fold, and one shepherd."[901] "My sheep hear My voice, and I know them, and they follow Me. And I give unto them eternal life; and they shall never perish, neither shall any man pluck them out of My hand."[902]

It's important that we each learn our true Shepherd's voice, otherwise we are easily deceived by the counterfeit. Someone who only considers money, power, or fame, is a hireling and doesn't own or care about the sheep. When he sees the wolf coming, he flees and the wolf catches and scatters the sheep.[903]

There is the story of Jesus' young friend Lazarus, mentioned in previous chapters, brother to Mary and Martha. He died and was placed in a tomb for four days. Jesus finally came and told them to remove the stone from the tomb. He lifted His eyes to heaven and said, "Father, I thank You that You have heard Me. And I know that You always hear Me, but because of the people who are standing by I said this, that they may believe that You sent Me."[904] Then Jesus cried out with a loud voice, "Lazarus, come forth!"[905] Lazarus rose from the dead and walked out of the tomb at the command of Jesus voice.[906]

Six days before the Passover when Jesus was to be killed, He prayed out loud again, and said, "'Father, glorify Thy name'. Then came there a voice from heaven, saying, 'I have both glorified it, and will glorify it again.'"[907] The people who were there heard the voice and some said it was thunder, others said it was an angel. Jesus told them the voice came for their sakes and not His.[908]

We should understand that Jesus has power over life and death. He certainly had the power to stop His own death at the crucifixion as He told the disciples the Father would send twelve legions of angels to save Him if He asked. But His death had to happen so the scriptures would be fulfilled.[909]

Jesus, as God in human form, was born to be the final Passover Lamb of God. As we read before, just as the blood of the lamb was placed on the houses of all the Israelites in Egypt so death would "Pass Over" them to spare their first born,[910] only the Blood of Jesus is the sign for eternal death to pass over the entire Earth to save those who trust in Him.

On His final day, Jesus stood before the Roman governor, Pontius Pilate, who questioned Him asking, "Are You a king then?" Jesus answered, "You say rightly that I am a king. For this cause I was born, and for this cause I have come into the world, that I should bear witness to the truth. Everyone who is of the truth hears My voice."[911] The Voice of God is Truth.

Finally, nearing death, "about the ninth hour (three o'clock), Jesus cried out saying, 'Eli, Eli, lama sabachthani?' That is, 'My God, My God, why have You forsaken Me?'"[912] "And when Jesus had cried out with a loud voice, He said, 'Father, into Your hands I commit My spirit'. Having said this, He breathed His last."[913]

At that moment on the cross, Jesus became the sin of the world and His mortal body bore the death penalty for all humanity. Because of His holiness, God the Father could not be joined with sin, so the Spirit of God left His only begotten Son. Jesus the man was alone for the first time, and completely forsaken as His earthly body died.

Every word spoken by the LORD has several meanings. In those last moments, Jesus became the serpent on the pole. During Israel's wandering in the wilderness, the people complained against God because they were tired of the food He provided. So, the LORD sent poisonous snakes to bite them, and many died. The people repented to Moses, and God instructed him to make a bronze serpent and lift it up on a pole, so all who looked on it lived.[914]

The serpent on the pole represented the poison of sin. It was the creature that had brought sin to the world in the Garden of Eden, and it was the only thing cursed by God.[915] Jesus became the symbol of the cursed serpent on the cross and allowed Himself to receive the punishment for all humanity. Jesus told His disciples, if He were "lifted up from the earth", He will draw all peoples to Himself.[916] All those who look on Jesus' crucifixion, and believe in His death and resurrection, can transfer the poison of our sin to Him to be saved and live forever.

Ironically, the symbol of the serpent on the cross is still the symbol of the Medical Industry today. Many of our medical experts don't understand this to be a symbol of our crucified Savior, Jesus Christ, who takes away the sin of the world. And through His sacrifice He still brings eternal salvation and healing.[917]

But the voice of God didn't stop even after Jesus died and rose from the dead. Later, a Jewish priest named Saul worked hard to have Jesus' followers arrested and executed. He felt they were blaspheming the God of Israel by claiming Yeshua (Jesus) as the Messiah and the Son of God.

During that time, Saul had a heavenly visitation where suddenly a light shone around him and he fell to the ground. A voice said to him, 'Saul, Saul, why are you persecuting Me?' And he said, 'Who are You, Lord?' Then the Lord said, 'I am Jesus, whom you are persecuting'".[918] The men with Saul heard the voice but didn't see anyone.[919] This same Saul later became known as Apostle Paul who wrote most of the New Testament.

In another city, the Lord gave instructions to the apostle Peter. This passage has brought some confusion and dissension and needs to be clarified. At the time, Peter was hungry and waiting for lunch when he had a vision. In it he saw a sheet with all sorts of animals and insects.[920] Then a voice spoke to him, "Rise, Peter; kill, and eat. But Peter said, 'Not so, Lord, for I have never eaten anything that is common or unclean.'" The voice repeated three times and said, "What God hath cleansed, that call not thou common."[921]

Then the Spirit of God told Peter three men would come and he was to go with them.[922] He was escorted to the household of a Roman Centurion named Cornelius with his family and friends. Peter reminded them that it was unlawful for a Jewish man to keep company with those of another nation. But God showed him that he should not call any man common or unclean.[923] This was the first ministry to the Gentiles to preach the good news of the resurrection of Jesus Christ and the remission of sins.[924]

Peter was still preaching when "the Holy Spirit fell upon all those who heard the word. And those of the circumcision who believed were astonished, as many as came with Peter, because the gift of the Holy Spirit had been poured out on the Gentiles also. For they heard them speak with tongues and magnify God."[925] This is such a fantastic story of salvation and the baptism of the Holy Spirit offered to everyone who will accept.

In telling this story, often Christian teachers miss the point and interpret it as God cancelling His law on food bans which were designed to keep the human body healthy. God gave Moses instructions to avoid certain meats because they are toxic.[926] This story is not about God changing His law but about God's people reaching those who don't know God's law and eat unclean foods, whether physically, intellectually, or spiritually. At that time, it was forbidden in Jewish custom for Jews to eat with people of another faith which the animals in the vision represented.

After several conversions, the apostles and elders held a meeting how to treat the new Gentile converts. Peter spoke to tell them God used his mouth as His voice to give the Gentiles the Holy Spirit also.[927] He told them God had made no distinction between them and the Gentiles and had also purified their hearts by faith.[928]

They were to teach the Gentiles, those learning about God, the basics of His laws, the milk of the word, so they wouldn't become overwhelmed with the Do's and Don'ts all at once. But from there, the new disciples were to continue learning the commandments of God for a healthy spirit and body. Peter said, "For Moses has had throughout many generations those who preach him in every city, being read in the synagogues every Sabbath."[929]

In today's modern Christianity, we rarely hear or teach the basic laws of the Ten Commandments written by God's own finger.[930] Not surprisingly, many of us are filled with sin, sickness, and brokenness, drinking only the milk of the Gospel of God without the wisdom of how to live a holy and healthy life. Paul said that everyone who only drinks milk is like a baby and unskilled in God's word of righteousness.[931]

Paul also said the Holy Spirit is still warning us, as in the days of Moses and the Old Testament prophets, with the same message. That we must still listen to God's voice today, not to harden our hearts as during the rebellion of the trials in the wilderness.[932] Paul further tells us, unless we have faith to obey, we cannot come into His rest.[933]

Most of the Christian teaching I've heard for these many years has been about the grace of God. And yes, that is a most important and wonderful gift, but like Moses and the prophets, the New Testament also brings us "Fear of the LORD".[934]

Paul described the day of Moses at the mountain that burned with fire, blackened, dark in a storm, with the sound of a trumpet and the voice of words. Those who heard it begged that the voice of God would stop speaking. They could not endure what was commanded. The sight was so terrifying that even Moses said, "I exceedingly quake and tremble".[935]

Paul continued, "But you have come to Mount Zion, to the city of the living God, the heavenly Jerusalem. You have come to thousands upon thousands of angels in joyful assembly, to the church of the firstborn, whose names are written in Heaven. You have come to God, the Judge of all, to the spirits of the righteous made perfect, to Jesus the mediator of a new covenant, and to the sprinkled blood that speaks a better word than the blood of Abel."[936]

And Paul warns us there is a condition of loyalty for Christians to receive the promises of God. "See to it that you do not refuse Him who speaks. If they did not escape when they refused him who warned them on Earth, how much less will we, if we turn away from Him who warns us from Heaven?"[937]

Being a believer in God is a two-way relationship. Many are taught God loves us unconditionally and will save us from all our crimes against Him without repentance or discipline. If we really had the "Fear of the LORD", we would continually strive to put Him above our self-absorption and personal addictions. And we would be too terrified to ignore Him or double-cross Him for fear of losing Him now and for eternity.

But the sad reality is that many of us love ourselves more than Him. A distortion of our own value often leads to depression with unresolved feelings of what we think we deserve but can't get. Eventually the futility of that way of thinking leads to anger, bitterness, and in extreme cases, to mental illness. Peter said it well, "Abstain from fleshly lusts which war against the soul".[938]

Many Christians believe they are saved, but there are conditions when we give our lives to Jesus to receive eternal salvation. You may have heard the expression, "once saved always saved". And although nothing external can separate us from the love of God,[939] we still have a choice to reject Him at any time. The Bible describes a person doing that like a dog returning to its own vomit.[940]

We must examine ourselves carefully to make sure we really have surrendered our hearts to Him, because the only way we could lose our salvation is if we never really accepted it in the first place. Each of us has been given the gift to choose through free will. God reads our hearts not our words.

The saddest and worst state of being is when we cannot grasp the overpowering love of God, and therefore don't know how to love Him back. Often the voice of the LORD, His Word, is sensed as a threat to our personal sense of control instead of the awe and reverence we would feel when we really know how He eternally loves us.

Let's try to focus on what Paul teaches, "Wherefore we receiving a kingdom which cannot be moved, let us have grace, whereby we may serve God acceptably with reverence and godly fear, for our God is a consuming fire."[941]

Finally, we reach the most symbolic book in the Bible called Revelation. It is filled with heavenly visions and voices experienced by the apostle John. How important are words? As in the beginning when the voice of God spoke all things into existence, the book of Revelation describes voices worshiping God and proclaiming things to come.

There will be a time that everything in existence will worship God. "And every creature which is in Heaven, and on the earth, and under the earth, and such as are in the sea, and all that are in them, heard I saying, 'Blessing, and honour, and glory, and power, be unto him that sitteth upon the throne, and unto the Lamb for ever and ever.'"[942]

John wrote that he was in the spirit and heard a voice like a great trumpet saying, "I am Alpha and Omega, the First and the Last." John turned to look at who was speaking and saw seven golden lampstands and in the middle was "one like a Son of Man", clothed with a garment down to the feet and with a golden sash wrapped around the chest. The hair on His head was white like wool, as white as snow. His eyes were like a flame of fire. His feet were like fine brass, as if refined in a furnace, and His voice as the sound of many waters."[943]

The Lord Jesus spoke the things for John to write as both warnings and blessings to His churches and to individual believers. The most intimate words from Jesus are, "Behold, I stand at the door, and knock. If any man hear My voice, and open the door, I will come in to him, and will sup with him, and he with Me".[944] His most wonderful invitation still stands today for anyone who will open the door to their heart and allow His Spirit to join with our spirit.

Do you know that in the first book of the Bible, God gave us a rainbow as a promise to mankind and to all living creatures, that He would never destroy the earth by flood again?[945] Then in the last book, an Angel, which many believe to be Jesus, appears wearing that rainbow on His head. He "cried with a loud voice, as when a lion roars. When He cried out, seven thunders uttered their voices".[946]

According to the book of Revelation, after many judgments are poured out, the seventh Angel sounded. "And there were great voices in Heaven, saying, the kingdoms of this world are become the Kingdoms of our LORD, and of His Christ, and He shall reign for ever and ever."[947]

Then after a terrible war in the heavens,[948] an Angel tells us, "Now salvation, and strength, and the Kingdom of our God, and the power of His Christ have come, for the accuser of our brethren, who accused them before our God, day and night, has been cast down. And they overcame him by the blood of the Lamb and by the word of their testimony, and they did not love their lives to the death."[949] It will cost God's people a great sacrifice, but the Kingdom of God will prevail!

The book of Revelation also describes the great war against the Babylonian systems and the Beast. A voice was heard in heaven saying, "Come out of her, My people, lest you share in her sins, and lest you receive of her plagues."[950] This is a strong warning: choose the side of the LORD now.

In the end, after the war to end all wars, John writes, "And I saw Heaven opened, and behold a white horse, and He that sat upon him was called Faithful and True, and in righteousness He doth judge and make war. His eyes were as a flame of fire, and on His head were many crowns; and He had a name written, that no man knew, but He Himself. And He was clothed with a vesture dipped in blood: and His name is called The Word of God. And the armies which were in heaven followed Him upon white horses, clothed in fine linen, white and clean."[951] To be a part of that army we must give Him our love, our life, and our allegiance.

John continues to tell us, "Out of His mouth goes a sharp sword (which is the word of the LORD, His Voice) that with it He should strike the nations. And He Himself will rule them with a rod of iron. He Himself treads the winepress of the fierceness and wrath of Almighty God. And He has on His robe and on His thigh a name written: KING of Kings and LORD of Lords."[952]

After the war between good and evil is over, a loud voice spoke, "Behold, the tabernacle of God is with men, and He will dwell with them, and they shall be His people. God Himself will be with them and be their God."[953] Yes, it is a happy ending for those who join the army of the Living God in obedience to His voice of truth!

We all know where there is a good army, there is also a bad army. When we are disobedient to our LORD, then we fight against Him. There is no such thing as being neutral, as we only stand in the way of either side. We must understand that God's war is not against humanity, as Paul wrote, "For we wrestle not against flesh and blood, but against principalities, against powers, against the rulers of the darkness of this world, against spiritual wickedness in high places."[954]

Jesus has a strong message to those of us who don't want to be involved and appear neutral, pretending to be in the middle. "I know your works, that you are neither cold nor hot. I could wish you were cold or hot. So then, because you are lukewarm, and neither cold nor hot, I will vomit you out of My mouth."[955] By these words Jesus is saying we are cast out of His covenant and His inheritance, no longer a part of His family. That means, anyone whose name is not written in the Book of Life will be cast into the Lake of Fire,[956] which is the second death. Again, we must take a stand. Which side of the eternal fence are we on?

HEART OF GOD

The Heart is a physical organ but is often described as the center of something. In the same way, God is the center of all things. Our hearts are the center of our being and with it we experience emotions, courage, and understanding. When we are in love, we feel it in our hearts, as we also feel heartache associated with negative emotions.

What do we know about God's heart? We are made in His image; therefore, it makes sense that we feel with our hearts like He also feels. The Bible describes the emotions of God's heart as very much like our own.

Generations after the fall of man, "Adonai saw that the wickedness of humankind was great on the earth, and that every inclination of the thoughts of their heart was only evil all the time. So, Adonai regretted that He made humankind on the earth, and His heart was deeply pained."[957]

Just as we can feel a broken heart, God's heart was aching with sorrow because of mankind's rejection of Him and their downfall. This caused Him great pain, just as it would for any good parent when their children turn away from them, head toward trouble, and need to be stopped.

God, having no other choice but to destroy all Life because it had become too corrupt, told Noah who was righteous in God's eyes, to build an Ark for his family and at least two of every creature, male and female.[958] After months of flooding the earth and time for dry land to resurface, Noah, his family, and all the creatures finally left the Ark.[959]

MALE AND FEMALE

Was God discriminatory when He told Noah to gather a male and female of every kind? No! It was His order for creation to duplicate itself through birthing a like-species and to replenish the earth after all oxygen breathing life had drowned. The most elementary knowledge of existence is that only a male and female can produce another life, regardless of what man-made science tries to prove.

Here I need to add the importance of the order of the male and female. Each has their distinctive roles. In several bird cultures, the male goes through great lengths to build a nesting home for the female. Only if she approves will she agree to produce offspring with him. This is also true with other species. Traditionally in many cultures, human females have trusted men to provide homes, and when she feels safe, she then joins him in starting a family. Even though they have different roles, they are still completely dependent on one another for the species to survive and flourish.

In the beginning of creation, God had given the same blessing to both the human male and female without distinction. He told them both, "Be fruitful, and multiply, and replenish the earth, and subdue it. And have dominion over the fish of the sea, and over the fowl of the air, and over every living thing that moveth upon the earth."[960]

But later, we read about Eve's gullibility in listening to the serpent and she ate the fruit that the LORD told Adam was dangerous.[961] She then gave it to Adam and he also didn't refuse it and ate.[962] Because Eve had not listened to the warning, her order of authority was diminished and instead of ruling and reigning with her husband, she came under his submission.

There has been an underlying current even to the present day from men in blaming women for the fall of mankind, but it's rarely mentioned that the instruction not to eat the forbidden fruit was given by God to Adam only and happened before Eve was created. Yes, Eve's mistake is that she trusted the serpent over her husband and ate first.

The serpent was intentional and knew Eve's exploitable nature, in that she could only trust what was said to her as she had never heard a lie before. The serpent explained so well, that the instruction God had given to Adam was misunderstood, "And the serpent said unto the woman, 'Ye shall not surely die: For God doth know that in the day ye eat thereof, then your eyes shall be opened, and ye shall be as gods, knowing good and evil.' And when the woman saw that the tree was good for food, and that it was pleasant to the eyes, and a tree to be desired to make one wise, she took of the fruit thereof, and did eat, and gave also unto her husband with her; and he did eat."[963]

This unsuspecting trait in the female is still in women today as they are more likely to believe falsehoods from men often called, "sweet nothings". This is why God gave Moses instruction that children were to be under their father's care and protection until he gave consent to their marriage.

With daughters, God gave additional instructions there was to be a bride price, like today's dowry, but the early church twisted this ritual. The financial gift was not supposed to be paid by the bride's family but by the intended husband to prove his true intent and worth in providing for her and their future children.[964] But even with a bride price for the woman's value, some cultures have mistaken this transaction to treat the bride as a commodity or as an owned servant, rather than an honored and valuable family member bearing God's gift of continuing their family blood-line through children.

In today's Western society, many fathers give up their role as protector over their daughters, while other men rob the father of his consent and blessing using the woman's body without these important financial and spiritual commitments. Losing the true value of a bride in bearing children, many women settle for domestic servitude with little security.

We can wonder what Earth would be like today if Adam had said "No" to Eve's offer to also eat the forbidden fruit since God gave the ban directly to him. Some say it was because Adam didn't want Eve to suffer alone. But knowing childish human nature it was more likely that he didn't want Eve to have more knowledge than him and the serpent knew that also.

Whatever the case, trust between the male and female was broken, and Adam made excuses for himself on that day by blaming the woman and God, as many men still do to this day.[965] We can see the results in the wounding and death tolls through domestic violence. As the physically weaker ones, women and children are usually the victims.

Adam's original role was to assign a function to every creature God had created, by naming them. These functions were to bring the earth into proper order. We could say Adam was given the job as General Manager of Earth which was in perfect harmony with God's plans.

Eve was to help Adam in that position. Her role was to reproduce humanity through birthing and raising new managers. God didn't give Eve a new role after her disobedience, since male and female were made to bring forth like species, but He told her she would now conceive and birth in pain and sorrow. She would also be dependent on her husband, and he would rule over her.[966]

It's possible this happened because for the first time, they both understood lies and betrayal, and Adam didn't trust Eve anymore. Eve was left with an inheriting sense of guilt which often women still struggle with today. And through Adam's disobedience, he lost the pure communication of God's wisdom in properly naming the functions of the animals they were supposed to manage. Even today we hear men cursing God, the land, and everything in creation. By not understanding the creative authority they release in the power of their words, Earth became a mess.

God didn't want a society of slaves, but the burden of rebellion caused just that. When Adam placed more importance on the will of his wife above the instruction of God, the woman became an instrument of worship to men now obsessed with sexual favors from women. This has caused the male to become a slave TO sex. Many men with the gift of music and song created to worship and love God, have replaced Him for the love of women. We can hear that in the vast variety of love songs dedicated to women instead of God.

On the other side, women had become slaves OF sex, replacing their importance of childbearing and co-managing earth and their household to instead become an instrument of beauty and pleasure. This has been a main factor in the destruction of their children who are often perceived as a burden and responsibility hindering personal indulgence.

As the male implemented his strength and rulership over the female, the female exploited her seductive influence over the male, with both looking to each other as their source for happiness that only God can give. This has led to many dysfunctional relationships, as sexual unions often become ways to manipulate one another for personal gain, instead of building God's kingdom together.

The serpent in the Garden of Eden was a voice for Satan, so what was his agenda? Knowing how easy it was to manipulate the female who had influence over the male, Satan set out to stop the increase of their future children.

Why is Satan's war against children? The Bible tells us, God's people are His army.[967] The earth is a battlefield between the forces of light and darkness. In any war, the immediate goal is always to take out the opposing forces, the soldiers of your enemy. The decimation of human children is the most strategic plan in hindering the growth of the Kingdom of God.

By causing division between the man and woman, Satan succeeded in getting fathers to take their focus off the protection and training of their children allowing them to become easy prey. In example, when we look closely at the Roe v. Wade, U.S. Supreme Court abortion decision of 1973, the basis of the law was to remove the father's rights to his preborn children, thereby also removing his physical and spiritual protection.

Satan's grand plan all along was to cause rifts between the male and female to divide them, so there would be less chances for them to raise healthy workers for God. The war against parents and children today through the promotion of infertility, abortion, same sex unions, and promiscuity are the battle strategies Satan has been using to keep control over this earth, by eliminating as many of God's warriors as possible.

God gave the serpent and Eve a prophetic warning after she ate from the forbidden fruit. He said to the serpent, "I will put enmity between thee and the woman, and between thy seed and her seed; it shall bruise thy head, and thou shalt bruise his heel."[968] In that warning there has been a constant war between them, and the battle is for humanity's children. God said, "Children are an heritage of the Lord: and the fruit of the womb is His reward."[969]

Protecting children and the mothers bearing them, should be our first duty in loving God. The apostle James, the brother of Jesus said, "Pure religion and undefiled before God and the Father is this, to visit the fatherless and widows in their affliction, and to keep himself unspotted from the world."[970]

By the time of Noah's generation, life on earth had become so corrupted, the LORD found it necessary to destroy everything and start again. He chose Noah, the purest man through Adam's son Seth's blood line, to build an Ark for his family and the animals that God would bring to the Ark before flooding the entire earth.

When the Ark was built and prepared according to the LORD's exact instructions, it is important to understand that God gave Noah a specific order in how they were to enter. I believe God wanted to restore the rightful order of His creation. The LORD said to Noah, "Come into the Ark, you and all your household, because I have seen that you are righteous before Me in this generation. You shall take with you seven each of every clean animal, a male and his female; two each of animals that are unclean, a male and his female; also seven each of birds of the air, male and female, to keep the species alive on the face of all the earth."[971]

God told Noah to bring a male and his female into the Ark together. When Noah and his family entered the Ark, Noah didn't heed that order for his family, and he entered the Ark with his three sons, Shem, Ham, and Japheth. Then the women entered: Noah's wife and the three wives of his sons, instead of God's order to enter two by two as male and female.[972]

After the flood subsided, the LORD was even more specific in the order of how they were to exit the Ark and step into the new world that had been completely washed of rebellion and sin. The detailed instruction God gave Noah was "Go out of the Ark, you and your wife, and your sons and your sons' wives with you."[973] But again, Noah didn't listen, and the men came out of the Ark first, the same way they went in. The Bible tells us, "Noah went out, and his sons and his wife and his sons' wives with him".[974]

Why is this important? Because God had planned for the human male and female to regain their position as one. Jesus confirmed that in marriage the two would become one flesh.[975] Instead, in this seemingly small act, Noah retained the dominance of human males over females for future generations which was not God's original plan.

And it became worse. Remember when God created Adam and Eve and blessed them, and told them to populate the earth and control it? They would have dominion over all earth's life forms, the fish of the sea, the birds of the air, and everything that moves on the earth.[976] Together Adam and Eve, and their descendants were to manage the earth, bringing it to order. Their food was to be only seed-bearing fruit and nuts.[977]

But because Noah ignored God's order, he and his sons stepped into the new world first, and again God gave another blessing. But this time it was to the men only as a blessing of violent dominance. The LORD said to the men, "Be fruitful and multiply, and fill the earth. And the fear of you and the dread of you shall be on every beast of the earth, on every bird of the air, on all that move on the earth, and on all the fish of the sea. They are given into your hand. Every moving thing that lives shall be food for you."[978]

Without the female half of God's heart together with the male, the blessing had been changed from one of life giving and order to one of fear and violence from predator to prey. Without men and women being equally yoked together, pulling the plow as the saying goes, now men would rule with men, in constant competition for dominance. The second order God changed was that men and animals would now become predators, the stronger preying on the weaker. And perversion for the pursuit of self-preservation and gratification began again.

Some may not see the seriousness of the mess this original loss of order has placed on humanity and creation, but placing women at a lower level of control has incapacitated both sexes. And although women have tried to restore societal and political equality to their plight, the real problem is a heart issue which can only be fixed one way which we'll read about in a moment.

Today, in Western society, we see the results of too many single mothers raising generations of children without the protection, provision, and spiritual naming and blessings from fathers to give them goals and function into who they're supposed to be. Only the male carries the anointing to impart that blessing to his children.[979] At the same time, we see too many men with wasted lives in prisons, addictions, and homelessness, without the nurture, love, and encouragement from healthy protected mothers and wives.

Without the completeness and strength of the other's true roles, neither gender is able to reflect their perfect half of God's image as sons and daughters of the Most High God whom they are created to be. As humans, we miss the perfect plans for restoration of the LORD's earthly kingdom because of our crippled lives. God created humankind's heart as His own, but only together from the combined heart of the male and the female can the image of God be complete to spread the deepest love of our LORD's heart.

To Noah's credit, the first thing he did after leaving the Ark was to remember the LORD and make a thanksgiving offering of every kind of clean animal. God smelled the pleasing aroma and said in His heart that He would never again curse the ground because of man, even though mankind's thoughts were evil, nor would He again destroy every living thing as He had done.[980]

Then God placed a rainbow over the earth to be a sign of His new covenant of survival to all life.[981] He said, "I will remember My covenant which is between Me and you and every living creature of all flesh, the waters shall never again become a flood to destroy all flesh. The rainbow shall be in the cloud, and I will look on it to remember the everlasting covenant between God and every living creature of all flesh that is on the earth."[982]

God made this promise to humankind and all the living creatures. This covenant is so important, and second blessing was made to the human males, Noah and his sons, first.[983] The reason this is significant today is that people professing same-sex unions cover themselves with God's symbol of amnesty, the "Rainbow," to remind God that He has a covenant with them not to destroy the earth regardless of their sins.

But they fail to acknowledge the later covenant and instructions God gave to Moses regarding marriage of a male and female only. They also fail to consider the physical judgments of disease and death that God pronounced on sexual unions outside of that.[984] Whether people have their genders altered through chemical or surgical means does not fool or void God's laws.

Certain sins carry a death penalty that are often executed through sickness and disease. The only possibility to escape is to stop sinning and ask for God's forgiveness and healing. Why are the penalties so harsh, we may ask? Because again, the "Heart of God" that is supposed to be expressed through a covenantal love union of male and female is corrupted, and God cannot allow this lopsided reflection of Himself to multiply, affecting future generations.

The ones who have suffered most are the children for which marriage laws were designed to protect. Since the human female is designed to bear and nurture children, the male is designed to care for them materially and spiritually as Adam was given the role of nurturing the land.[985] This is why the highest rate of poverty is in the homes of single mothers as they often can't perform the role of both parents properly, splitting their focus on the children's care and their careers. Even harder for the children is when the emotional and spiritual protection and care from the husband and father is cut off. It's a main reason divorce is repulsive to God; He calls it violence.[986]

When two people of the same sex marry, there are often prior children involved. Which of their children will receive their father's material, and especially, spiritual inheritance? God's wisdom in inheritance laws is thrown out. Even so, when no children have been born to either of them, God's bigger plans to build His Kingdom has been prevented through the generational bloodlines of descendants not even conceived, having the same result as the sin of aborting unborn children.

Job said about Yahweh, "He is wise in heart and mighty in strength."[987] Then Job's friend Elihu said, "If He set His heart upon man, if He gather unto himself His Spirit and His breath, all flesh shall perish together, and man shall turn again unto dust."[988] Even with His incredible power, God is patient and merciful, waiting for us to turn back to Him.

Yahweh called David, Israel's second king, "a man after Mine own heart, which shall fulfill all My will."[989] Here is a king who wanted to do all of God's will and shared God's heart, vision, plans, and purposes. But like all humans, he was still prone to personal sin which cost his family dearly. Yet, God richly honored David, promising him that his descendants would rule forever. That promise was kept in the human part of Jesus' bloodline. In Him, God's government is established on the throne of David forever.[990]

In the Song of Solomon, some Bible scholars liken God in this passage about King Solomon. It reads, "look at King Solomon wearing the crown which His mother crowned Him on the day of His wedding (to His people), the day His heart rejoiced". [991] God experiences joy in His heart.

It continues, "You have ravished My heart, my sister, my spouse. You have ravished My heart with one look of your eyes".[992] By this powerful statement, we see that the heart of the Almighty Creator, like a man, is capable of passionate desire for His bride, Israel, which includes each one of us who say "YES" to His spiritual proposal of love.

All love flows from His heart. God is "in Love". "For I am married to you. I will take you … and I will give you shepherds according to My heart, who will feed you with knowledge and understanding."[993] God is our spiritual husband, provider, and teacher.

Later, we read that King Solomon built a temple for Yahweh in Jerusalem. When he finished, the LORD said to him, "I have heard the prayer and plea you have made before me. I have consecrated this temple which you have built by putting My name there forever. My eyes and My heart will always be there".[994]

Just as the New Testament tells us, when we accept Christ into our hearts, we become the Temple of the Living God, and He consecrates us by putting His Name in us and His eyes and heart will always be there.[995] God is faithful.

But God's promises to King Solomon came with conditions. The government of Israel was to keep God's commandments, especially in serving Him only. The men were not to marry wives from foreign religions, since their worship of sexual favors from women would often lead them to worship their wives' pagan gods.[996]

And of course, Yahweh was right. Even though Solomon had personal visitations from God, he not only disobeyed once, but married three hundred wives and had seven hundred live-in girlfriends called concubines.[997] By acquiring them as part of his kingdom, Solomon also acquired their native tribes, foreign kingdoms and religions that became part of Israel, making King Solomon the most powerful and richest of kings.

But Solomon, who was given the honor of building a temple for the God of creation, also had temples built all over Israel for the foreign gods of his wives.[998] An altar was even built to Molech, the demon god who demanded human sacrifice of Israel's children to be burned alive by fire.[999]

Solomon, just as the first Adam, gave his spiritual authority to women, who gave it to their demonic idols through their worship, just as Eve had given her authority to the serpent. Again, this split God's heart. It didn't take long, just a few generations later, when Israel was divided, then invaded, their rulers captured, and God's Temple in Jerusalem destroyed.

As Israel and their surrounding nations did in biblical times, we are doing it again today through terminating the lives of our most vulnerable preborn babies. One third of our younger generations are dead, and an uncountable number of their descendants were never conceived. They had no chance of fulfilling God's purposes in building His Kingdom.[1000] And He feels outrage, grief, and mourning when His judgment must come.

Israel's terrible crimes against God's image by plundering, abusing, and killing their own weakest, for personal satisfaction or gain, had become worse than the nations around them.[1001] During Ezekiel's time, God allowed Jerusalem to be invaded by Babylon and their leaders killed or taken as slaves. History proves repeatedly the great devastations and loss when we refuse to listen to God's warnings against shedding innocent blood.[1002]

Toward the end of Jerusalem's seventy-year captivity, the heart of God was split even more. The Babylonian king, Ahasuerus, ruler over the known civilized world at that time, became upset with his queen, Vashti. This king signed an official law making all husbands masters of their homes under threat of divorce.[1003] This was a serious social and financial loss to women, legally robbing them of all rights including wealth, property, and children. This law also overturned the honored God-given status of women as wives and co-partners, to be legally classified as servants.

What we often don't realize is that many of our Western legal and social laws are based on God's instructions given to Moses written in the Torah (the first five books of the Old Testament) and explained by Israel's prophets and apostles. They were also modified as deemed needed by Jewish oral laws and other political dynasties of Babylon, Rome, and Western legal systems.

The ancient Babylonian law regarding husbands as masters in their homes is still in effect in most of the Muslim world today, at the risk of death to some women, who are still viewed as legally owned servants. And it was carried over into Western culture when Christian marriage ceremonies included a woman's legal vow to obey her husband.

But Jesus said God's perfect law didn't allow divorce except for adultery. His exact words to the men of His day were: "Moses because of the hardness of your hearts, permitted you to divorce your wives, but from the beginning it was not so." "From the beginning of the creation, God made them male and female. For this reason, a man shall leave his father and mother and be joined to his wife, and the two shall become one flesh; so then they are no longer two, but one flesh. Therefore, what God has joined together, let not man separate." "Whoever divorces his wife and marries another commits adultery against her. And if a woman divorces her husband and marries another, she commits adultery."[1004]

Most likely, our Lord's intention and hope for a broken marriage is for the love of that couple to be restored, just as Jesus waits for us to return to Him. Jesus' rules have been hard even for Christians. In my opinion, I don't believe Jesus expects us to live under emotional or physical abuse, and in those cases as well as abandonment, there should be legal separation.

Under modern Church law, divorce and remarriage are accepted. But again, by His instructions, the matter may be that Jesus wants us to wait for the offending partner to come to their senses and turn to Him to be saved. In a perfect world, people would find the strength to wait for restoration, but as it was and still is, most of us only have the strength to be concerned for our own welfare.

As leaders in the first church, Paul instructed husbands to love their wives, and wives are instructed to respect their husbands.[1005] Peter told men to honor and treat their wives with understanding, "That your prayers may not hindered".[1006] If both were to follow Jesus' instructions, they would put each other's needs ahead of themselves. But again, we are often so far from perfect. The best gift Jesus taught us is kindness to one another. And even that gift is hard to practice when we place our desires first.

Some religions teach that marriage is eternal, and a man and woman married through an earthly ceremony are bound together forever, regardless how ill-suited their relationship was during their lifetimes. But Jesus was clear when He said, "For in the resurrection they neither marry, nor are given in marriage, but are as the angels of God in heaven."[1007] Jesus words set people free from marriage vows not ordained by God. We can only imagine the horror of having to live with someone eternally who abused us during our life cycle. Apparently, marriage and childbearing are only earthly events.

Many Western societies, including the United States, followed the Bible's advice in marriage laws, and divorce was only allowed in cases of adultery or wrongdoing. But in 1959, the US Supreme Court changed family law, by allowing "No Fault Divorce". This led to a rush of older men leaving the wives and children of their youth, to marry younger less burdensome women who saw the benefits in relations with financially established older men.

Most of the ex-wives didn't work outside the home, but this legal rebuke of Jesus words forced a migration of women in the western Christian world to enter the workforce in mass to support themselves and their children. It also led to the Women's Rights Movement, as divorced women were now seeking equal treatment and pay.

Again, Satan succeeded in further dividing the male and female. His main goal was and still is, to cripple the army of the Lord. Children of divorced parents were now at more risk of abandonment, becoming easier prey to predators and even faced extermination. Abortion of pre-born children was legalized just a few years later in 1967 in some States and 1973 in all. How this must have grieved the heart of God.

Going back to the law of male dominance, it may sound like a good idea to some but was never God's intention or any part of His heart, as He has given all people free will. His first gift to each of us is partnering with Him and with each other through choice, regardless of gender, race, or culture, to build on our beautiful differences for a paradise here on Earth as it is in Heaven.[1008]

Traditionally some churches put a limit on women preaching or even teaching, but Jesus didn't seem to hold this tradition as He chose a woman outside the Jewish faith as His first missionary. She had been married several times and was then living with a man not her husband, yet Jesus revealed Himself to her first as the promised Messiah. Then she gathered a whole town to come and meet Him.[1009] Apparently her pulpit was the town square.

In this age of fallen mankind, when the whole world is in more turmoil than in our remembered history, it will take God's entire army: Male, female, young, old, rich, and poor, of many tribes and languages to reap the harvest of souls for His Kingdom. The Bible tells us even "a child shall lead them."[1010]

King David understood the heart of God: He wrote, "When my father and my mother forsake me, then the LORD will take me up."[1011] The Book of Proverbs often called the Book of Wisdom, tells us, "My son, hear the instruction of thy father, and forsake not the law of thy mother."[1012] Noting both are important.

Jesus came to set humanity free and restore God's original order in all things on the earth. Paul explained it so well when He said, "There is neither Jew nor Greek, there is neither bond nor free, there is neither male nor female: for ye are all one in Christ Jesus."[1013] In God's eyes, we are equally valuable.

But it's important to recognize and celebrate our differences. Men carry unique roles as fathers, protectors, providers, and guides to the proper roles for their children. While women provide childbearing, nurturing and societal life skills. Children struggle without the benefits of both genders as parents. Both sexes carry a part of God's heart, and we cannot take away from either. Nor can we turn one into the other as weird modern science tries to persuade us to do.

Paul tells us, "The husband is head of the wife, as also Christ is head of the church; and He is the Savior of the body."[1014] This is to protect her and their children as Christ protects the church. God made her to be a helpmate to her husband to take care of the garden God has given them. That is whatever part of society God has placed them in to grow the Kingdom of God, but not their own selfish plans.

Can we ignore the prophet Joel's words when God told him, "I will pour out My Spirit upon all flesh; and your sons and your daughters shall prophesy?" This word from God is also repeated in the New Testament, the book of Acts.[1015]

Moses reminded the people of Israel in the desert, "Take heed to yourself, and diligently keep yourself, lest you forget the things your eyes have seen, and lest they depart from your heart all the days of your life. And teach them to your children and your grandchildren, especially concerning the day you stood before the LORD your God in Horeb, when the LORD said to me, 'Gather the people to Me, and I will let them hear My words, that they may learn to fear Me all the days they live on the earth, and that they may teach their children."[1016]

Over time many religious leaders of all faiths have minimized the importance of the role of women as teachers of God's wisdom even though He instructed daughters to be taught also. In doing so we often miss the female strength of God's heart as He created humanity male and female, both incomplete without the other.

Because of this division, children often pay the price as fodder for the enemy's camp as we count the climbing casualties of the almost seventy million missing children in the US alone who weren't given the right to be born, and the millions of others caught in snares. Without utilizing the fullness of the male and female's spiritual gifts, as a whole, the church is not operating at the full power of the Holy Spirit revealing the fullness of God's heart.

The reason I'm bringing up this difficult topic, is that in my opinion this uneven church and home life has crippled Western society with people of all walks of life rebelling against all forms of restrictions, resulting in rampant divorce, runaway children, and increased tolerance to sin. Without the true importance of roles and spiritual functions together as male and female, the man-made Kingdom of God will always be a single-parent household bringing forth a dysfunctional army.

This one-sidedness has also put undue pressure on men, as they can't effectively operate in their full potential, without the spiritual anointing of the female part of God's heart. As the saying goes, "two heads are better than one". Working as a team, making decisions together, they can move much further with amazing synergy, meaning "the whole is greater than the sum of its parts", instead of leaving the burden on men alone,

So how do we fix this division between male and female, as well as many others, where a sense of superiority rules even in our churches through divisions of gender, class, age, property, race, or anything else stunting the growth of the Kingdom of God. We must put our differences aside and honor one another and the differing gifts of God placed in us, since each person is made in our Lord's image completely unique. Do we dare question His motives and plans?

The Lord is quick to point out that His kingdom is of every tribe and language.[1017] That means God does not hold favoritism, on any self-imposed divisions human societies tolerate. His love knows no bounds and He has plenty of it for all of us. I often tell people I'm His favorite one, but the truth is, I know full well that to God all believers are His favorite ones in different stages of spiritual development.

We must also remember that Jesus looked on the multitude of people and had compassion on them and said, "The harvest truly is plenteous, but the labourers are few; Pray ye therefore the Lord of the harvest, that he will send forth labourers into his harvest".[1018] As Christians we each need to grow in reflecting His image to the world as we gather in those who are lost by sharing His words. The only way to do that is for every believer to open our mouths and speak.

Several years ago, I had a dream that I was part of a village where all the women and children were on a road walking together toward a mountain to pray. From the mountain, we saw the men of our village carrying battle gear of rifles and other weapons heading off to war. I learned from that dream, how important it is for women and children to pray for men, as roles in the natural are often what is happening in the spiritual.

There should be no competition between us as we all fight the same enemies of darkness, but with different tools and talents assigned to us as male, female and individuals. We must also teach our children how to pray. "For the weapons of our warfare are not carnal but mighty in God for pulling down strongholds."[1019]

FATHERS AND CHILDREN

The other major division fragmenting the image of God's heart on Earth is between fathers and children. Do you know the first time the word love was mentioned? It was between a father and his son, Abraham and Isaac.[1020]

Modern day acceptance of rampant fornication and convenient divorce leaving a legacy of abandoned and wounded children has caused a huge chasm that seems impossible for all sides to cross. This parental breakup must be healed for society to flourish.

There is the generational devastation caused to the children of divorce. Malachi asks us, "Has not the one God made you? You belong to Him in body and spirit. And what does the one God seek? Godly offspring. So be on your guard, and do not be unfaithful to the wife of your youth."[1021]

Thankfully God always offers redemption after separation and ruin. In His promise to mankind, Malachi said, "He shall turn the heart of the fathers to the children, and the heart of the children to their fathers." [1022] This last Old Testament passage also speaks about the restoration of Father God's heart to His children, as fathers who return to Him will once again accept their own children, raised in a fatherless society.

There is a curse without this redemption between father and child as we see too many homeless adults wandering aimlessly, missing the revelation of their purpose through a father's naming and blessing. The sign of this redemption would be the coming of the spirit of Elijah to prepare the way for the great and terrible "Day of the LORD". The angel Gabriel told the parents of John the Baptist that he would be given that role to prepare the way for the Messiah.[1023]

Jesus told His disciples, "He that hath seen Me hath seen the Father".[1024] By accepting Jesus, we become one with the heart of our Father God. This godly union restores the powerful relationship between the human parent and child that can only be achieved through God's love.

As Father God said, "They shall be My people, and I will be their God. And I will give them one heart and one way, that they may fear me forever, for the good of them, and of their children after them."[1025] "I will rejoice over them to do them good, and I will plant them in this land assuredly with My whole heart and with My whole soul."[1026]

Wow, the promises of God cannot be broken! He isn't a man that He can lie.[1027] His heart is to unite us as one people loving one God joyously to become the perfect beings He created us to be formed in

His image. He gives us every good and perfect gift to accomplish all He promised.[1028] The only way we can lose out on this great deal … is to reject Him.

When Peter preached the good news of Jesus' resurrection, redemption, and forgiveness for the first time in Jerusalem, three-thousand people became disciples, and of the multitude who believed, they were of one heart and of one soul.[1029]

God's great plan of redemption is through accepting Jesus' offer, then we become one with Him and with each other, sharing His heart. This is true unity. Jesus said that through this union, everyone would know that we are His disciples, when we show we have love for one another.[1030]

One of Jesus most beautiful promises to us as individuals is, "Come unto me, all ye that labour and are heavy laden, and I will give you rest. Take my yoke upon you, and learn of me, for I am meek and lowly in heart and ye shall find rest unto your souls."[1031]

What an awesome truth! To know that our King Jesus does not beat us up, but He came as a servant, to take our burdens and give us peace. In doing so, He longs to change our hearts to match His, and follow His example selflessly serving others. His command to us is to love one another.

Apostle Paul gives men an example of godly parenting when he wrote, "Fathers, don't irritate your children and make them resentful; instead, raise them with the Lord's kind of discipline and guidance."[1032]

Often, the separations between us seem to be impossible for any of us to fix, but not impossible for our Lord. As I wrote before, the prophet Joel shares this momentous promise from God: "It shall come to pass afterward, that I will pour out My Spirit upon all flesh; and your SONS and your DAUGHTERS shall prophesy."[1033]

We cannot misinterpret God's words and since this will be a mighty act of God, no human or demon will be able to stop our children from giving all glory to God. On that day, we will look up and be amazed.

MIND OF THE LORD

By now we must know that God thinks and feels like us since we are made in His image. Like any good father, He deserves respect. And like any king, He demands it. There is a story of a young man who cursed and "blasphemed the name of the LORD". The people took him to Moses to find out the "mind of the LORD." The LORD told Moses to have all the people stone the young man.[1034] Many people today use the LORD's name as a curse word, without knowing they are in extreme danger because they have cursed themselves.

If you or your children have a disease, please ask yourself if you are under this curse of death or any other curse, and repent, meaning to stop and ask His forgiveness and mercy. God hasn't changed and without repentance, His laws are still in effect. "For the wages of sin is death but the gift of God is eternal life in Christ Jesus our Lord."[1035]

I even hear Christians and Jews take liberty with God's holy name by claiming they have no self-control and have already been forgiven. How dare we? What if others were using our names in profanity, would we not be offended? And don't we take people to court for slander? If we cursed the judge, wouldn't they throw us in jail for contempt? How much greater the offense against the God and King of the Universe? Be careful. Ignorance of the Law is no excuse, and our pathetic arguments won't save us from torment here on earth or in the next part of our existence.

In the story of Israel's high priest Eli, he and his sons kept the best parts of the offerings the people brought for God, to eat or use for themselves.[1036] His sons also laid with women who would come to the holy Tabernacle.[1037] The LORD told Eli that because of their sins, they would be replaced by "a faithful priest, that shall do according to that which is in Mine heart and in My mind."[1038] Yes, God thinks and reasons, and He chose Samuel who was offered to serve Him before his mother conceived him.[1039]

King David asked God, "What is man that You are mindful of him, and the son of man that You visit him?[1040] David then said, "He has given food to those who fear Him, He will ever be mindful of

His covenant." "The LORD hath been mindful of us, He will bless us, He will bless the house of Israel."[1041]

But there is always a two-way commitment. When the people sin against Him, the LORD will punish them. He said, "Though Moses and Samuel stood before me, yet my mind could not be toward this people, cast them out of my sight, and let them go forth."[1042]

Why was God angry? It was because of something we are still doing today in Israel, in the United States, and several other nations who call themselves His people. God said, "They built the high places of Baal, to cause their sons and their daughters to pass through the fire to Molech, which I did not command them, nor did it come into My mind that they should do this abomination".[1043] This was the same crime we are doing today, now called "Abortion".

God's people then, as His people today, worshiped other gods in self-gratification of lusts and comforts. In our western culture, we have taught our children to honor harlots and sexual deviance. Even though most of us don't burn incense to goddesses and idols today, we honor them with our time and wealth. "Did not the LORD remember them and came it not into His mind?"[1044] "Therefore the LORD has kept the disaster in mind, and brought it upon us, for the LORD our God is righteous in all the works which He does, though we have not obeyed His voice".[1045]

Knowing the mind of God, His will, and His thoughts, is so deep. We can understand somewhat by reading His Words in the Bible. But there is a more excellent way for each of us to know Him personally, through the union between us and the Spirit of God. The apostle Paul tells us, "He who searches the hearts knows what the mind of the Spirit is, because He makes intercession for the saints according to the will of God."[1046]

Paul also had encounters with God and said, "Oh, the depth of the riches both of the wisdom and knowledge of God! How unsearchable are His judgments and His ways past finding out! For who has known the mind of the LORD."[1047] "Let this mind be in you which was also in Christ Jesus."[1048] "For God hath not given us a spirit of fear, but of power, and of love and of a sound mind".[1049]

There is a communication between our minds filtered through the Holy Spirit and our human spirit. The same Spirit who raised Jesus from the dead lives in each true believer.[1050] Then we are no longer our own but joined with His Spirit living inside us, who thinks and speaks through us when we allow Him.

"'This is the covenant that I will make with them after those days', saith the LORD, 'I will put My laws into their hearts, and in their minds I will write them'".[1051] There is only one way to receive this promise of really understanding God's laws and sharing His mind, and that is to receive the baptism of the Holy Spirit, meaning that we are immersed in Him, sharing His thoughts.[1052]

Paul said, "Be mindful of the words which were spoken before by the holy prophets, and of the commandment of us the apostles of the Lord and Savior."[1053] We need to live by the words of the Bible, both the Old and New Testaments, and that takes self-discipline and a desire to keep them.

I used to listen to a radio program hosted by a knowledgeable Christian psychologist; unfortunately, I don't remember her name. She made the claim that depression and mental illness were the direct result of sin because every human being is given inward knowledge of breaking God's laws. And without accepting forgiveness that only comes through Jesus, the human mind cannot bear the weight of unresolved guilt. We must repent and forgive to be forgiven.[1054]

Several times throughout this book, I have quoted these most important words, so we fully understand the grave devastation caused by sin and how to free ourselves. "For the wages of sin is death; but the gift of God is eternal life through Jesus Christ our Lord."[1055]

James, the brother of Jesus, tells us, "Each one is tempted when he is drawn away by his own desires and enticed. Then, when desire has conceived, it gives birth to sin; and sin, when it is full-grown, brings forth death." But James also gives us the antidote to the poison of sin and the rewards we receive. He said, "Every good gift and every perfect gift is from above and comes down from the Father of lights."[1056]

If you want and need peace in your life, always do your best to do the right thing, treating others as you want them to treat you. This is what it means to fulfill Jesus' command to love God, our neighbors and ourselves. Some people try and trick God and themselves. They do all the right things as perceived in the Bible but have little of His selfless character of love and compassion. We can fool ourselves and others, but we will never fool God. Our works will prove if our hearts and minds are aligned with His.

Some of us may even judge God and believe Him to be cruel because we place so much importance on our temporary, earthly lives. We need to understand our value lies in our spirits, and what we will accomplish for God's Kingdom while we are here on earth. Remember the story of Lazarus, the beggar shared earlier? We can learn from that: Lazarus suffered unbearably during his physical life but after he died, his soul was given a place of honor with Abraham, while the selfish, rich man suffers in eternal damnation and fire.[1057]

Jesus warns all of us who place our value on earthly wealth: "Because you say, 'I am rich, have become wealthy, and have need of nothing' and do not know that you are wretched, miserable, poor, blind, and naked. I counsel you to buy from Me gold refined in the fire, that you may be rich; and white garments, that you may be clothed, that the shame of your nakedness may not be revealed; and anoint your eyes with eye salve, that you may see. As many as I love, I rebuke and chasten. Therefore, be zealous and repent.'"[1058]

We should be careful when we judge others who don't look like us. The Bible tells us, "Do not forget to entertain strangers, for by so doing some have unwittingly entertained angels."[1059] Every step we take here on earth is a test, and it's important to judge ourselves to see how we measure up to God's standards and strive to make improvements one step at a time.

Often unbelievers tell Christians, "Do not judge". But their understanding is completely wrong and harmful. We are each called to judge the sin, but not condemn the sinner. The apostle James tells us that those who turn a sinner away from their error, will save a soul from death by stopping their multitude of sins.[1060] Therefore, it's every believer's duty to God and the sinner, to tell them truth.

We cannot allow those who want to stay in sin, to keep others in bondage hurting themselves and everyone around them.

Personally, I am thankful when others give me wisdom, saving me from a heap of trouble when I'm about to do something foolish. Yet non-Christians continually tell us to stay silent. But what does God say: God told the prophet Ezekiel to warn the people that if they see destruction coming to someone and they don't sound a warning, the victim's blood is on their head.[1061] Likewise, if we see our brother or sister about to jump off a cliff it's our duty to stop them. God always gives us time to turn back to the protection and strength of His arm, until death closes the door. Do we love enough to warn them?

The most important thing a parent can do for their children is to teach them about Jesus.[1062] Over the years, I've met parents who refused to take their children to the houses of God, church, to learn His mind and words in this Christian nation. Instead, they made lazy excuses, saying they can worship God in their back yards, while silently letting entertainment raise their children to learn self-centered lusts.

Oh, how grievous it is to hear the heart-breaking prayers of parents as their children have completely turned away or broken down. Worse yet, is when parents blame God, after they refused to acknowledge Him, except to use His name in blasphemy, teaching their children to do the same.

But it's not too late, as parents we can also repent and change our personal behavior to reflect God's mind and heart. Our children are certainly worth the cost of dumping our pride and rebellion to turn to our Heavenly Father and His Son, Jesus Christ.

So what is the mind of God? To be the Shepherd of His people: leading, guiding and providing for His family and He longs for us to let Him. King David wrote, "The Lord is my Shepherd, I shall not want. He maketh me to lie down in green pastures: he leadeth me beside the still waters. He restoreth my soul. He leadeth me in the paths of righteousness for His name's sake."[1063]

WHAT IS A SOUL?

The Bible tells us God has a soul and so do each of us. As close as we can explain, our souls are the personhood of our being, the part of us that consist of our will and emotions, giving us individuality and understanding of choices. And each of us can win the souls of others through sharing God's words and love. "The fruit of the righteous is a tree of life, and he who winneth souls is wise".[1064]

When God first formed man, Adam, he was made from the dust of the ground and God "breathed into his nostrils the breath of life, and man became a living soul."[1065] The Bible describes people as living souls and tells us that in the time the descendants of Israel first went to Egypt, because there was a famine, "all the souls that came out of the loins of Jacob were seventy souls."[1066]

Then when God gave Moses His instructions for the people, He used very convincing language of the benefits in staying faithful to Him. "For I will have respect unto you, and make you fruitful, and multiply you, and establish my covenant with you … I will set My tabernacle among you, and My soul shall not abhor you. And I will walk among you and will be your God, and ye shall be My people."[1067]

In the same way, His intense passion is severe when we betray Him, "I will destroy your high places, cut down your images, and cast your carcasses upon the carcasses of your idols, and My soul shall abhor you".[1068] The LORD tests the righteous, but the wicked and the one who loves violence His soul hates".[1069]

God told Isaiah that even if His people kept all His special dates and feasts, but committed terrible sins, His soul will hate them: "They are a trouble to Me, I am weary of bearing them".[1070] This is even for those of us who attend church faithfully, but live ungodly lives at home. Or worse yet, we secretly harbor unforgiveness toward others or Him. Dare we mock God, pretending He doesn't see? "Be instructed, O Jerusalem, lest My soul depart from you, lest I make you desolate, a land not inhabited."[1071]

One of the saddest books is written by the prophet Jeremiah when the LORD told him about the coming invasion of Jerusalem.

God said, "I have forsaken Mine house, I have left Mine heritage, I have given the dearly beloved of My soul into the hand of her enemies".[1072] This was after the people were given many warnings but refused to stop sinning against God and their nation's weakest.

Jeremiah is often referred to as the weeping prophet because he spent many years warning Jerusalem's leaders, but only to see their total invasion and exile. He wrote, "If ye will not hear it, my soul shall weep in secret places for your pride; and mine eye shall weep sore, and run down with tears, because the LORD's flock is carried away captive."[1073] Jeremiah felt the emotions of the LORD.

Israel's sins were so bad, God told Jeremiah to stop praying for their good. Jeremiah was a true prophet of Israel, and he saw its destruction coming. And even though all the other prophets said there would be victory, Jerusalem was invaded, and their leaders with their families were taken captive to Babylon.[1074]

But as always, because of the LORD's covenant with Abraham, Isaac, and Jacob, His promise was to bring them back to the land although it took seventy years of captivity. God said, "Yea, I will rejoice over them to do them good, and I will plant them in this land assuredly with My whole heart and with My whole soul."[1075]

Moses instructs us to love God "with all your heart, with all your soul, and with all your strength".[1076] Throughout history after great suffering and wars, when the people returned to Him, God restored them as He promised. "So they put away the foreign gods from among them and served the LORD. And His soul could no longer endure the misery of Israel".[1077]

The books of Psalms and Proverbs tell us about our souls; "I will praise You, for I am fearfully and wonderfully made. Marvelous are Your works, and that my soul knows very well." "Praise the LORD, O my soul!"[1078]

God Himself tells us about a special One: "My Servant whom I uphold, My Elect One in whom My soul delights! I have put My Spirit upon Him, He will bring forth justice to the Gentiles".[1079] This was about Jesus and Isaiah wrote: "Yet it pleased the LORD to bruise him, He hath put Him to grief, when Thou shalt make His soul an offering for sin."[1080]

Jesus was the soul God conceived as the ultimate sacrifice for each of us. This is so great a deed that most of us in our selfish nature can't even grasp the magnitude of what Jesus gave up. Every one of us has a hard time giving up even the smallest thing in comparison. "Because He poured out His soul unto death, He was numbered with the transgressors, and He bore the sin of many, and made intercession for the transgressors".[1081]

The week before Jesus was to die, He told His disciples "Now is My soul troubled; and what shall I say? Father, save Me from this hour: but for this cause came I unto this hour."[1082] Then the night Jesus was arrested, He said to His closest disciples Peter, James, and John, "My soul is exceedingly sorrowful, even to death. Stay here and watch with Me."[1083]

Even though Jesus knew His role as the Lamb of God, was to die through this most horrible and humiliating way of crucifixion, the human part of Him felt all the emotions of pain and grief as any of us would feel. How many of us could willingly go to the slaughter?

The apostle Peter quoted King David's prophecy about the resurrection of the Messiah to come. He said, "His soul was not left in hell, neither His flesh did see corruption."[1084] The people who heard Peter believed and were baptized. "And the same day there were added unto them about three thousand souls."[1085]

Jesus talked about the human soul when He said, "For what shall it profit a man if he shall gain the whole world, and lose his own soul? Or what shall a man give in exchange for his soul?"[1086]

Many years ago, before my encounter with the LORD, I had an accident resulting in a near death experience, where my body died. Immediately I found myself in a place where there was only the brightest light that stretched out infinitely. I had no body, only a self-aware consciousness, as a living soul. I felt as if I had always been there in a state of pure bliss, with no need for anything.

Some religions believe this place is called Purgatory, where people are given another chance to enter Heaven. Perhaps this is a place to learn the truth about Him for those who are destined to enter Heaven but die before they're ready. In my case, I loved God as a child, but rejected Him in my teens and adulthood because of religious confusion told to me by other trusted adults.

I was only there for a moment before returning to my body and present trauma. Then in an instant, my consciousness (soul) was sent back to my body. But because of a lack of understanding, I spent many years thereafter in the "school of Hard Knocks" also known as foolish living, until I finally understood and surrendered my will to God. This supernatural experience caused me to search for deeper answers for the truth about life, death, and finally God. After this event, for the first time, I no longer feared death.

Paul, who gave his life in the service of God, wrote, "I will very gladly spend and be spent for your souls, though the more abundantly I love you, the less I am loved".[1087] "And the very God of peace sanctify you wholly. I pray God your whole spirit and soul and body be preserved blameless unto the coming of our Lord Jesus Christ".[1088]

Paul added, "For the word of God is quick, and powerful, and sharper than any two-edged sword, piercing even to the dividing asunder of soul and spirit, and of the joints and marrow, and is a discerner of the thoughts and intents of the heart." "Now the just shall live by faith, but if any man draw back, my soul shall have no pleasure in him."[1089]

The apostle James tells us "He who turns a sinner from the error of his way will save a soul from death and cover a multitude of sins".[1090] Isn't that what Jesus is still doing today, by using us to spread His word through His love, compassion, and mercy?

Peter tells us, "Since you have purified your souls in obeying the truth through the Spirit in sincere love of the brethren, love one another fervently with a pure heart".[1091] He also warns us to, "abstain from fleshly lusts which war against the soul". "For ye were as sheep going astray but are now returned unto the Shepherd and Bishop of your souls."[1092]

Why is the LORD so concerned with our souls? We are each created as a part of Him, to have His Spirit living in us, sharing our souls, mind and body with His. This is a perfect union between God and mankind and can only be achieved through our soul's free will.

SPIRIT TO SPIRIT

We first hear of this spiritual union when John the Baptist was in the wilderness and people came to him to be baptized in the Jordan River, where he preached a baptism of repentance for the remission of sins. He said, "There comes One after me who is mightier than I, whose sandal strap I am not worthy to stoop down and loose. I indeed baptized you with water, but He will baptize you with the Holy Spirit."[1093]

After that Jesus came to the Jordan River and was baptized by John. "Immediately, coming up from the water, He saw the heavens parting and the Spirit descending upon Him (Jesus) like a dove."[1094]

Later still, Jesus told the priest Nicodemus that a person must be "Born Again" of the Spirit to enter the Kingdom of God. Nicodemus questioned how to do that.[1095] The only way is to freely give control of our lives to Jesus, making Him our Lord and not just our Savior. By surrendering our wants, desires, skills, and possessions as well as our rights to offenses through repentance, we are able to accept God's forgiveness and salvation.

Finally, we are offered the honor to become the temple of the Holy Spirit for God to live in us, entering an eternal spiritual union. Like a marriage to become one with our spouse, there is a voluntary consummation, between the Spirit of God and our human spirit.[1096]

The Bible tells us there are two kinds of baptisms. While Apostle Paul was in Ephesus (an ancient city in Turkey), he met some disciples of Jesus and asked them, "'Did you receive the Holy Spirit when you believed?' They answered, 'No, we have not even heard that there is a Holy Spirit.' So Paul asked, 'Then what baptism did you receive?' 'John's baptism,' they replied. Paul said, 'John's baptism was a baptism of repentance. He told the people to believe in the one coming after him, that is, in Jesus.' On hearing this, they were baptized in the name of the Lord Jesus. When Paul placed his hands on them, the Holy Spirit came on them, and they spoke in tongues and prophesied."[1097]

The baptism of the Holy Spirit is so powerful that "God did extraordinary miracles through Paul, so that even handkerchiefs and aprons that touched him were taken to the sick, and their illnesses were cured, and evil spirits left them."[1098] This was the hand of God, displayed through Paul in the power of the Holy Spirit.

The Holy Spirit is a very real entity as are other spirits. Those who practice the occult and use idols or things for healing and spiritual power, invite the spirits of fallen angels and creatures to work through them. These spiritual entities also known as demons, are in rebellion to God as they take control of our souls and bodies with their inferior power for supernatural works in so called magic. These were the third of heaven cast down to Earth which still plague us today.[1099]

But we can choose to pledge our loyalty to Jesus Christ as our Lord through faith, with repentance and by renouncing these evil entities. Our King Jesus already paid with His body, blood, and life to cleanse us of every mistake. We can then invite the Holy Spirit to live in us and through us. This is what it means to be "Born Again".

This is also why God says He is a jealous God, and He goes as far as to call His people prostitutes for worshiping demons and having a spiritual relationship with them.[1100] His first command to Israel is,

"You shall have no other gods before Me".[1101] Allowing demons to inhabit us is a serious offense as we become spiritually and physically infested, replacing the Holy Spirit to have control over us, often leading to physical and mental disease.

Dabbling in the occult and other ways of breaking God's laws usually leads to many kinds of sin, especially immorality. The sicknesses we face in the natural through sexually transmitted disease are a physical manifestation of the sickness in our souls caused by betrayal of our God through sin.[1102] The apostle Paul said, "For the wages of sin is death", as he described our earnings in rebelling against God. But he added, "The gift of God is eternal life in Christ Jesus our Lord",[1103] giving us eternal hope.

We may think when we allow demons access to our lives and our bodies that we gain power and control. But the opposite is true. We become slaves to Satan, used by his minions to build an opposite kingdom of evil which shows no mercy. And we open doors to sickness and death in ourselves and everyone around us, especially our children.[1104]

Then finally, if we haven't repented in this earthly life and accepted the blood sacrifice of our Savior, the Lord Jesus Christ, our names will not be found written in the Book of Life. Our consciousness (our souls) will end in the Lake of Fire through the second death, along with the rebellious entities we have served. Then death and hell will also be cast into the Lake of Fire to exist no more.[1105]

Yes, all life is a series of choices. Choosing whom we will serve is the greatest one.[1106] Blaming God or others for our bad decisions won't hold up in any court. Neither will excuses hold up in the Court of Heaven when the Judge of All opens the Book of Life, and our names are not written there.[1107]

Many people accept Jesus in name only but refuse to submit to the Holy Spirit's leading; instead, they opt to stay in control and do incredible damage to His name. Could this be what it means to "blaspheme the Holy Spirit" for which Jesus warned there is no forgiveness? Such as when a person claims to be the voice of, and do the acts of, the Holy Spirit, but in reality work in complete rebellion and perversion?[1108]

King Herod was an example of that when God's judgement was swift against him after having some of Jesus' disciples arrested. Herod sat on his throne and gave a speech. "The people kept shouting, 'The voice of a god and not of a man!' Then immediately an angel of the LORD struck him because he did not give glory to God. And he was eaten by worms and died."[1109]

As Christians we should not only carry Jesus' name but accept the Spirit of God's invitation to become His living temple. When we allow Him access, our lives are completely transformed as we move from earthly gratification to spiritual enrichment. This relationship is consensual and allows God access to accomplish the purposes for which we were created. Paul wrote, "What agreement has the temple of God with idols? For you are the temple of the living God. God has said: 'I will dwell in them and walk among them. I will be their God, and they shall be My people.'"[1110]

I once met a man who was very angry with God because his young son had died. The man said he was ready to die and wanted to go to heaven where his son was but wanted nothing to do with God or the Son of God. I told him he couldn't go to Heaven without Jesus, because Heaven is the place where God lives.

Would you invite someone to live at your house when they want nothing to do with you? The most important part of the salvation message is that God gives each of us a choice to turn away from our bitterness and unbelief to accept Him and become part of His family.

So why do we need to repent? Jesus said, "If you love me, keep my commandments".[1111] Often teachers of the New Testament disregard the Old Testament and teach all God's laws were replaced by one love commandment.

But like any child, we start out not knowing how to do anything, until we're taught how to eat, talk, walk, yet we still act like babies. Then we move on to higher skills in reading, writing, math, and science. How many years do we spend in basic school to learn earthly skills? And how few years do we spend learning about our God, creation, and eternity? For some of us, it's an hour per week if that.

The result is that we spend a lifetime breaking the laws of God, which carry a death sentence. But the good news is that Jesus already paid the penalty by dying for us. Our part is to acknowledge our sin and ask forgiveness to allow His payment to set us free. If we continue to argue that we are not guilty when we are, we will be caught up in the Court of Heaven with Satan as our prosecutor, and no advocate to plead our case. There is NO salvation without repentance.[1112]

And then only with the salvation of Jesus Christ and the baptism of the Holy Spirit, allowing God Himself to live in us, sharing our soul, spirit and body, can we have a full and true relationship with our eternal Father. The key to this union is surrender. Are we willing to give up the most precious thing we own, our free will and control, to allow the Holy Spirit to rule and reign in us and with us?

Through the knowledge and power enabled in a partnership with the Holy Spirit we accomplish the greater works of God assigned to us when we were created. King David wrote "You formed my inward parts; You covered me in my mother's womb … Your eyes saw my substance, being yet unformed. And in Your book they all were written, The days fashioned for me, When as yet there were none of them."[1113]

CHAPTER FIVE

Author of Emotions

GOD IS LOVE

It's amazing to read how many scriptures there are commanding us to love the LORD our God, love one another, and love oneself. So what is love? There are many viewpoints. Let's explore what the Creator of Love means by it.

A description of "Love" is "a strong complex emotion or feeling causing one to appreciate, delight in, and crave the presence or possession of another; to please or promote the welfare of the other; devoted affection or attachment". One of the descriptions of "Emotion" in the dictionary is "the power of feeling". "Love can be an emotion to feel; a noun as something to possess; a verb as a call to action; an adjective to describe something."[1114] All these descriptions are about something positive.

The word "Love" is first used in the story of Abraham. He had gained peace with his neighbors, and he called on the name of the LORD, Yahweh "the Everlasting God".[1115] Since the time of Abel, it was a required practice to offer blood sacrifices of animals. One day God asked for the best from Abraham to test his loyalty, by giving the life of his son Isaac, "whom you love", as a burnt offering. For the first time the Bible acknowledged an earthly love relationship, and it was between a father and son.[1116]

Because of disobedience in the garden of Eden by humanity's first parents, Adam and Eve, love between a man and woman had become tainted with self-interests. And because of the death penalty placed upon mankind, fatherhood gave Abraham immortality through his son Isaac and future descendants he would bear. Abraham had an older son, Ishmael, the son of a slave girl named Hagar. The legitimate heir Isaac, was loved and valued, while Ishmael was eventually banished.[1117]

The story tells us God asked Abraham to sacrifice his son Isaac to test his loyalty. But just when Abraham lifted the knife to kill Isaac on the altar, God stopped him and supplied a ram for the sacrifice.[1118] Only payment in blood could cleanse sins where judgment was punishable by death. A thousand years later, God the eternal Father sacrificed His own Son, Yeshua, whose immortal blood satisfies the penalty of breaking God's universal laws for all mankind forever.[1119]

Because of his willingness to follow God, even to sacrificing his beloved son Isaac, Abraham received God's favor and authority to become the father of nations.[1120] It's also a story to remind us, that to be a follower of God, it can cost us everything.[1121]

The second time the word "Love" is mentioned follows the beloved and promised son Isaac who passed on that love to his wife Rebekah.[1122] She gave birth to twin sons, Esau and Jacob. Isaac loved his son Esau, but it was for selfish gain, since Esau was a hunter and provided his father with fresh meat.[1123]

Esau was like his father, considering a meal more important than the position and authority God had given him as the first-born son. Esau sold his birthright to his brother Jacob for a stew of lentils and bread.[1124] God's favor in his inheritance for generations to come, was not as valuable to Esau as a meal.

But Jacob whose name was later changed to Israel, became the founder of the most influential nation as God's chosen people. It meant so much to him that with the help of his mother Rebekah, he even tricked his father Isaac for the first-born blessing.[1125] God later said, "Yet I loved Jacob, and I hated Esau."[1126]

Malachi warns us not to be like Esau and bring God the lame and blind of our sacrifices, meaning our left-overs, even in our works. Do we offer God our discards, even with our spare time? Then we demand to be blessed and blame Him when He doesn't answer our prayers?[1127]. We should each ask ourselves if we treat God in this way.

Jacob didn't receive the full love of his father, and he passed that divided love on to his two wives, Rachel he loved and Leah was unloved.[1128] The two sisters and their two handmaidens bore Jacob twelve sons and a daughter. Jacob, whose name was changed to Israel, loved Rachel's eldest son Joseph more than the others.[1129]

Down through the pages of history, as we follow this human perspective, love seems to be a contagious emotion as well as learned behavior based mostly on selfish value. These divisions of love have caused problems between the tribes and families to this very day.

This powerful emotion passed down from Father God also reveals to us His desire for human love. We saw the example of love from a husband to his wife, then the love of a father to his son. Now God says He gives His mercy to those who love Him, and we prove our love by keeping His commandments which means listening to His advice for us.[1130]

Would a ruler require love? Yet God does, as a husband requires love from his wife and a father from his children, so God requires love from His people, just as we need love from our families and close friends. You shall "love the LORD your God with all your heart, soul, and strength."[1131]

In His kindness, God teaches us to love through His commandments, "Do not seek revenge or bear a grudge against anyone among your people but love your neighbor as yourself. I am the LORD your God." "The foreigner residing among you must be treated as your native-born. Love them as yourself." [1132]

Why would God instruct His people to love others unless this is how He loves us and treats anyone who wants to be part of His family? Moses wrote that the LORD chose the descendants of the people He loves so He can keep passing on the inheritance He promised to the generations before them.[1133]

Oh, what an evil action to kill our own unborn children, robbing them and God of their destinies to receive the inheritance that He promised, even generations before they were born! If we only realized that we are killing God's plans and destroying His gift of love to our family line and to the nations of the earth. The LORD clarifies through Moses that He doesn't love us because we are the best, but because He keeps His promises of mercy for a thousand generations made to our forefathers who kept His commandments.[1134]

Who are these forefathers? The most notable are Adam and Eve, Seth, Enoch, Noah, Shem, Abraham and Sarah, Isaac and Rebecca, Jacob with Leah and Rachel. Then the promises were continued to Israel's descendants and those grafted into the Kingdom of Israel through the blood of the promised Messiah, Yeshua of Nazareth.[1135]

Many people say they don't care if God loves us, then wonder why their lives are a mess. Or they may own many worldly goods but lack the peace to enjoy them. God's promises are to those of us and our offspring, who love Him. "He will love you and bless you and multiply you, He will bless the fruit of your womb and the fruit of your land, your grain and your new wine and your oil, the increase of your cattle and the offspring of your flock, in the land of which He swore to your fathers to give you."[1136] He said, "That I may cause those who love Me to inherit wealth, that I may fill their treasuries".[1137]

With the LORD and people, to be successful and thrive, there must be a two-way relationship. Just as it is here on earth between a husband and wife, parents to children, siblings to siblings, friends to friends. God gives many promises of how He shows His love and also what He expects in return: "And now, Israel, what does the LORD your God require of you, but to fear (revere) the LORD your God, to walk in all His ways and to love Him, to serve the LORD your God with all your heart and with all your soul and to keep the commandments of the LORD and His statutes which I command you today for your good".[1138]

His commandments are simple, yet in our selfish humanity they can often be difficult for us to follow. "He defends the cause of the fatherless and the widow, and loves the foreigner residing among you, giving them food and clothing. And you are to love those who are foreigners, for you yourselves were foreigners in Egypt."[1139] Because of many migrations, all of us are the descendants of foreigners, which the LORD is reminding us. Although in our modern times, we must also protect our homes and be careful to distinguish between immigration and invasion, so we don't lose our children's inheritance.

These are just a few of His instructions, all filled with His love in compassion, mercy, and wisdom. But in my experience, I have found that many of us, like little children, have the most creative ways of subverting God's instructions then blame Him when things go wrong!

I mentioned him before but would like to reiterate once again because of his vast treasures, a thousand wives and concubines, and immense influence this man had! He is a good example of our human failures ... Can you guess who it is? King Solomon, born to King David and Bathsheba. He was loved by the LORD and became the world's most powerful and wealthy king because of God's continuous favor. Like Moses, he had incredible personal visitations with our powerful God. But his addiction to women was stronger than his love and loyalty for the LORD, and he defiled the land with demons by building temples to foreign gods for his wives, which led God's people all over Israel into worshiping idols even generations later.[1140]

I have often heard people say the LORD loves unconditionally and that's true in the sense that God is Love and He cannot go against His nature. "But", and there is a "but" … Yahweh is a perfect judge and God of justice. The only real deciding factor of right versus wrong is recorded in His instructions given to Moses. They start out with the Ten Commandments, [1141] and are then broken down in the books of Exodus and Leviticus.

Although God loved King Solomon, his rebellion against God's commandments allowed evil to prevail, poisoning the people and the land for generations. As a good Father, God cannot allow sin which produces sickness and death to continue without end.[1142] "It is a fearful thing to fall into the hands of the living God."[1143]

King David tells us, "For the LORD is righteous."[1144] "He loves righteousness and justice. The earth is full of the goodness of the LORD."[1145] "For the LORD loves justice and does not forsake His saints, they are preserved forever. But the descendants of the wicked shall be cut off."[1146]

Even though the House of David, just as all the other tribes, had its share of sin, the Bible says that God, "chose the tribe of Judah, the mount Zion which he loved."[1147] "The LORD loveth the gates of Zion more than all the dwellings of Jacob."[1148]

So, what is the secret ingredient for God's continual love and favor? In Psalm 91, one of the most comforting songs, God said, "Because he hath set his love upon Me, therefore will I deliver him, I will set him on high, because he hath known My name."[1149] The secret to receiving God's love is to love God back.

Like all humans made in His image, God also requires love for His well-being, and He created us as a life form with His extreme passions and the ability to return spiritual love? The Bible is full of love truths, God says, "I love those who love Me, and those that seek Me early shall find Me."[1150] Yes, GOD is LOVE!

This aspect of God's passion is written throughout the Song of Solomon, as a man deeply in love with a woman. In this story, Jewish scholars believe the Shulamite woman represents Israel, while Christians often believe she represents the Church. Still others understand it as a love affair between God and individual believers.

Here are some verses of love between them: "Let him kiss me with the kisses of his mouth. For thy love is better than wine."[1151] The woman eagerly petitions His mouth for His precious words. "Tell me, you whom I love, where you graze your flock and where you rest your sheep at midday. Why should I be like a veiled woman beside the flocks of your friends?"[1152] She wants to know why we should hide ourselves from Him and those He feeds and loves.

He answers, "I have compared thee, O my love, to a company of horses in Pharaoh's chariots."[1153] In ancient times, the king's horses were the most prized and valued. "He brought me to the banqueting house and His banner over me was love."[1154] His banquet contains all our provision covering us with His banner of love. Can anything dare to come against us without His permission?

The woman responds of her need for more because she is lovesick for Him. "Sustain me with cakes of raisins, refresh me with apples, for I am lovesick."[1155] When we feel such strong love towards God, He passionately draws near to us, just as two lovesick people who can't get enough of one another. King David had this kind of spiritual relationship with Him. In one of his psalms he wrote, "O God, You are my God. Early will I seek You. My soul thirsts for You. My flesh longs for You in a dry and thirsty land where there is no water."[1156]

The LORD responds, "Rise up, my love, my fair one, and come away."[1157] He calls to each of us who's hearts yearn for His presence, as deep calls unto deep, Spirit to spirit.[1158] He then reminds us the winter is past and it's time to bring forth the harvest.[1159] What does this mean? We are now ready to reproduce what He's put in us, bearing fruit to bring others into His Kingdom. Jesus last words to His followers were, "Make disciples of all nations".[1160] We can start with those around us.

This command isn't a forced response but comes out of pure, spiritual love. Like a man who longs to give his wife a baby produced by their union of love He calls to each of us. For those of us who answer the call, He longs to enjoy our beauty in the secret place of who we really are. Not as the world sees us, but as a love-stricken husband who only sees our amazing spiritual beauty.

As God chasers, like the Shulamite woman, there are times when we feel distanced from Him. Then we look for Him when we're ready. She said, "I will rise now, and go about the city, in the streets and in the squares, I will seek the one I love. I sought him, but I did not find him."[1161] Our hesitation and distraction costs us more heartache, but when we keep persisting, He is never far, drawn to our heartfelt love for Him, He cannot resist us either. And so we find Him again. More and more we dare not let Him go, recognizing our complete dependence on Him.[1162]

The songs of love go back and forth between us and the Lover of our souls throughout the rest of the verses in the Song of Solomon. Few of us can understand this relationship fully even between human love. How can the Creator of all, love us like this? God says to us, "You have ravished my heart, My sister, my spouse. You have ravished my heart with one look of your eyes".[1163]

Then, like the Shulamite woman, our soul finally surrenders to our beloved God's love for us. "Set me as a seal upon Your heart, as a seal upon Your arm. For love is as strong as death, jealousy as cruel as the grave. Its flames are flames of fire, a most vehement flame. Many waters cannot quench love, nor can floods drown it. If a man would give for love all the wealth of his house, it would be utterly despised."[1164]

"LOVE" is such a powerful testimony of the emotion our Creator placed in us. This emotion is in Him first and then placed in everyone called by His name, made in His image, and created for His glory.[1165]

Scriptures consistently describe God's amazing love for the nation of Israel, which has been honored above all others because of the covenant made to His faithful ones, Abraham, Isaac, and Jacob. "I am the Lord your God, The Holy One of Israel, your Savior. I gave Egypt for your ransom, Ethiopia and Seba in your place. Since you were precious in My sight, you have been honored and I have loved you".[1166]

God violently proves His jealousy whenever Israel would make agreements with their enemies instead of trusting Him. Their rebellion against Him would always lead to His people committing spiritual adultery by worshiping their enemies' idols, and always to their detriment. Yet He continually rescues those who are remorseful because of His unfailing love.[1167]

In another verse revealing the passion of our lovestruck LORD for Jerusalem, He says, "I remember you, the kindness of your youth, the love of your betrothal, when you went after Me in the wilderness, in a land not sown."[1168] But God's people are often fickle and insist on turning away to follow the things we feel we have control over. Unlike us, He patiently waits for us to return and heals us. But often after tremendous loss on our part which causes us to repent.

God's love and mercy are so great, and even though He has absolute cause to abandon us, He takes us back, adjusting His command when it comes to remarriage. 'If a man divorces his wife, and she goes from him and becomes another man's, may he return to her again? Would not that land be greatly polluted? But you have played the harlot with many lovers, yet return to Me, says the LORD."[1169]

Some of us commit spiritual adultery with occultic demons through fortune-telling by psychics, tarot cards, astrology, yoga, spirit guides, witchcraft, Ouija boards, crystals, worshipping other persons or objects, some music and movies, even wealth. We can easily become contaminated by these sources of spiritual power other than the power of the Holy Spirit. God warns us, we and our families will be plundered by the rebellious spirits we empower. These dangerous demonic entities we chase after, believing we get power and control from them, really hate us, and bring sickness and death to ultimately control us instead.

And God, our true love, asks us an eternal, life-determining question: "What will you do in the end?" Without Him, there is nothing good. Eternal damnation is existence completely cut off from the only eternal source of light, love, and life, which is God. Who will we choose?[1170]

When hearing stories in the Old Testament, people often interpret God as angry and vengeful. But because of His enormous love, He continuously warns us what will happen when we separate ourselves from Him. And He keeps drawing us back to Himself through all the pain, chaos, and destruction we ourselves allow through our own bad behavior. Who needs a spouse or family member who betrays us at every single turn? It was mankind through Adam and Eve who chose to decide for themselves, against the command of God, to acquire the knowledge of good and evil. Now each of us must continually make that decision.

Our Creator describes His people as a beautiful and delicate woman.[1171] But like an unfaithful wife, He cannot reward our unfaithful behavior. He reminds us that our spiritual lovers, those we place above Him, will leave us abandoned, abused, and ultimately, we'll be destroyed.[1172]

As this prophecy is to the nation of Israel, it's also to all nations and people who have claimed Yahweh as our God. Oh Israel, America, and the Western nations: Why won't you listen? As the LORD spoke through the prophet Ezekiel, He is still speaking today.

God says, "Because you poured out your lust and exposed your naked body in your promiscuity with your lovers, and because of all your detestable idols, and because you gave them your children's blood, therefore I am going to gather all your lovers, with whom you found pleasure, those you loved as well as those you hated. I will gather them against you from all around and will strip you in front of them."[1173]

He continues, "I will sentence you to the punishment of women who commit adultery and who shed blood. I will bring on you the blood vengeance of my wrath and jealous anger. Then I will deliver you into the hands of your lovers, and they will tear down your mounds and destroy your lofty shrines. They will strip you of your clothes and take your fine jewelry and leave you stark naked. They will bring a mob against you, who will stone you and hack you to pieces with their swords."[1174]

As an angry husband, God removes His hand of protection and favor, leaving us completely vulnerable both as individuals and as nations. Our idols and their priests will not save us, because we have turned away from His love.[1175] Does He destroy us to get even? Absolutely not! Our destruction comes because in our rebellious state we destroy everything He has created as beautiful, including our future children who are God's gift to us to build His Kingdom and keep us strong.[1176]

God calls His people the LORD's army.[1177] The more terrible our sins become the more we empower His enemies. Does a General destroy his future soldiers? Yet we kill our own and He must stop us.

But as said before, to those who survive with a repentant heart, the LORD's mercy endures forever.[1178] He said, "I will establish my covenant with you, and you will know that I am the LORD. Then, when I make atonement for you for all you have done, you will remember and be ashamed and never again open your mouth because of your humiliation."[1179] The atonement was Jesus, the Lamb of God. "For God so loved the world that He gave His only begotten Son, that whoever believes in Him should not perish but have everlasting life".[1180]

Our tears of true repentance move His never-ending compassionate heart to cover our nakedness, our shame and guilt with His wings. He renews His spiritual covenant of love and marriage like a man to a woman. "You became Mine", says the LORD God.[1181]

Whether we sin because it feels good for a moment, or we make excuses that we have no control over our bad behavior, God says we are worse than prostitutes since they get paid, but those running to sinful pleasure make payments to their lovers.[1182]

What few people understand is our sins allow demons (fallen angels) unhindered access to our human souls through spiritual infestation, using our bodies as their vessels and making us their slaves. Our only reward is that sin may make us feel temporarily satisfied or numb, but like addictive drugs, it eventually robs us of all self-worth and control, leaving us in torment and sickness. The apostle James said, "When desire has conceived, it gives birth to sin, and sin when it is full-grown, brings forth death."[1183]

But there is hope! After we are infested and plundered to the point of emptiness, God beckons us to return to our first husband, our LORD. Even after all the spiritual prostitution and lies giving every other thing credit for His gifts to us, God doesn't break His covenant and He says, "I will heal their backsliding, I will love them freely, for My anger has turned away."[1184] "The LORD your God in your midst, the Mighty One, will save. He will rejoice over you with gladness, He will quiet you with His love, He will rejoice over you with singing."[1185] But again this is always a choice on our part. Will we let Him?

So how big is God's love? I have met people who felt their sins were too terrible, and God could never forgive them. This is where we come to the Good News (the Gospel) of the Savior of the World![1186]

HIS LOVE IN THE NEW TESTAMENT

Let's look at the ONE who is the human image of God in the flesh, according to the testimony of the apostle John. He begins by telling us, "In the beginning was the Word, and the Word was with God, and the Word was God."[1187] We will explore how God's powerful emotion of love translates to human emotion through the earthly life of Jesus.

Two of the major principles Jesus taught was to love the LORD our God with all our heart and love our neighbors as ourselves. We often call this the New Covenant, but it is really the summation of the Ten Commandments in the laws God had given to Moses. The first five teach us how to love God, and the second five, how to love others.[1188]

Jesus taught us more on applying God's commandments: "Love your enemies, bless them that curse you, do good to them that hate you, and pray for them which despitefully use you, and persecute you."[1189] That's a tall order which all of us struggle to uphold. Yet Jesus made Himself the living example of the Father's perfect love by allowing His own crucifixion. Through His selfless sacrifice, Jesus expects all His believers to take up the cross given to us and follow Him.[1190]

An example of this Scripture in action is to revisit the story of a rich man who was given that offer. He kept all God's commandments, and one day he knelt before Jesus and asked what else he needed to do to be saved. Jesus looked at him and loved him, then asked the man to give up his vast wealth and follow Him. Sadly, the man declined, he wasn't ready to trade his earthly riches, even though this personal invitation was made by the very source of universal power and eternal life, Yeshua the Messiah.[1191] He still makes that offer to each one of us today, but the sacrifice is always different and based on what we love over Him. Do we love Him enough to give Him what we value the most?

Another key point about God's amazing love is in the story of the sinful woman who washed Jesus' feet with her tears. She wiped them dry with her hair, kissed them, and anointed them with expensive fragrant oil.[1192] Jesus was confronted about her actions, and His answer was, "'Therefore I say to you, her sins, which are many, are forgiven, for she loved much. But to whom little is forgiven, the same loves little.' Then He said to her, 'your sins are forgiven.'"[1193]

We can apply these powerful words to our Lord as He hung on the cross as the replacement for all the sins of the world, past, present, and future, while He said, "Father forgive them, for they know not what they do."[1194] THIS IS AMAZING! In one short sentence, the only person given authority to judge the entire world absolved each and every one of us from every sin, which is every crime against the Father. But we must claim this pardon by accepting His forgiveness and forgiving others.[1195] It sounds easy but can only be done through faith in Jesus alone.

In Western society, we often revere a mother's love, and discount the role of men as parents, but here we see the most powerful love of the Father. Jesus said, "For the Father loves the Son and has given all things unto His hand and shows Him all things that He Himself does. And He will show Him greater works than these, that you may marvel."[1196] "Therefore My Father loves Me, because I lay down My life that I may take it again."[1197]

The most recited Bible verse in Christianity is: "For God so loved the world that He gave His only begotten Son, that whoever believes in Him should not perish but have everlasting life."[1198] In this instance of self-sacrifice, the Son represented the Father to save the world. In these modern times of great rebellion, fewer children can say they follow the orders of their fathers even in small matters, let alone lay down their lives.

Several times in the book of John, the command that Jesus, as the human image of God the Father, gave to His followers was: "Love one another; as I have loved you, that ye also love one another."[1199] This is the perfect example we are to follow to fulfill all the Father's commandments summed up to: Love the LORD and love one another. Jesus continues to say His followers will be known by keeping these most basic laws.[1200]

Another powerful statement made by Jesus is, "If anyone loves Me, he will keep My word, and My Father will love him, and We will come to him and make Our home with him".[1201] Has anyone ever thought it's possible to have the Spirit of the God of the universe living in us, inhabiting our bodies as living temples, calling us to partner with the Godhead, Spirit to spirit?

It's too huge a possibility and can barely be imagined! That is, until we invite the living God into our hearts, the center of our being. And as we surrender more and more, He can take over and transform us through the new birth process from the inside out, creating us in His spiritual image.[1202] Do we want this? Wow, how can we refuse this most exciting offer? What else is there to live for? Yet so many of us continue to want only our own weak and flawed self-rule.

Perhaps most of humanity doesn't trust Him. But this next verse explains God's character through His example of complete sacrifice, "Greater love hath no man than this, that a man lay down his life for his friends."[1203] God is Love! We can fill in the blanks to suit our own thinking, but there was no greater love in all creation, in all time, than given by the Son of God, Yeshua. He is the complete human image of God the Father. He laid down His mortal body to destroy every sin committed by humanity: past, present, and future, so we don't have to pay for breaking the universal laws in place since the foundation of the world.

This amnesty is given to anyone who believes and accepts the offer to become His. In return, Jesus requires our love and allegiance. This gives us a covenantal contract with the King of kings, born again into the most royal and most noble of families. What a terrible waste for anyone to miss out by not accepting this amazing proposal. Yet many people refuse God's offer, and end their lives dying in their sins, believing they alone should be god over their petty existence.

If you haven't already accepted Him, what are you waiting for? Don't wait until you feel you need Him, or are in an unexpected, tragic accident! It may be too late. Or sadder still, are you waiting to atone for your own sins to achieve human perfection? It is just not possible. The most deceptive words people believe are: "I'm a good person". How many criminals have said the same? The Bible tells us, "For all have sinned and come short of the glory of God".[1204]

On another level, many in our Christian circles are taught, or choose to believe, that all it takes is a simple confession with our mouths to achieve salvation. But God reads our hearts, not just our words, which can be deceiving even to ourselves.

Our Lord Jesus requires so much more from us. Does the Holy Spirit live in us? Jesus said He will judge the hearts true intent by our fruit.[1205] In our own spheres of influence, we are called by Jesus to be like Peter, as He petitions each of us with this age-old request, "Do you love Me? Feed My lambs … Tend My sheep … Feed My sheep".[1206]

LOVE IN ACTION

In recruiting us for godly work in His Kingdom, here are some scriptures of how God equips us in, through, and with LOVE:

1. If God is for us, who can be against us?[1207]
2. Who shall separate us from the love of Christ? Shall tribulation, or distress, or persecution, or famine, or nakedness, or peril, or sword?[1208]
3. We are more than conquerors through Him who loved us.[1209]
4. Neither death nor life, neither angels nor principalities nor powers, neither things present nor things to come, neither height nor depth, nor any other created thing, shall be able to separate us from the love of God, which is in Christ Jesus our Lord.[1210]

5. Eye has not seen, nor ear heard, nor has it entered into the heart of man, the things which God has prepared for those who love Him.[1211]

6. So now abide faith, hope, and love, these three, but the greatest of these is love.[1212]

7. The grace of the Lord Jesus Christ, and the love of God, and the communion of the Holy Spirit be with you all.[1213]

8. The fruit of the Spirit is love, joy, peace, patience, gentleness, goodness, faith, meekness, and self-control.[1214]

9. To know the love of Christ which surpasses knowledge, that you may be filled with all the fullness of God.[1215]

10. Therefore be imitators of God as beloved children. Walk in love, as Christ loved us and gave Himself for us.[1216]

11. And this I pray, that your love may abound yet more and more.[1217]

12. That their hearts may be comforted, being knit together in love.[1218]

13. Above all these things embrace love, which is the bond of perfection.[1219]

14. Remembering without ceasing your work of faith, labor of love, and patient hope.[1220]

15. May the Lord make you increase and abound in love for one another and for all men.[1221]

16. But let us who are of the day be sober, putting on the breastplate of faith and love, and as a helmet, the hope of salvation.[1222]

17. Now the goal of this commandment is love from a pure heart, from a good conscience, and from sincere faith.[1223]

18. The grace of our Lord overflowed with faith and love which is in Christ Jesus.[1224]

19. Follow after righteousness, godliness, faith, love, patience, and gentleness.[1225]

20. For God has not given us a spirit of fear, but of power and love and self-control.[1226]

21. Follow the pattern of sound teaching which you have heard from me in the faith and love that is in Christ Jesus.[1227]

22. Flee youthful desires and pursue righteousness, faith, love, and peace, with those who call on the Lord out of a pure heart.[1228]

23. A crown of righteousness is laid up for me, which the Lord, the righteous Judge, will give me on that Day, and not only to me but also to all who have loved His appearing.[1229]

24. Hospitable, a lover of what is good, self-controlled, just, holy, temperate.[1230]

25. Older men should be sober, serious, temperate, sound in faith, in love, in patience. Older women should be reverent in behavior, teachers of good things, that they may teach the young women to love their husbands, to love their children.[1231]

26. For God is not unjust so as to forget your work and labor of love.[1232]

27. Let us consider how to spur one another to love and to good works.[1233]

28. For whom the Lord loves He disciplines.[1234]

29. Let brotherly love continue.[1235]

30. Blessed is the man who endures temptation, for when he is tried, he will receive the crown of life, which the Lord has promised to those who love Him.[1236]

31. Listen, my beloved brothers. Has God not chosen the poor of this world to be rich in faith and heirs of the Kingdom which He has promised to those who love Him?[1237]

32. Whom having not seen, you love.[1238]

33. Above all things have unfailing love for one another, for because love covers a multitude of sins.[1239]

34. Whoever keeps His word, truly has the love of God is perfected in him.[1240]

35. Whoever has the world's goods and sees his brother in need, but closes his heart of compassion from him, how can the love of God remain in him?[1241]

36. My little children, let us love not in word and speech, but in action and truth.[1242]

37. Anyone who does not love does not know God, for God is love.[1243]

38. No one has seen God at any time. If we love one another, God dwells in us, and His love is perfected in us.[1244]

39. We have come to know and to believe the love that God has for us. God is love. Whoever lives in love lives in God, and God in him.[1245]

40. There is no fear in love, but perfect love casts out fear, because fear has to do with punishment. Whoever fears is not perfect in love.[1246]

41. We love Him because He first loved us.[1247]

42. If anyone says, "I love God," and hates his brother, he is a liar. For whoever does not love his brother whom he has seen, how can he love God whom he has not seen?[1248]

43. Whoever believes that Jesus is the Christ is born of God, and everyone who loves the Father loves the one born of the Father.[1249]

44. Grace, mercy, and peace will be with you from God the Father and from the Lord Jesus Christ, the Son of the Father, in truth and love.[1250]

45. May mercy, peace, and love be multiplied to you.[1251]

46. From Jesus Christ, who is the faithful witness, the firstborn from the dead, and the ruler of the kings of the earth. To Him who loved us and washed us from our sins in His own blood.[1252]

47. Those whom I love, I rebuke and discipline. Therefore be zealous and repent.[1253]

There are many other scriptures telling us that the key to 'power in godliness' is to love God and love others. One of the most important scriptures to defeat the enemy and the root of evil within us, and teach others so they too can be set free, is found in the Book of Revelation: "And they overcame him by the blood of the Lamb, and by the word of their testimony, and they loved not their lives unto the death."[1254] This is the holiest sacrifice and gift of pure love to our God that He desires from each of us, as we learn to lay down our lives at His request to follow Him.

DOES GOD HATE?

One of history's most famous physicists, Sir Isaac Newton, explained the third Law of Motion, "For every action there is an equal and opposite reaction". That also applies to (E)motion. We've been reminded by the many Bible scriptures that the LORD is a passionate spiritual lover. But the Bible is also clear there are times the LORD says He "hates." Thankfully, it's seldom mentioned in comparison to His love!

Hate is the equal and opposite reaction to "Love." It began in us, with the prince of rebellion and lies who appeared as the serpent in the garden. He still manages to trick us into eating disobedience ever since our first parents, Adam and Eve, ate from the Tree of Knowledge of Good and Evil.[1255] To this day, those traits are still in our generational DNA.

The seed of hate grew inside the first parent's first-born son, Cain. He killed his brother Abel in a jealous rage, because God disapproved of his offering but accepted Abel's instead.[1256]

Generations later we find this same hate of sibling rivalry in another older brother. "Esau hated Jacob because of the blessing with which his father blessed him, and Esau said in his heart, 'The days of mourning for my father are at hand, then will I slay my brother Jacob.'"[1257]

In a third biblical account about brothers' rivalry, Jacob's favorite son Joseph was hated and nearly murdered by his brothers, but they decided to sell him into slavery instead. "When his brethren saw that their father loved him more than all his brethren, they hated him."[1258]

Where does this jealous hate come from? God says mankind was made in His image, so we must carry all His emotions and character as well as His form.[1259] Our Father God's strong warnings in His commandments are: "You shall have no other gods before Me. You shall not make carved images, bow down to them, nor serve them. For I, the LORD your God, am a jealous God."[1260] Here we read this jealousy we humans feel is a very real attribute of God.

God gave strict warnings to His people not to imitate the way the pagan nations worship their idols. When they conquered and possessed the land, God told them not to inquire about their gods, saying they will worship the same. For every practice He hates, they have done to their gods, including burning their children in fire to idols.[1261]

He also said, "You shall not set up a sacred pillar, which the LORD your God hates".[1262] These symbols are forbidden by God but can be seen around the world. Even here in the United States, we have huge standing monuments in many cities, including our nation's Capital.

When humans create gods with their own hands from natural materials, are they really saying, "I am like God and can make my own gods to serve me?" Isn't this what we do with things we place above our eternal Creator and Father God? Yet, humanity can't create anything without using materials God already created. All we can produce is a childish imitation.

The Bible is so important, filled with the words and deeds of God's prophets throughout generations to instruct people what God is saying to us, "Oh, do not do this abominable thing that I hate!"[1263] The people were burning offerings to self-made idols, often combined with sexual perversions.

There are many ways in our modern Western society where we burn offerings by using our money on perversion such as pornography, prostitution, and other forms of sexual immorality. This often leads to throwing the precious product of those acts - aborted dead children - into the flames of bio-waste dumps. It's amazing how little humanity has changed. God's people, Jews and Christians alike, are still sacrificing their children to gods of perversion today.

Something else to consider are the reasons some men impregnate women, then coerce them to kill their own child in the womb, a way for those men to feel like God with the power over life and death? Yes, Father God sacrificed His Son Jesus who was then resurrected and is alive today! But our human children are still dead. They were never able to fulfill their destiny.

Then there are the women. Can a mother hate her own child? Tragically, some do. And many women choose a man's approval by offering the life of their child to the god of convenience, at the expense of their baby's life and future. Don't kid yourself ladies! Let's be honest and search our hearts on whom we choose to obey; is it God or our lovers?

Some even claim abortion as a holy act, acknowledging their belief in the sacrifice of their dead children to atone for their own sins. These things are very deep to consider, but we must look under every rock for our foul motives, because most of the time they are selfish and produced by jealousy and fear, especially when it comes to destroying the life of another.

King Solomon wrote "These six things the LORD hates. Yes, seven are an abomination to Him: A proud look, a lying tongue, hands that shed innocent blood, a heart that devises wicked plans, feet that are swift in running to evil, a false witness who speaks lies, one who sows discord among brethren."[1264]

These things go against God's commandments because they hurt others. And as the Bible clearly states, God's greatest laws of instructions to humanity are summed up in two which Jesus confirmed. "'You shall love the LORD your God with all your heart, and with all your soul, and with all your mind, this is the first and greatest commandment. And the second is like it, you shall love your neighbor as yourself. On these two commandments hang all the Law and the Prophets."[1265]

Over and over, the Bible teaches us how to keep these commandments, telling us what is acceptable and what isn't. "For I, the LORD, love justice; I hate robbery and wrongdoing."[1266] God hates self-righteous offerings taken at the expense of others against their will, through manipulation or trickery. "Let none of you imagine evil in your hearts against his neighbor; and love no false oath. For all these are things that I hate, saith the LORD."[1267]

How terrible is rebellion? Many people make up their own imaginary god who loves everyone in the whole world regardless of their relationship with Him. In their own eyes, they persuade themselves that God must allow people into heaven because they are "a Good Person" according to their simplistic, earthly standards.

But until we understand God's truth and accept Jesus' sacrifice, we are condemned and will die in our sins. Jesus said, "He that believeth on Him is not condemned: but he that believeth not is condemned already, because he hath not believed in the name of the only begotten Son of God."[1268]

We must ask ourselves; do we really believe Him? Or will we be one left out when the Lord Jesus closes the door, leaving us outside saying, "Lord, Lord, open to us!". But He will answer, "I know you not."[1269] Are you giving Him your life's service or just lip service? He is counting the difference.

Because of their wickedness, perversions and sins, God told the tribes of Ephraim, "I hated them. Because of the evil of their deeds, I will drive them from My house. I will love them no more. All their princes are rebellious."[1270] God says He even hates their holy days and offerings, because they're defiled by worshipping ungodly things too.[1271] Are we also doing that? Just attending Church or Synagogue won't save us. Even today, many people hate the pastors and preachers who try to correct them by speaking God's truth: "Hate the evil and love the good, establish judgement".[1272]

The strongest word of God's hate was given to Jacob's brother, Esau. God said, "I loved Jacob, and I hated Esau and laid his mountains and his heritage waste".[1273] I often hear people say, God is love and He loves everyone. But Esau is one person God has singled out by name and said He hated. Can any of us imagine being hated by God? For years I wondered why.

We can find our answer in the book of Malachi, when God again makes a profound statement about separation. "For the LORD God of Israel says that He hates divorce, for it covers one's garment with violence. Therefore, take heed to your spirit, that you do not deal treacherously."[1274] For a man and woman, who have become one through a covenantal union, then to be separated is destructive. This is why the LORD hates divorce, especially when it separates us from Him.

In reading about Esau's birth and life, God had a generational promise and commitment to him as Isaac's first-born son, to receive a double portion naturally and spiritually to become the future leader of God's people.[1275] But Esau squandered that amazing birthright and sold it to his brother Jacob to satisfy his stomach for a meal.[1276] His contract, responsibilities and blessings from God meant too little to him.

Like some marriages today, with vows, promises and agreements, an adult human male and female join together, spiritually and physically, intimately learning every strength and weakness of the other. An unfaithful spirit will use that personal information for their own gain, then discard their spouse to satisfy their hunger for an outsider's quick meal. This leaves the betrayed person with a deeply wounded heart, feeling plundered, violated, and emotionally bleeding. The LORD calls this kind of betrayal, violence, and treachery.[1277] How we treat the ones we vowed to love, is how we treat Him. God hated Esau for his uncaring and unfaithful heart.

We must each check ourselves! Are we mocking God by taking His promises for granted by selling our birthright for temporary gratification? Perhaps that's why we see so many of America's sons and daughters on the streets, with nothing left but dirty bags to call their own.

I can envision the possibility of my own life ending there if the Lord Jesus hadn't rescued me in His amazing mercy. But my part was to repent, as it is with all of us, to ask forgiveness and be willing to turn away from mocking and blaming our God and others. That's all it took for the Holy Spirit to begin cleaning me up and setting me on a righteous and healthy path of eternal life and rewards, now and forever.

Jesus said, "No one can serve two masters, for either he will hate the one and love the other, or else he will be loyal to the one and despise the other. You cannot serve God and mammon."[1278] We either serve God and allow Him to control our lives, or without Him we serve money to take control for ourselves. Many of us don't understand how fleeting riches are, and after the few years we have in these mortal bodies, we can't take anything material with us when we die.

Once we make a commitment to Jesus to allow Him to enter our lives, we come into a spiritual marriage with our Lord. Paul said it this way, "Husbands ought to love their wives as their own bodies. He who loves his wife loves himself. After all, no one ever hated their own body, but they feed and care for their body, just as Christ does the church. For we are members of His body." There is also an instruction to women on how to treat their husbands, "The wife must respect her husband".[1279] In this same way, Christians as the Bride of Christ should respect our Lord.

And through this spiritual contract, nothing can take us away from God. The apostle Paul put it so beautifully when he wrote, "For I am persuaded that neither death nor life, nor angels nor principalities nor powers, nor things present nor things to come, nor height nor depth, nor any other created thing, shall be able to separate us from the love of God which is in Christ Jesus our Lord."[1280] This is His most powerful promise to us.

BUT there is one thing and one thing only that can separate us from God, based upon our own human "free will," which allows us to choose sin over JESUS! We can choose to leave Him by turning away, rejecting Him. And even though He waits in sorrow for us to return, there may come a time when it's too late because we won't remember who He is to desire His faithful love. This is grievous for our Lord, and why He hates anything that will turn us away from His passionate love for us and the destruction that follows an apathetic Esau heart.

HIS FIERCE JEALOUSY

People often have a hard time picturing God as jealous. But the Bible clearly states, "For I, the Lord your God, am a jealous God".[1281] When we enter a relationship with Him, we begin to understand the intense emotion He feels for us. Those who don't know Him are confused, and don't believe He would bother with them at all. Or others, in their own self-importance, believe God is jealous of them.

Some of the meanings of jealousy are: "Fearful or wary of being supplanted; Apprehensive of losing affection or position; Vigilant in guarding something; We are jealous of our good name; Intolerant of disloyalty or infidelity".[1282]

To really get to know Him, we must understand His fierce jealousy. "For the Lord your God is a consuming fire, a jealous God".[1283] Is the Lord's jealousy the same as we feel? We have all felt intense jealousy for love, possessions, or position. We will look at more statements God makes and remember that we are made in His image, therefore the basis of emotions we carry, come from Him. Although God is always in perfect control over His emotions, we are like little children often swayed by the dictates of our selfish interest.

Chapter Five in the Book of Numbers goes into detail on the legal rights of a jealous husband if he suspects his wife of committing adultery. It says that a husband can take his wife to the priest, and she is given a drink filled with curses. If she is guilty, she will suffer reproductive disorders.[1284] Most of us don't understand these curses and claim we are free from God's laws, but even today, many women suffer from several reproductive problems and disease. If we are to believe God, a woman's sexual sins against His natural laws are often the root cause.

In the story of King Solomon, he had one thousand wives and concubines given to him as virgins, and there were no sexually transmitted diseases.[1285] But apparently when a woman has more than one male partner, she can become a conduit for disease. The reproductive curses in the Bible regarding adultery applied to the woman.

Which may be why throughout history, many societies have had a low respect towards promiscuous women rather than men. Even in modern times, there are several derogatory names applied to women with several lovers, including calling them female dogs as a norm, while men are often admired. In some countries women are still stoned to death by neighbors or become victims of honor killings by family members for the crime of adultery or sex outside of marriage.

But the man was also sentenced to death if he defiled another man's wife. The book of Proverbs even tells us they risk destroying their liver.[1286] We should be more concerned about God's warnings since there aren't any medical doctors that can save us from God's judgements.

Although modern society often admires a man's sexual conquests, the Bible gives him strict warnings to stay away from immoral women.[1287] Perhaps a man's heart is more vulnerable than we are led to believe. When we see the devastation in men's lives in higher rates of homelessness, addictions, and prison life, we can see there is major damage to their emotions. Perhaps the real issue in men unable to raise themselves up in healthy ways is because of a broken heart.

In the Bible, a curse of death is also applied to men in sexual relations with other men.[1288] This curse often leads to terminal disease. Again, the wages of sin, not heeding God's warnings, can cause an early death. Paul wrote, "Flee sexual immorality. Every sin that a man does is outside the body, but he who commits sexual immorality sins against his own body."[1289]

Which brings me to the next point, and that is God sees His people who turn their love away from Him to lust for others or things, as an adulterous wife. And she (His people, His church) is judged the same way with curses on her womb. The prophet Ezekiel confirms this prophecy to Israel, "I will judge you as women who break wedlock or shed blood are judged. I will bring blood upon you in fury and jealousy".[1290] We don't have to look far at the results of sex with multiple partners to see it often leads to diseases, even terminally.

But there is a greater spiritual curse on churches that worship other gods, committing spiritual adultery, and that is sickness and barrenness as God cannot allow them to reproduce indefinitely. This is why we find once great churches, especially in the nation of Turkey which used to be the world's center of Christendom (where the seven churches in the book of Revelation were located) and in Europe, are now either empty or taken over by other religions.

Isn't it time we took God at His word? Instead, we often put our faith only in our limited knowledge of modern medicine and science to counteract the natural laws of God's order. We even have the audacity to blame God, and ask why He allows evil, when He warns us repeatedly, "The wages of sin is death but the gift of God is eternal life in Christ Jesus our Lord."[1291]

Worse yet, God said, the penalties for our physical and spiritual betrayals are passed down to our children to the third and fourth generations.[1292] Could the parent's or forefather's betrayals be the reason why innocent children carrying our DNA die of cancer or other premature death?

We can look to the story of King David's and Bathsheba's first child, who was conceived in adultery and murder. No matter how much David prayed and fasted, God didn't spare the baby's life.[1293] King David's sin was so severe, he had taken Bathsheba who was another man's wife, got her pregnant, then he purposely sent Bathsheba's husband into battle to die so he could marry her.[1294]

Not only did their baby die, but the prophet Nathan told King David, "The sword shall never depart from your house", meaning there would never be peace in his family line.[1295] In total, four of David's sons died violently. And to this day, the House of Judah, the Jewish people, have been in constant peril since Nathan's prophecy. This was a curse and the consequence of a king's actions generations before. But Yeshua came to break every curse by paying the death penalty for all nations when we finally accept Him.

The Bible continues to tell us how the descendants of Judah became worse in their sins. "Judah did evil in the sight of the Lord, and they provoked Him to jealousy with their sins which they had committed, above all that their fathers had done."[1296]

We read in Proverbs (known as the book of wisdom), "Jealousy is the rage of a man, therefore he will not spare in the day of vengeance." "Wrath is cruel and anger a torrent, but who is able to stand before jealousy?"[1297] The Song of Solomon says; "Jealousy is cruel as the grave, the coals thereof are coals of fire, which hath a most vehement flame."[1298]

But we serve a gracious, mighty, and good King. Moses records God proclaiming His name and describing Himself as "merciful, gracious, longsuffering, and abundant in goodness and truth".[1299] And that His jealous anger won't last, "So will I make my fury toward thee to rest, and my jealousy shall depart from thee, and I will be quiet, and will be no more angry."[1300] "I will bring back the captives of Jacob, and have mercy on the whole house of Israel, and I will be jealous for My holy name".[1301]

"Therefore, wait for Me, says the Lord, until the day I rise up for plunder … to gather the nations to My assembly of kingdoms, to pour on them My indignation, all My fierce anger. All the earth shall be devoured with the fire of My jealousy. Then I will restore to the peoples a pure language, that they all may call on the name of the LORD, to serve Him with one accord."[1302]

The apostle James tells us when we are a friend of the world, we become an enemy of God and he asks, "Do you think that the scripture says in vain, 'The Spirit who dwells in us yearns jealously?'"[1303] "Draw near to God and He will draw near to you. Cleanse your hands, you sinners, and purify your hearts you double-minded".[1304]

Paul acted as a match maker, in telling us to be pure for our Lord, he said, "I am jealous over you with godly jealousy, for I have espoused you to one husband, that I may present you as a chaste virgin to Christ."[1305]

Yes, our LORD is a jealous God as a husband is toward a wife with whom he is madly in love. How it grieves Him when we reject Him. We can't even imagine the great sorrow, multiplied by the billions of us who turn away. And how closely He safeguards those of us who are devoted to Him. We can each hold on to these amazing words from God to remember: "Yes, I have loved you with an everlasting love. Therefore, with lovingkindness I have drawn you."[1306] This is His eternal promise. Amen.

AROUSING GOD'S ANGER

Does God get angry? Yes, He does! The Bible first describes God's anger when He appeared in the burning bush to Moses and gave him instructions to speak to Pharoah.[1307] But Moses complained as most of us do, that he wasn't a good speaker and he told God to send someone else.[1308] The Bible says, the LORD was angry, like an impatient father. He then appointed Moses' brother Aaron to be the speaker for Moses.[1309]

The next time God's anger arose was after the Israelites were rescued out of slavery from Egypt and they started to complain. This time it was about the food, the Manna from heaven the LORD had provided for them. They wanted the variety of meats and fresh vegetables they ate during their slavery. Isn't that like us to prefer being slaves to our appetites over our freedom? But the destructive consequence of their complaints was that the outer edge of their camps caught fire.[1310] Just like God's people today, the further away from Him we place ourselves especially by complaining, the more danger we are in.

Even more telling of the human-like emotions of our God is the story of Moses' siblings, Miriam and Aaron, who complained against their brother Moses because his wife was an Ethiopian. The LORD heard them and called all three out to meet with Him as He appeared in the cloud. When the cloud lifted, Moses' sister, Miriam the instigator, was covered in leprosy. Not only was the LORD appalled by their questioning Moses' leadership, but Miriam's punishment lasted seven days for all to see that her white skin became even whiter in leprosy. This is the first story of God's extreme anger at racism and His judgement against it.[1311]

The tribes of Israel had a hard time living up to their potential as God's people after their liberation. Some of the slaves who had been freed from the perversions of Egypt were lured back into lusting after false gods, for personal power and sexual pleasure. They joined with the women of Moab and their demon god Baal of Peor. Yahweh's protection left them, plague broke out, and the offenders were killed.[1312]

Perhaps we should question the diseases we get and stop the sins God warns us about. Instead, we pay billions for new medicines, and continue to keep doing what God has repeatedly told us would lead to sickness and death. Paul's words still hold true: "The wages of sin is death, but the gift of God is eternal life in Christ Jesus our Lord".[1313]

After forty years of wandering the desert, all the people who had left Egypt as adults and had witnessed God's wonders, had died, except Caleb and Joshua. Moses' last words to the new generations were to remind them about God's anger when their parents refused to go into the promised land even though the LORD had given it to them.[1314]

God's instructions to them were the same; they were to conquer the land from those who had defiled it with sexual perversion and innocent blood. Instead of another worldwide flood destroying everything because of unredeemable corruption, God pronounced judgment over certain regions and cities where He told Israel to kill everyone, human and beast. He said to them, that it was not because they were so good that He was having them drive out these nations, but because the existing people had become so wicked.[1315]

Moses is careful to tell this new generation of Israel, they will make God angry and will also be destroyed if they act corruptly and worship man-made images.[1316] He reminded the people how God almost destroyed them before, but he pleaded for their lives and fasted forty days without food or water, and the LORD listened to him and relented.[1317] This is incredible and shows us the power of prayer to save those who are about to be destroyed. God listened to Moses and spared them.

Since that time, the Jews have been reciting a daily Hebrew prayer, translated as, "Hear, O Israel, the LORD our God, the LORD is one. You shall love the LORD your God with all your heart, with all your soul, and with all your strength"[1318] as is written in the book of Deuteronomy. Further teachings include God's most beautiful blessings of protection, health, and provision to His people if they follow His instructions and come with a strong warning if they don't.[1319]

Throughout the Bible and even today, God doesn't punish without sending prophets and pastors to sound warnings when people move away from His perfect mark. Like a protective father, He is forced to deal with rebellious people who would spread unhealthy behaviors to others. Even family members, as we've all learned from the old saying, "One rotten apple spoils the barrel".

God, our Father, looks at the big picture. Yes, He is angry at rebellion, but says "I have no pleasure in the death of the wicked, but that the wicked turn from his way and live. Turn ye, turn ye from your evil ways, for why will ye die, O house of Israel?"[1320] He is still saying that today.

We often wonder why God allows suffering in the world. According to Him, it's our rebellion that causes Him to turn away from us as He said, "My anger shall be kindled against them in that day, and I will forsake them, and I will hide My face from them, and they shall be devoured, and many evils and troubles shall befall them, so that they will say in that day, 'Are not these evils come upon us, because our God is not among us?'"[1321]

The greatest threat to us as humans comes when we worship idols and other gods. Not only does our LORD turn away, but demons replace Him in our lives, and in our homes and communities. "And the anger of the LORD was hot against Israel, and He delivered them into the hands of spoilers that spoiled them, and He sold them into the hands of their enemies round about, so that they could not any longer stand before their enemies."[1322]

This is where Western nations, which were established on the covenant of the Judeo-Christian God, now find ourselves. We have become debtor nations at the mercy of unbelievers who have ravished our lands for personal gain. Many of those we've elected to represent us don't know our LORD. The love of money and all its power have become our nations' gods.

There is the very serious Bible story of a man named Uzzah. He put his hand on the holy Ark of the Covenant which contained the two tablets of the Ten Commandments given to Moses by God. While it was being moved to Jerusalem, the oxen stumbled and Uzzah reached out to steady the Ark. He died instantly. The Bible said it was the LORD's anger which killed him.[1323]

King David, who had given the order to move the Ark to Jerusalem, learned the "fear of the LORD" through His holiness that day.[1324] So David left the Ark in that place until he was ready to pick it up again.[1325] Three months later, David brought animal sacrifices because blood was needed to cover all their sins. And with intense worship, loud shouts, and the blast of trumpets, they carried the Ark to the City of David, as their king danced before the LORD with all his might.[1326]

Also in this story, David's wife named Michal, accused him of showing off by dancing for the women instead of God. Her mockery against David's worship to God, caused her to be barren, which was considered a curse, and for a king's wife it meant her royal family blood line was cut off completely.[1327]

We can take a serious lesson from these stories. How often are we clueless, blaspheming God, cursing His name, or using it for perversion or mocking, and then blame Him when our families are covered in trouble, disease and even death? Mocking God or those who serve Him is extremely serious at our own peril. We are called to pray instead.

Isaiah, one of Israel's greatest prophets, said in his plea to God, "Oh that thou wouldest rend the heavens, that thou wouldest come down, that the mountains might flow down at thy presence.[1328] Then when God showed Himself to Isaiah, he recognized his vulnerable humanity in the presence of God and an angel came to cleanse Isaiah's lips with a fiery coal.[1329] We should all be warned standing before our God, to rend open our hearts and allow His cleansing fire to come down and purify the words we speak to Him.

In another story of the LORD's anger over the nation's sin, God not only gave Israel the leadership they deserved but He allowed those leaders to make bad decisions against the people. We usually blame those in authority for causing our problems, but this next story clearly shows the correlation between the people's sins and their leaders' mistakes.

Because of God's anger towards Israel's behavior, it caused King David to take a census out of pride to number the people when God didn't tell him to. The consequence was an angel sent by God brought a plague on Israel that killed seventy thousand men.[1330]

Who taught us that Angels only bring peace and happiness? Through art, they are often depicted as naked toddlers or beautiful women with wings. But the Bible tells us they are messengers sent to God's people to tell them about important events.[1331] Others are sent to release mass destruction after God's many warnings, as we just read.[1332]

"For the LORD will strike Israel, as a reed is shaken in the water. He will uproot Israel from this good land which He gave to their fathers, and will scatter them beyond the river, because they have made their wooden images, provoking the LORD to anger."[1333] History proves this happened and Israel was scattered. We also see a continuous repeat of this through the generations of many wars when properties are destroyed, and the inhabitants displaced.

God, our loving Father throughout the Book of Kings, continually sent prophets to warn the kings of every generation against the practice of idol worship.[1334] The results were always the same, where

God allowed enemy forces to invade until Israel was finally removed from their land completely.

We may wonder why idol worship is so offensive to the LORD. What we fail to realize is that God is at war with non-human enemies, rulers and principalities of rebellion who fight against Him. Idol worship gives them power over lands and people. In effect, we equip God's enemies to destroy us, privately in our homes with families, and territorially as people groups and nations.

Paul tells us, "For we do not wrestle against flesh and blood, but against principalities, against powers, against the rulers of the darkness of this age, against spiritual hosts of wickedness in the heavenly places."[1335]

We can see that even today in the free world where countries hold elections, we sometimes prefer to elect those who tickle our ears with comforting words while blinded to the reality of corruption and crime. So, God allows wicked people to rule over us, until their bad decisions cause so much pain the people can't take anymore and cry out to God for relief. And as always, throughout the Bible's history, our merciful Father sends deliverers … until finally, we will see the return of the one true King, our Messiah Yeshua, who will reign in truth, justice, compassion, and love.[1336]

So how evil did God's chosen people Israel become? Well, in their affluence and independence, they grew more selfish, and began burning their children as sacrifices to the demon gods of the nations around them. In their warped beliefs, they used the death of their children to appease these gods for favor and protection, instead of honoring Yahweh, the life-giving God of Israel. It was also a convenient way for them to not have to share their time and resources taking care of their children.

A good example is when the people of Israel left Egypt with much of their gold and riches. The LORD told them to give the gold to the next generation. Perhaps He commanded that because He knew wealth would be a snare for the adults, which it was. They disobeyed and took the gold off their children and gave it to Aaron the priest to build a golden calf to worship. In their even greater insult to Yahweh, they gave this man-made beast the credit for delivering them out of slavery in Egypt.[1337]

In these modern times, we've resorted to the practice of human sacrifice again, using laws written by powerful people to convince mothers it's their right and privilege to kill the living child inside her womb. This also allows fathers to shirk their responsibilities. We pretend ignorance that God hasn't breathed His breath of Life into these little humans making them a living soul, until they take the first breath of earths air outside the womb, and therefore they aren't alive yet.

How dare we take such liberty with God's word. The Bible states, "The Lord God formed man of the dust of the ground, and breathed into his nostrils the breath of life, and man became a living being."[1338] Can we be sure God's breath isn't released the moment the male sperm unites with the female egg, making them one new being? And if we're not sure, dare we take that chance? Human life is too mysterious and wonderful for us to destroy what God created in His own image.

Whatever the foul external excuses, perhaps the spiritual bottom line is that parents, sanctioned by modern law, believe they can use their children's blood to pay for their sins just as our forefathers did in ancient days. God's laws cannot be revoked, and the Bible says: "The blood pollutes the land and no atonement can be made for the land, for the blood that is shed on it, except by the blood of him who shed it".[1339] Since it's the DNA of the parents that create the child, some believe they can murder their children as a substitute to pay God's death penalty against them, so they can continue the lust of their sins.

Each of us has an inner knowledge of our sins against God. But will God accept the blood of our children instead of our own? Here is the Bible's answer: "The fathers shall not die for the children, neither shall the children die for the fathers, but every man shall die for his own sin."[1340]

Contrary to what some believe, the blood of our children will not save us from eternal hell. Instead, our savagery can lead us there because of selfishness and cowardice in destroying God's greatest gift to us, our children. The Bible says, "Children are an heritage from the LORD, the fruit of the womb is a reward."[1341] Destroying them will also cost us terrible shame, regret and loss for momentarily satisfying our bellies just like Esau.

In other ways to make God angry, just like the growing popularity in Western cultures today, ancient Israel resorted to consulting spiritual advisors and mediums. They prostituted themselves to evil spirits, which are fallen angels who chose to follow Satan. Jeremiah tells us God's warning, "The children gather wood, the fathers kindle the fire, and the women knead their dough to make cakes for the queen of heaven, and to pour out drink offerings unto other gods, that they may provoke Me to anger."[1342]

God spoke to His prophet Ezekiel to tell Israel, "Moreover you took your sons and your daughters, whom you bore to Me, and these you sacrificed to them (the demon gods) to be devoured. Were your acts of harlotry a small matter, that you have slain My children and offered them up to them by causing them to pass through the fire?"[1343] Do we notice that God claims them to be HIS children?

Humanity's cruelty and depravity knows no bounds as Israel fell further away. "They left all the commandments of the LORD their God, and made them molten images, even two calves, and made a grove, and worshipped all the host of heaven, and served Baal. And they caused their sons and their daughters to pass through the fire, and used divination and enchantments, and sold themselves to do evil in the sight of the LORD, to provoke Him to anger."[1344] Is this what many of God's people, Christians and Jews who say they follow the Bible, are doing today?

Yet, our gracious LORD provides atonement even for these crimes when we truly repent. There is only one blood that can atone for our sins, and that's the blood of Jesus, the Lamb of God. Because it's the only blood that became eternally alive in the resurrection of God's first born.[1345]

Throughout Israel's and the Christian nation's history, God blesses His people until they get comfortable and fall into the temptation of lust, greed, and power, forcing God's hand of protection to lift. Again and again the people end up in misery with famine, plagues, and wars until they turned back to our LORD for mercy.

When Nehemiah returned from Babylon to Jerusalem to restore the walls of the city and the work was finished, Ezra and the priests taught God's commandments during the Fall holy feasts of the LORD.[1346] They also gave a history lesson on God's graciousness, telling the people that despite their forefather's rebellion, God is quick to forgive.

The priests repented of Israel's past sins and prayed to the LORD saying, "They refused to obey, and they were not mindful of Your wonders that You did among them, but they hardened their necks. And in their rebellion, they appointed a leader to return to their bondage. But You are God, ready to pardon, gracious and merciful, slow to anger, abundant in kindness, and did not forsake them."[1347]

Finally, the returning Jewish families made a new contract with God to restore and keep His laws, promising renewed faithfulness in a recommitted covenant.[1348] God is the perfect lawgiver and judge. He cannot allow evil to continue indefinitely without the consequence of punishment. He is quick to forgive, but only when we sincerely ask forgiveness and stop our rebellion. There are those who won't give in to truth and continue to bring destruction upon themselves and everyone around them.

Here is what King David had to say to God: "Your hand will find all Your enemies. Your right hand will find those who hate You. You shall make them as a fiery oven in the time of Your anger. The LORD shall swallow them up in His wrath, and the fire shall devour them."[1349]

In reading the words of David, he spent a lot of time soul-searching and honestly assessing his human weaknesses. If ever a man loved God, it was David, yet he suffered with sexual lust for a married woman. And as recently mentioned, we know the tragedy he brought upon one of his most faithful, mighty men so he could selfishly satisfy his own wicked desire. It can be hard for us to understand why God called David, "A man after My own heart who will do all My will."[1350] But this is a great example of the power of repentance and forgiveness available to all of us.

Even with David's depression, self-debasing and pleading for mercy, he leaves us all with the brightest hope of our amazing and loving Father, for all who will turn back to Him. David wrote, "Hide not thy face far from me, put not thy servant away in anger. Thou hast been my help, leave me not, neither forsake me, O God of my salvation."[1351] David continued, "His anger endureth but a moment, in His favour is life: weeping may endure for a night, but joy cometh in the morning."[1352]

WHEN JESUS WAS ANGRY

This is where we come to our God in human flesh. We must remember Jesus was God on earth. Many believe that the love of Jesus is always gentle and nice with people. Of course, as Lord, Jesus is master over His emotions even during the times He let His anger break out.

Such as the time Jesus healed the withered hand of a man on the Sabbath day and the religious leaders plotted to have Him killed over this. They felt threatened that Jesus was replacing their authority, power, and money, since they required an offering for healing. No financial business was allowed on the Sabbath and Jesus' services were free. Jesus "looked around at the religious leaders with anger, being grieved by the hardness of their hearts".[1353]

In another example, Jesus related a third person story about a master of the house who prepared a great banquet and invited his friends and people he knew. But they all had excuses not to come and he was angry. Then he sent his servant to gather all sorts of strangers, the poor, maimed, lame and blind, wherever he could find them so the house would be filled.[1354]

Then Jesus said that none of the invited ones would taste His supper. He was telling us this story about Himself inviting the Jewish religious leaders into the House of God, but they refused. So, He became angry and invited ordinary people instead, the outcasts and the Gentiles.

Jesus also prophesied several judgements against people and cities revealing God's anger. His judgements were especially strong to those who held spiritual and political authority. He then rebuked the cities where most of His miracles took place, but their leaders didn't repent.[1355]

"Woe unto thee, Chorazin! woe unto thee, Bethsaida! for if the mighty works, which were done in you, had been done in Tyre and Sidon, they would have repented long ago in sackcloth and ashes."[1356]

"Woe unto the world because of offences! For it must needs be that offences come; but woe to that man by whom the offence cometh!"[1357]

"Woe unto you, scribes and Pharisees, hypocrites! For ye shut up the Kingdom of Heaven against men, for ye neither go in yourselves, neither suffer ye them that are entering to go in." [1358]

"Woe unto you, scribes and Pharisees, hypocrites! for ye devour widows' houses, and for a pretense make long prayer: therefore ye shall receive the greater damnation."[1359]

"Woe to you, scribes and Pharisees, hypocrites! For you travel land and sea to win one proselyte, and when he is won, you make him twice as much a son of hell as yourselves."[1360]

"Woe unto you, ye blind guides, which say, whosoever shall swear by the temple, it is nothing; but whosoever shall swear by the gold of the temple, he is a debtor!"[1361]

"Woe to you, scribes and Pharisees, hypocrites! For you pay tithe of mint and anise and cummin and have neglected the weightier matters of the law: justice and mercy and faith. These you ought to have done, without leaving the others undone. Blind guides, who strain out a gnat and swallow a camel!"[1362]

"Woe unto you, scribes and Pharisees, hypocrites! For ye make clean the outside of the cup and of the platter, but within they are full of extortion and excess."[1363]

"Woe to you, scribes and Pharisees, hypocrites! For you are like whitewashed tombs which indeed appear beautiful outwardly, but inside are full of dead men's bones and all uncleanness. Even so you also outwardly appear righteous to men, but inside you are full of hypocrisy and lawlessness."[1364]

"Woe to you, teachers of the Law and Pharisees, you hypocrites! You build tombs for the prophets and decorate the graves of the righteous. And you say, 'If we had lived in the days of our ancestors, we would not have taken part with them in shedding the blood of the prophets.'" [1365]

Jesus continues his severe judgments against the religious leaders: "So you testify against yourselves that you are the descendants of those who murdered the prophets. Go ahead then and complete what your ancestors started! You snakes! You brood of vipers! How will you escape being condemned to hell?"[1366]

"Therefore I am sending you prophets and sages and teachers. Some of them you will kill and crucify, others you will flog in your synagogues and pursue from town to town. And so upon you will come all the righteous blood that has been shed on earth, from the blood of righteous Abel to the blood of Zechariah son of Berekiah, whom you murdered between the temple and the altar. Truly I tell you, all this will come on this generation."[1367] Clearly Jesus was angry and pronounced judgement against these leaders. And the judgements all came to pass.

There is the story of Jesus entering the Temple of God in Jerusalem during the time of the Passover. This was one of the Temple's most profitable seasons, as Jews would come from all over to prepare animal sacrifices, commemorating the Passover in Egypt when the blood of the lamb was applied to all Israeli houses to save them from death.

But Jesus found all manner of business happening in the Temple with the buying and selling of sacrificial animals. This story is a clear case of the Lord's anger, as He made a whip with rope to drive out the people with their livestock, and He overturned the tables of the money changers.[1368] Then He said to them, "Take these things away! Do not make My Father's house a house of merchandise!"[1369] What a sight that must have been and a good reminder to all of us, to keep HOLY the things of God.

GOD'S PAIN AND SORROW

The first time the word sorrow is mentioned is by God. He told Eve that because she listened to the serpent in the Garden of Eden and ate the forbidden fruit of knowledge, her sorrow and pain would be multiplied through childbirth.[1370] So obviously God knows sorrow, as Eve was made in His image. This is an emotion in God as well.

For mankind, it went downhill from there as our first parents' descendants grew more wicked. The seeds of good mixed with evil continued to breed together. They had forgotten God's goodness and came against His beautiful plan of increasing life and bringing order. The desire for each to build his own kingdom ruled. Rebellion, murder, idolatry, and every thought they had was evil, everything was corrupted.[1371] So much so, the Bible says, "The LORD was sorry He had made man on the earth and was grieved in His heart."[1372]

How sad for our Creator, when the Bible says God grieved at mankind's bad choices of selfishness and cruelty, just like any good father would do. Although very little is written about that time, it must have been extremely evil if God felt there was no other way than sending the great flood to destroy much of what He had created.[1373] Out of all humanity, God only spared the family of Noah to continue His plan for the earth.

Generations later, we read about Jacob (whose name was later changed to Israel), pleading with his older sons not to allow his youngest son, Benjamin, to be put in danger in Egypt. He stated that if he lost Benjamin, sorrow would cause his death. Jacob's heart was so tender towards his youngest son.[1374] This is a good example of our Father God's heart toward us, His children.

Four hundred years later, after a new government in Egypt enslaved the descendants of Israel, God sent Moses to deliver them and told him, "I know their sorrows". How could God know unless He feels sorrow Himself? As usual, God always devises a plan to deliver His people once they can't help themselves. Certainly, He feels our pain which causes sorrow, like any good parent feels for their hurting child.[1375]

There is a story about Nehemiah, who was captured after the fall of Jerusalem and taken to Babylon as a child. He became a top servant to the King of Babylon, where he heard the report that Jerusalem was in ruins. Nehemiah began to pray and cry out to God, for many days, asking God to restore Israel.[1376]

Finally, the King of Babylon saw Nehemiah's sorrow and promoted him as Governor of Jerusalem, providing everything to rebuild the city.[1377] One might wonder, "Was Nehemiah capable of such passionate sorrow for a city he hadn't seen since a child, or was it God's own supernatural sorrow?" Often God places His passion and concern in a person's heart, and they can't think about anything else until the task of healing is accomplished.

Then there's King David, who God said was a man after His own heart.[1378] Yet David struggled with sin, as previously noted he committed adultery and murder. But David knew the wrong he had done, the sins he had committed, and paid a severe price for his mistakes. David wrote, "How long shall I take counsel in my soul, having sorrow in my heart daily? How long shall mine enemy be exalted over me?"[1379]

How does this happen to us? David again writes, "Their sorrows shall be multiplied that hasten after another god". "Many sorrows shall be to the wicked, but he that trusteth in the LORD, mercy shall compass him about."[1380]

So that's the key! Whenever we place importance on anything above our God, making "Me, He, She, They, or It" our idols of worship, we suffer in sorrow. This emotion is such a big part of God, it's possible that we each share a portion of what He Himself feels when we turn away, grieving Him and hurting ourselves in the process.

Here are some additional verses, to remind us of His great compassion and tenderness towards us, not wanting us to live in sorrow: "The blessing of the LORD, it maketh rich, and he addeth no sorrow with it."[1381]. "He who sows iniquity will reap sorrow, and the rod of his anger will fail."[1382] "Therefore remove sorrow from thy heart and put away evil from thy flesh."[1383]

And this is to God's people who turn back to Him, "It shall come to pass in the day that the LORD shall give thee rest from thy sorrow, and from thy fear, and from the hard bondage wherein thou were made to serve."[1384] "The ransomed of the LORD shall return and come to Zion with songs and everlasting joy upon their heads. They shall obtain joy and gladness, and sorrow and sighing shall flee away."[1385]

Herein is one of the most important verses in the Old Testament, revealing the suffering and sorrow of the Anointed One, describing the Messiah. "He is despised and rejected by men, a Man of sorrows and acquainted with grief. And we hid our faces from Him. Surely He has borne our griefs and carried our sorrows. Yet we esteemed Him stricken, smitten by God, and afflicted. But He was wounded for our transgressions, He was bruised for our iniquities, the chastisement for our peace was upon Him, and by His stripes we are healed."[1386]

Seven hundred years after this prophecy was spoken by Isaiah, it happened to Jesus of Nazareth who was accused, beaten, and crucified. Our Messiah, our Savior God, cloaked Himself in human flesh to take our sin, our pain, our grief, our sorrow, to defeat the enemy and overcome even death, which had its claim on humanity. But no more, because Yeshua conquered all and took the keys of Hell and Death from Satan who tricked mankind out of the promise of eternal life in God's perfect garden.[1387]

One day while in prayer, the LORD allowed me to sense a fragment of the world's sorrows that He carries on His shoulders, which no one ordinary human being could possibly carry. Oh, how grievous a burden for our LORD, yet He will make a complete end of it. Already He overcame death and hell by dying on the cross followed with His resurrection. But during this lifetime, each of us carries our own burdens. And the Spirit of God is part of each of us, sharing our every pain as we willingly lay down self-rule, and accept His offer to rule and reign with Him.[1388]

The prophet Daniel was overwhelmed by his encounter with the LORD and the future he was allowed to see. He said, "My LORD, by the vision my sorrows are turned upon me, and I have retained no strength."[1389]

The prophet Jeremiah cried out in emotional pain, feeling the anguish of the LORD. He mourns, "O my soul, my soul! I am pained in my very heart! My heart makes a noise in me, I cannot hold my peace because you have heard, O my soul, the sound of the trumpet, the alarm of war."[1390] "Wherefore came I forth out of the womb to see labor and sorrow, that my days should be consumed with shame?"[1391]

The LORD spoke to the people through Jeremiah's warnings about the coming invasion and Israel's exile. He said, "Why do you cry about your affliction? Your sorrow is incurable. Because of the multitude of your iniquities, because your sins have increased, I have done these things to you."[1392]

Yet over and over, God relents and promises to restore Israel. After two thousand years of being dispersed throughout the world, we see that has continued to happen, even today!

"Therefore, they shall come and sing in the height of Zion, and shall flow together to the goodness of the LORD, for wheat, and for wine, and for oil, and for the young of the flock and of the herd: and their soul shall be as a watered garden; and they shall not sorrow any more at all … For I will turn their mourning into joy, and will comfort them, and make them rejoice from their sorrow."[1393] "For I have satiated the weary soul, and I have replenished every sorrowful soul."[1394]

MAN OF SORROWS

Now we look at the life of Jesus who was the Word of God made flesh and the Word was God.[1395] Jesus was an extremely emotional being. One story to confirm that, is about the death of Lazarus, his beloved friend. Even though Jesus knew he would raise Lazarus from the dead, Jesus wept because his friends were grieving, and possibly because of their lack of faith in Him.[1396] He shares our burdens, our pain, and our grief, even when it is completely unfounded. Oh, how He loves us!

Later Jesus wept over Jerusalem with these sorrowful words, "If you had known, especially in this your day, the things that make for your peace! But now they are hidden from your eyes. For days will come upon you when your enemies will build an embankment around you, surround you and close you in on every side, and level you, and your children within you, to the ground. And they will not leave in you one stone upon another, because you did not know the time of your visitation."[1397]

Jesus continues with an aching heart, "O Jerusalem, Jerusalem, the one who kills the prophets and stones those who are sent to her! How often I wanted to gather your children together, as a hen gathers her chicks under her wings, but you were not willing! See! Your house is left to you desolate; for I say to you, you shall see Me no more till you say, 'Blessed is He who comes in the name of the LORD!'"[1398]

In the garden of Gethsemane, Jesus knew His earthly body was going to be put to death. He also knew He would conquer Hell and death, rising from a corruptible body into a glorified, eternal one. Yet He struggled with the violent sacrifice He was to undergo, also grieving over the sorrow His disciples would experience, and Jerusalem's coming destruction.[1399] He said to them, "My soul is exceedingly sorrowful, even to death. Stay here and watch with Me."[1400]

Jesus had already forewarned His disciples that He would be killed, and on the third day be raised up.[1401] He said, "Ye now therefore have sorrow: but I will see you again, and your heart shall rejoice, and your joy no man taketh from you."[1402]

Then on His way to Golgotha, carrying the cross of His death, Jesus turned to the women following and grieving over Him.[1403] He said, "Daughters of Jerusalem, weep not for me, but weep for yourselves, and for your children."[1404] Jesus foresaw the destruction that would come to this majestic city and the Jewish people living there.

So, what is the purpose of all this sorrow and pain we may ask? Paul stated it well when he wrote, "Now I am happy, not because you were made sorry, but because your sorrow led you to repentance." "Godly sorrow brings repentance that leads to salvation and leaves no regret, but worldly sorrow brings death."[1405]

In the end of God's instructions of hope to us, John records these wonderful, comforting words, "God shall wipe away all tears from their eyes, and there shall be no more death, neither sorrow, nor crying, neither shall there be any more pain. For the former things are passed away."[1406]

THE GREATEST IS COMPASSION

So why would a God who is all powerful, all encompassing, all consuming, ever-present, everywhere, and eternal, give us chances over and over again? What is this strange trait He has passed on to humans and even animals? If atheists are right and emotions are no more than chemical reflexes, how can anyone describe the intensely self-sacrificing and emotional act of "Compassion"?

Moses begged the God of Israel, Yahweh, who had performed such amazing wonders to deliver them out of Egypt, to show Himself. God allowed Moses to see His form as He passed by and described Himself in His character and function. God said, "I will make all My goodness pass before you, and I will proclaim the name of the LORD (Yahweh) before you. I will be gracious to whom I will be gracious, and I will have compassion on whom I will have compassion."[1407]

We can only imagine this most wondrous sight as Yahweh told Moses who He was: "Now the LORD descended in the cloud and stood with him there and proclaimed the name of the LORD. And the LORD passed before him and proclaimed, "YHVH, YHVH" translated as, "The LORD, the LORD, merciful and gracious, longsuffering, and abounding in goodness and truth, keeping mercy for thousands, forgiving iniquity and transgression and sin, by no means clearing the guilty, visiting the iniquity of the fathers upon the children and the children's children to the third and the fourth generation."[1408]

As beautiful and terrifying as this encounter was that revealed God's compassion, there was also a stern warning by God, as the unrelenting Judge. Moses told the people of Israel that in the future their children would forget God and be scattered but they will always have His promise. "The LORD your God will turn thy captivity, and have compassion upon thee, and will return and gather thee from all the nations, whither the LORD your God has scattered thee."[1409]

Here is also the most valuable promise given to Moses, hidden as a 'Pearl of Great Price.' "For the LORD shall judge His people, and repent Himself for His servants, when He seeth that their power is gone, and there is none shut up, or left."[1410]

This is incredible! The LORD told Moses in advance that He will repent for us when His people become too weak. The incredible part is what happened fifteen hundred years later. God in the flesh as Jesus Christ, took all of humanities sins on the cross and the punishment of the cruelest death through crucifixion, to repent for all mankind. And He said, "Father, forgive them for they know not what they do."[1411] This was the most compassionate act ever performed and God never stops, even today.

What a faithful God we serve! Because He made a promise to three men, He continues to keep His word. "The LORD was gracious to them, had compassion on them, and had respect unto them, because of His covenant with Abraham, Isaac, and Jacob, and would not destroy them, neither cast He them from His presence as yet."[1412] "For the LORD your God is gracious and merciful, and will not turn away His face from you, IF ye return unto Him."[1413]

The LORD sends repeated warnings to His people to keep His laws, through history's prophets and pastors. He continues even today, because of His compassion for His people and their homes.[1414] But unfortunately, many people didn't listen then or in modern times today. Then enemies come against us, who don't have God's compassion on anyone including the young, old, and weak.[1415]

Our LORD gives us so many promises, with such faithfulness and beauty in His character. Why wouldn't everyone run to this loving, compassionate God to find shelter, love, joy, peace, rest, hope, and all that's good and beautiful? The Bible is often criticized by those characterizing a brutal God, but they are so far from understanding the truth of who He is and what He says!

In their bitter and selfish rage, some work hard to keep others from knowing the LORD. And there are those who allow temporary pleasure and power for this very temporary, earthly existence to blind their vision of the eternal reality we all face, with or without our loving God.

These verses from the Book of Psalms tell us about the wonderful leader our God really is: "He, being full of compassion, forgave their iniquity and destroyed them not. Yea, many a time turned He His anger away."[1416] "Thou, O LORD, art a God full of compassion, and gracious, long suffering, and plenteous in mercy and truth."[1417] "He hath made His wonderful works to be remembered: the Lord is gracious and full of compassion."[1418] "Unto the upright there ariseth light in the darkness." "He is slow to anger and great in mercy."[1419]

Our God also describes Himself as an everlasting parent who must chastise us, but never gives up on us. "Can a woman forget her nursing child, and not have compassion on the son of her womb? Surely they may forget, yet I will not forget you."[1420] "I will return and have compassion on them and bring them again, every man to his heritage and every man to his land."[1421] "It is of the Lord's mercies that we are not consumed, because His compassions fail not. But though He cause grief, yet will he have compassion according to the multitude of His mercies."[1422]

Finally, here is the most amazing promise to us, that He will again have compassion on us and conquer our sins. "You will cast all our sins into the depths of the sea."[1423] "As far as the east is from the west, so far has He removed our transgressions from us."[1424] Wow, here is the promise that our crimes and faults won't exist anymore. But ... there is a "but". Our Father continually trains and teaches us to be just like Him. When we refuse to listen, we receive the same treatment as others who are rebellious. "Thus says the Lord of hosts: 'Execute true justice, show mercy and compassion, everyone to his brother.'"[1425]

There is no greater book written in the world, that describes true compassion in action more than the New Testament through the life of Yeshua of Nazareth, who was also named Immanuel, meaning "God with us".[1426] He was born to a teenage girl named Miryam (Mary), by the spiritual seed of God, the first-born Son through the Holy Spirit. In this man, God came down to earth to become fully human.[1427]

Jesus was the Torah (Truth) and Jesus lived the Torah. The Book of John explains, "In the beginning was the Word, and the Word was with God, and the Word was God. He was in the beginning with God. All things were made through Him, and without Him nothing was made that was made"[1428] "He was in the world, and the world was made through Him"[1429] "And the Word became flesh and dwelt among us, and we beheld His glory, the glory as of the only begotten of the Father, full of grace and truth".[1430]

Some Bible teachers say we only need to keep two commandments, "Love the Lord your God and your neighbor as yourself." And that we can throw out the rest of God's instruction given to Moses, written in the Old Testament. But these words from God to Israel, was the "Word" John was talking about. During Jesus time, the New Testament hadn't been written yet, and all His stories were examples how to help us keep God's laws in the Old Testament, practically teaching the laws of love and compassion.

Ignoring God's full set of instructions has led many of God's people, Jews and Christians alike, to be totally ignorant of even the basic Ten Commandments which Western civilization was built upon. And they have no understanding that the other six hundred and three instructions that break them down are the basis of God's ordered society.[1431]

Instead, we choose faulty human leaders, many who don't even know God, to write hundreds of thousands of man-made laws to keep order of which none of us can possibly know them all, let alone keep them. Man's knowledge, without God's wisdom, only creates chaos and lawlessness.

Even in our modern Christian nations, God's basic instructions for humanity are disappearing from all houses of influence. Leadership in government, education, and media have been rapidly throwing us back into another period of "Dark Ages" as when the word of God had disappeared.

During those days in history, God's laws were hidden, and the majority of people purposely weren't taught to read. They also were not taught to know God's truth and were unable to discern right from wrong. Just as today in modern society, the light of truth has become dim because the Law of God (His lamp) has been kept low. "For the commandment is a lamp and the law a light, the reproofs of discipline are the way of life."[1432] Leaving each person to decide what's right for themselves is like allowing children to raise themselves into productive citizens. How's that been working for us?

OUR COMPASSIONATE KING

There is no better human life reflecting the persona of God than the life of Jesus. He walked among us to be that perfect example and role model for us to follow. So often we resort to doing what we clearly know is damaging, then make excuses repeating the mantra, "I'm only human". Yet Jesus came to show us that we can rise above our weaknesses and temptations, by choosing to become more like

Him. And yes, it's a process of growing up spiritually. As children don't have a choice staying children, neither do true children of God have a choice to stay in spiritual immaturity.

Jesus said, "If you love Me, keep My commandments". "He who has My commandments and keeps them, it is he who loves Me. And he who loves Me will be loved by My Father".[1433] Jesus wouldn't have said this if God's laws were harmful or impossible. Perhaps instead of viewing the Old Testament instruction manual God gave to Moses as an impossible list of 'Do's and Don'ts', we should look to them as a complete owner's manual for spiritual advice on abundant and healthy living, individually and as a community.

We can all agree we are not God, and in our current human state it's impossible to keep God's laws flawlessly.[1434] But Jesus said, "Follow Me" and He made certain to keep every law handed down to Moses as our example.[1435] Shouldn't we each do our best to learn what God's commandments are, and keep them to the best of our ability? We can only do this by reading the entire Bible and listening to teachers who do the same.

As instructed by God, going to church is important for fellowship, and there are great teachers, but usually there is only time for short messages. Without knowing God's words for ourselves, we're left to repeat the errors of other human teachers who can also be limited by personal interpretations and experiences.

Often, we hear the excuse that God's laws aren't valid anymore because our compassionate Jesus died to erase our sins, so we won't suffer eternal punishment under the old law, when we repent. Yes, this is true.

A powerful example of complete forgiveness is in the story of the second thief on the cross. Jesus promised him they would be together in Paradise.[1436] But because of the thief's crimes against man's laws, his earthly body still received punishment and he was still executed by barbaric crucifixion. Jesus did not save the thief from an agonizing earthly death, but a spiritual one.

As a Church, we must ask ourselves: "How has ignoring God's laws in our biblical teachings affected us?" In the United States today, sexual sin has led to killing one third of our children, and one third of teenage girls have debilitating sexually transmitted diseases. Half of American mothers are single, leaving an epidemic of fatherless children raised by women only or other men not their fathers, or gang leaders who use them as mules and prostitutes. Our prisons are filled with fatherless men who had no father to teach them their true functions with loyalty, compassion, and courage using God's instructions for healthy lives and families. Things go drastically wrong when we leave God's law and order behind.

God gave man the ability to duplicate himself through his seed. He gave woman the miraculous blessing of bringing new "life" into the world. Wow! What incredible favors and privileges! How were women conned into believing the fruit of their womb, God's greatest reward (our children), are a curse to be abandoned or destroyed?[1437] And when did men turn from understanding their most valuable strength is their ability to reproduce their image on earth through an ongoing legacy of future generations? God calls children a man's arrows, as his private army.[1438]

Reproduction is God's greatest blessing and investment that He gave all LIFE.[1439] Instead, many men choose Esau's thinking, trading their children for a bowl of stew of temporary sexual and financial gratification. And women have been taught to fear the miracle of human life they were designed to carry, trading them for short term beauty and security.[1440]

When Christian nations, passed laws to allow the killing of unborn children, these laws devalued human life as free beings made in the image of God. Instead, unborn children became the legal property of another, the woman carrying the child. This mindset has created a new class of slaves in children, with their value downgraded and exploited for the marketable buying and selling in free labor, sexual perversion, child sacrifice and even human body parts. There is no end to human cruelty for personal gain.

So how do we turn back to God's law of compassion that is required of us? Our best examples are from the life of our Messiah Yeshua. He led the way in keeping the Father's laws of love and life. Jesus was, and is, the ultimate extremist. Everything He did was to teach us how to keep two basic commandments. All other laws have been written down to show us how to accomplish that.

Jesus taught us how to love the LORD our God with all our heart, soul, strength, and mind, and love our neighbors, treating them as we would ourselves, through His messages and by the way He lived His life.[1441] Moses tells us that to love God, means to serve Him.[1442] Jesus also taught and showed us how to serve others. The best teachings Jesus gave to us came through the Beatitudes in the Book of Matthew, Chapters 5 through 7. We should all study and practice them.

The following stories are some of the best examples of how Jesus proved His love, mercy, kindness, gentleness, compassion, and self-control. We will see His character in action as God in the flesh, as He shows us the way like a parent teaching His children by example in word and in deed.

The Bible tells us, "Jesus went about all the cities and villages, teaching in their synagogues, preaching the gospel of the Kingdom, healing every sickness and every disease among the people. But when He saw the multitudes, He was moved with compassion for them, because they were weary and scattered, like sheep having no shepherd."[1443] So He began to teach them many things."[1444] Many healings happen even today when people learn to live a healthy lifestyle doing right by God's standards, and Jesus came to teach us how to do that.

At one time, Jesus said to His disciples, "I have compassion on the multitude, because they have now continued with Me three days and have nothing to eat. And I do not want to send them away hungry, lest they faint on the way."[1445] So, Jesus taught His disciples how to feed all the people with only seven loaves of bread and a few fish.[1446] It was a miracle! These stories demonstrate how much God cares about His people, not only healing their disease, but also providing nourishment for our minds, bodies, and souls so we aren't sick in the first place.

One of the most important lessons we learn from Jesus is the gift of "forgiveness". When someone asks us to forgive them, we are to freely do it, just as God forgives us again and again. This doesn't mean those who do us wrong don't have to live with the consequences of their bad actions, or that we are to trust them to always do the right thing. But we absolutely should not hold on to the offenses, to the sins that God Himself forgives whenever the person has true remorse for their crimes.

Jesus told many stories to a simple people on how to practically follow His example. One of them was about a master who was moved with compassion to forgive a large debt owed by his servant. But this servant wouldn't release a smaller debt of a fellow servant who owed him.[1447] The master asked, "Should you not also have had compassion on your fellow servant, just as I had pity on you?" Then the master changed his mind, and had the unforgiving servant sent to the tormentors.[1448]

When we refuse to forgive others who are repentant, we place a continuous judgment on that person that is above God's compassion because He has already forgiven them. Are we above Jesus? He said we will not be forgiven unless we forgive.[1449]

I have met people who are full of bitterness, which can lead to disease because our bodies weren't made to sustain the long-term stress of negativity and torment. Please let go of your old memories of offenses against people. We cannot move forward until we do. Even worse, we will die in our sin of unforgiveness where the penalty is Hell, no matter how godly we believe we are.

Let's review some wonderful stories of God's healing compassion. Jesus and the disciples encountered two blind men on the road and because of His compassion, Jesus touched their eyes and immediately they could see and began to follow Him.[1450]

A man who was a leper asked Jesus if he were willing to heal him, "Then Jesus, moved with compassion, stretched out His hand and touched him and said to him, 'I am willing, be cleansed.'"[1451]

In this next story, Jesus cast out a demon from a boy with seizures after the boy's father appealed to Him for compassion.[1452] Jesus often cast out demons to heal the sick. Those demonic spirits caused a variety of physical and mental illnesses. Many people today don't believe in demons. But the Bible says one third of the beings in heaven were cast down to earth along with Lucifer, in rebellion against God. Where do we think they went?[1453]

Here is another exciting example of our Lord Jesus' great love and care for a widow in a funeral procession for her only son. The Lord saw her, had compassion, and told her not to weep. Jesus then told the dead son to get up from his coffin, and the young man rose and began talking! The story goes on to say that the people were afraid and began to glorify God.[1454] Can you imagine being there to witness that? And yet we hear stories of raising the dead in Jesus' name, happening even today.

Later Jesus tells the famous story of a man who was beaten and left on the road to die. 'Good' religious people pretended they didn't see him and left him there. But a Samaritan, someone outside the Jewish faith, had compassion. He washed the man's wounds, fed him, paid for his housing until he got better, and saved his life. Jesus was making a point that the Samaritan was really the good, godly neighbor regardless of his faith.[1455] The Bible is clear, "Faith without works is dead".[1456]

God's compassion runs in a variety of forms. Jesus shared another story of a father's love for his son who returned home after many years of squandering all his inheritance on earthly pleasures. "He arose and came to his father. But when he was still a great way off, his father saw him and had compassion, and ran and fell on his neck and kissed him."[1457] How can we understand such great love? As Yahweh said to Moses, "I will have mercy on whomever I will have mercy, and I will have compassion on whomever I will have compassion."[1458]

The apostles beautifully sum up God's request to us. Peter said, "Finally, all of you be of one mind, having compassion for one another, love as brothers, be tenderhearted, be courteous".[1459] And Jude adds, "But you, beloved, build yourselves up in your most holy faith. Pray in the Holy Spirit. Keep yourselves in the love of God while you are waiting for the mercy of our Lord Jesus Christ, which leads to eternal life. On some have compassion, using discernment. And others save with fear while pulling them out of the fire, hating even the garment stained by the flesh (their sins)."[1460]

These are such great examples of God's compassion. Often people think love and compassion in Christians means to always be "nice" and encouraging, helping all the time no matter how much sin a person is in and how much harm they cause. As Christ-followers, we are not to enable destructive behavior, allowing it to go unchecked by God's laws of love and truth.

Unrepentant bad behavior will grow into a huge unmanageable monster destroying everything (and sometimes everyone) in sight. James tells us that giving in to temptation leads to sin, and when sin is fully grown it produces death.[1461] Often churches do a poor job in showing the other compassionate side of Jesus, the one exposing evil, giving people a choice to repent and turn from their own destruction.

Jesus said to self-righteous religious leaders who wanted to kill Him, "If God were your Father, you would love Me, for I came from God and proceeded into the world. I did not come of My own authority, but He sent Me. Why do you not understand My speaking? Because you cannot bear to hear My word. You are of your father the devil, and you want to do the desires of your father. He was a murderer from the beginning, and does not stand in the truth, because there is no truth in him."[1462]

Rarely do we preach the extremist Jesus, speaking extreme truth of right and wrong. We must remember the enraged Jesus at God's holy temple, who made a whip and drove out the businesses which were there for a profit instead of prayer.[1463]

These amazing stories tell of our most passionate and compassionate God. And as John wrote two thousand years ago, "There are also many other things which Jesus did. Were every one of them to be written, I suppose that not even the world itself could contain the books that would be written".[1464] What a picture that would be! Perhaps our Lord's intent is that each one of us who follows Him, is a page in that book.

GOD LAUGHS

Does God actually laugh? Yes! The first place in the Bible we find His laughter is in the Book of Psalms. King David wrote that

God laughs when the leaders of nations plot against Him. He is still laughing today. HA! "Why do the nations rage, and the peoples plot in vain? The kings of the earth set themselves, and the rulers take counsel together, against the LORD and against His Anointed". "He who sits in the heavens laughs, the LORD ridicules them." They will face His anger.[1465]

The LORD also laughs as the wicked plot against His people. "The LORD laughs at him, for He sees that his day is coming. The wicked have drawn out the sword and have bent their bow, to cast down the poor and needy, to slay those on the upright path."[1466]

Then again King David wrote about the LORD coming to his personal defense as He does for each of us who love Him even today. "They belch with their mouth, swords are in their lips, for they say, 'Who hears?' But You, O LORD, shall laugh at them ... For God is my defense." [1467]

Finally, God gives an answer to scoffers for His laughter, in the form of wisdom. "Because you disdained all my counsel, and would have none of my rebuke, I also will laugh at your calamity. I will mock when your terror comes. When your terror comes like a storm, and your destruction comes like a whirlwind. When distress and anguish come upon you."[1468]

In another book of wisdom, Solomon tells us, "Sorrow is better than laughter, for by a sad countenance the heart is made better".[1469] It's important that we go through hard times, because hardship often produces regret and gives us a chance to meditate on our wrongs to repent and put things right.

Like all of God's emotions, His laughter is passed down to us as Jesus explains, "Blessed are you who hunger now, for you shall be filled. Blessed are you who weep now, for you shall laugh."[1470]

JOY OF THE LORD!!!!

Wow! Who wouldn't want to know Him. Why would anyone want to give Him up for statues, mantras, rituals, yada, yada, yada? They just don't know the truth about the happiest Superstar in existence!!!

On a human level, we can see a fragmented picture of what will happen at the return of our King Yeshua. King Solomon's coronation is a good, but tiny, example of that. "All the people went up after him, and the people played the flutes and rejoiced with great joy, so that the earth seemed to split with their sound."[1471]

Solomon was only human, so how can we even imagine when that day comes at the coronation of the King of kings, when all of creation will rejoice with great joy. This will be God's people, the animals, rocks, trees, fields, lands, and seas. As Jesus said when the people rejoiced over His entry into Jerusalem, "The stones would cry out".[1472]

So where does this ability for great joy come from? Throughout the Bible, we read about people singing and worshiping with great joy. There have been times I could hardly contain myself from jumping up from my seat to incite a riot of fervent praise because of the joy that overwhelmed me during worship, for the most beautiful person in existence! There are churches where many enter passionate praise and dancing, like King David did. I'm sure the Spirit of the LORD dances with them in whatever form we worship.

A few years ago, I attended a worship service at a church which was televised. The church was filled to capacity as never before. My cynical thought was that people only attended so that they could be filmed. But as we entered into serene worship, I had a vision of their souls reaching up to God. It was beautiful and divine. And I learned not to judge another person's worship and interaction with our heavenly Father.

King David knew the importance of releasing music and dance. He appointed Levite priests to be singers accompanied by stringed instruments raising their voices with resounding joy.[1473] "All Israel brought up the Ark of the Covenant of the LORD with shouting and with the sound of the horn, with trumpets and with cymbals, making music with stringed instruments and harps."[1474] David himself danced his way with abandonment to Jerusalem making a spectacle of himself.[1475]

Do I believe God is a person? Absolutely! Are humans made in His image? That's what the Bible tells us. The surge of joy we feel can only emanate from Him as a reflection of His personality. King David said to the LORD, "I know, my God, that You test the heart, and with uprightness You are pleased."[1476] God finds pleasure, He gets joy at our devotion to Him, like any one of us when we are appreciated and loved.

The times the Bible mentions the people as joyful and happy were always when the LORD was honored. After many days of feasting, King Solomon sent the people home with a joyful heart because of all the things the LORD had done for David, Solomon, and His people Israel.[1477]

Battles were won, and the people rejoiced when giving God the glory. King Jehoshaphat led every man of Judah and Jerusalem with joy because the LORD led them to victory.[1478]

Always, the people were blessed and happy when their kings returned to God and His laws. After several kings had led Israel astray, King Hezekiah reinstated the Passover and other holy festivals, because this was another banqueting season with much meat and the best foods for all the people. The people hadn't seen anything like this, since the time of King Solomon, and there was great joy in Jerusalem."[1479] "Then the priests and Levites went out and blessed the people, and their voices were heard. And their prayers came up to His holy habitation in the heavens."[1480]

In my many years of walking with God, I have often witnessed people associate prayer with bombarding God with self-centered and petty requests. Instead, we should take every opportunity to thank and praise Him, our King. What a novel thing it would be to ask our LORD what HIS prayer requests are.

When Queen Esther and her uncle Mordecai defeated Haman who wanted to wipe out all Jews from the face of the earth, God came to their rescue and gave her favor with her husband, the King of Babylon. And so Jews everywhere had extreme joy. They celebrated with banquets and a holiday, around the spring Passover season.[1481] Even today, this is a special feast day of Purim.

Then when the Jews returned to Jerusalem after being exiled in Babylon for seventy years, burnt offerings were made to the LORD for the first time in decades. There was so much emotion that the older ones, who had seen the first Temple before it was destroyed, wept out loud when the foundation of this temple was laid before their eyes. Many others shouted with joy, so the people couldn't tell if the noise was from shouts of joy or weeping that could be heard from a distance.[1482]

Finally, the Temple was restored, and the children of Israel celebrated the dedication of this House of God with joy during the Passover and Feast of Unleavened Bread. God had even turned the heart of the neighboring King of Assyria to help rebuild the house of the God of Israel.[1483]

After everything was completed, God's Word - the Law given to Moses was read - and the people's hearts were overwhelmed with emotion! Nehemiah and the priests responded with the compassion of God, saying "Go your way, eat the fat, drink the sweet, and send portions to those for whom nothing is prepared; for this day is holy to our LORD. Do not sorrow, for the joy of the LORD is your strength."[1484]

"On that day they offered many sacrifices and rejoiced because God had given them great cause for rejoicing. From far away the joyful celebration of Jerusalem was heard."[1485] These public sacrifices meant abundant food was shared with all the people. God is a person of great joy, which is strength to all who love Him. His joy is contagious. We should all begin to say: "A happy God is a happy life!"

In the Book of Job, God described His awesomeness revealing who He really is.[1486] It's a beautiful book about His powerful Majesty. There is no king like Him, He is Ruler over the kings of the earth.[1487] God Himself tells us about the beginning of creating Earth and how even the angels reflect His joy. He said, "When the morning stars sang together, and all the sons of God shouted for joy."[1488]

King David wrote many songs about "Joy" and that the LORD was his exceeding joy. He sang:

- ❖ May all those who seek refuge in You rejoice, may they ever shout for joy. Because You defend them. May those who love Your name be joyful in You.[1489]
- ❖ In Your presence is fullness of joy.[1490]
- ❖ Weeping may endure for a night, but joy comes in the morning.[1491]
- ❖ My soul will be joyful in the LORD. It will rejoice in His salvation.[1492]
- ❖ To the God of my joyful gladness, with the harp I will give thanks to You.[1493]
- ❖ The joy of the whole earth, is Mount Zion … The city of the great King.[1494]
- ❖ The pastures are clothed with flocks, the valleys also are covered with grain, they shout for joy, they also sing.[1495]
- ❖ Shout joyfully to God, all you lands! [1496]
- ❖ Let the field be joyful, and all that is in it. Then all the trees of the forests shall rejoice.[1497]
- ❖ Let the rivers clap their hands. Let the hills be joyful together before the LORD.[1498]

❖ Oh, let the nations be glad and sing for joy, for You will judge the people uprightly, and lead the nations on earth.[1499]

❖ Blessed are the people who know the joyful shout. They walk, O LORD, in the light of Your presence.[1500]

❖ Let us make a joyful noise to the rock of our salvation![1501]

❖ Those who sow in tears shall reap in joy.[1502]

❖ Let Israel rejoice in its Maker, let the children of Zion be joyful in their King.[1503]

These are amazing verses filled with the excitement of joy and hope. The Book of Proverbs gives us wisdom on how to live in the joy of the LORD. "Deceit is in the heart of those who plan evil, but counselors of peace have joy."[1504] "It is a joy for the just to do justice, but destruction will come to the workers of iniquity."[1505] "For God gives wisdom and knowledge and joy to a man who is good in His sight, but to the sinner He gives the work of gathering and collecting, that he may give to him who is good before God."[1506]

When isn't God happy? When everyone is wicked. The prophet Isaiah said, "The LORD shall have no joy in their young men, neither shall have mercy on their fatherless and widows. For everyone is an hypocrite and an evildoer, and every mouth speaketh folly."[1507] "Gladness is taken away, and joy out of the plentiful field. In the vineyards there shall be no singing".[1508]

There are even times the LORD calls for weeping and mourning, but instead the people created their own joy and gladness, saying, "Let us eat and drink, for tomorrow we shall die!"[1509] But human joy on its own is completely self-seeking, temporary, and always ends in disaster and waste.

Because we turn away from God's instructions on how to maintain ourselves and the earth properly, God said the music will stop and there is a cry for wine in the streets, all joy is turned to darkness, and the fun of the land is gone.[1510] Isn't that drastically obvious today as people turn away from the LORD, and turn to depressing music, violent video games, rock stars, media idols, alcohol, drugs, violence, fornication and suicide? We pretend to ignore the reality of being far away from God, and the pain and destruction that comes with a godless society.

But God is amazing! His goodness and mercy never leave us without a solution. And what is that we wonder? "The humble also shall increase their joy in the LORD, and the poor among men shall rejoice in the Holy One of Israel."[1511] What is God saying? We must let go of the love for the ordinary to become a person who doesn't place money, prestige, or things as priorities. Let Him be our Number One since He alone can give us true joy. Whether we're materially rich or poor, pure joy is a beautiful gift from God alone and cannot be bought with anything manmade.

Repeatedly, the Bible tells stories of how God blessed His people. But over time, a new generation was born who only learned about Him through stories and did not take Him seriously. They only trusted in their own work to produce their blessings. Without God's instructions, new generations raised in comfort and blessed by the faithfulness of their parents, fell quickly into corruption and perversion.

God always allows mankind to make their own choices. He would leave them to their own devices which always led to plundering one another, because jealousy has no limits, until their cities were destroyed. "On the land of my people will come up thorns and briers, yes on all the happy homes in the joyous city; because the palaces will be forsaken, the bustling city will be deserted."[1512]

Again, I say God is amazing. No matter the mess we make, He never leaves His people to suffer in misery permanently. Isaiah tells us a few chapters later how the wilderness, the wasteland, and the desert "shall blossom abundantly and rejoice, even with joy and singing … They shall see the glory of the LORD, the excellency of our God."[1513]

Here are more beautiful promises for God's people to receive the joy of the LORD. Even though they certainly didn't deserve His love, He still kept His word to their forefathers, Abraham, Isaac, and Jacob.

❖ And the ransomed of the LORD shall return and come to Zion with songs and everlasting joy upon their heads. They shall obtain joy and gladness.[1514]

- Sing, O heavens! And be joyful, O earth! And break forth into singing, O mountains![1515]
- For the LORD will comfort Zion. He will make her wilderness like Eden and her desert like the garden of the LORD. Joy and gladness will be found in it, thanksgiving, and the voice of melody.[1516]
- I will bring to My holy mountain and make them joyful in My house of prayer.[1517]
- Then you shall see and be radiant, and your heart shall thrill and rejoice, because the abundance of the sea shall be converted to you, the wealth of the nations shall come to you.[1518]
- To give to them beauty for ashes, the oil of joy for mourning, the garment of praise for the spirit of heaviness.[1519]
- Be glad and rejoice forever in that which I create, for I create Jerusalem for rejoicing and her people for joy.[1520]

If you've been to Israel, one of the biggest marvels you saw is how they took desert land and turned it into one of the richest farmlands on earth in such a short time since 1947. With so many years of rest, the land thrives, and everything God mentioned grows in abundance when Israel brought worship to Yahweh back to the land.

These scriptures tell us that God is in love with Israel. His earthly capital is Jerusalem. He chose the Jewish people to care for the land and be a blessing to the world by honoring Him.[1521] That includes teaching the nations His laws and instructions. When we look at societies today, we can see the Torah influence brought by the Jews who were scattered across the world, especially through the most famous Jew, YESHUA – JESUS!

Now let's see what the New Testament has to say about the "Joy of the LORD". It begins when the angel Gabriel appeared to the priest Zacharias to tell him that he and his wife Elizabeth would have a son. It would be a miracle, since they were past childbearing years.[1522] Gabriel said the boy would give them "joy and gladness, and many shall rejoice at his birth … and he shall be filled with the Holy Ghost, even from his mother's womb. And many of the children of Israel shall he turn to the Lord their God".[1523] This baby boy would grow up to be John the Baptist, a cousin to Jesus of Nazareth.

Six months later, the same angel Gabriel visited a virgin teenage girl, Mary, to tell her she also would have a son,[1524] and "that Holy One who is to be born will be called the Son of God". Mary said, "'How can this be since I do not know a man?' The angel answered her, 'The Holy Spirit will come upon you, and the power of the Highest will overshadow you. Therefore the Holy One who will be born will be called the Son of God.'"[1525]

Mary went to visit her cousin Elizabeth who was then six months pregnant. Elizabeth said to her, "Why is it granted to me that the mother of my Lord should come to me? As soon as the sound of your greeting came to my ears, the baby in my womb leaped for joy."[1526] Imagine that! A preborn baby feeling joy, filled with the Holy Spirit, who recognized God in the flesh, who was also a preborn baby in Mary's womb.

Finally, when the Son of Salvation was born in the city of Bethlehem, an angel of the LORD appeared with the glory of the LORD to shepherds who were out in the field at night. He said to them, "Listen! Do not fear. For I bring you good news of great joy, which will be to all people. For unto you is born this day in the City of David a Savior, who is Christ the Lord."[1527] Then suddenly a multitude of heavenly beings appeared praising God for the peace and goodwill that had just come into the world.[1528]

When wise men from the East followed a star that was foretold would bring the coming King of the world, they traveled to worship Him. "When they saw the star, they rejoiced with great excitement. And when they came into the house, they saw the young Child with Mary, His mother, and fell down and worshipped Him. And when they had opened their treasures, they presented gifts to Him: gold, frankincense, and myrrh."[1529]

Amazing! From the conception of the Son of God, at His birth, and throughout the New Testament, the Bible continually talks about "JOY". Often God is depicted as a stern deity, quick to punish at the smallest provocation. But Jesus is shown as a man who disciplined with love. He taught people how to be set free and live abundant lives, healing them from past and present afflictions. And He taught us how to help one another.

When Jesus began His ministry, the first instruction He gave to people was, "Repent, for the Kingdom of Heaven is at hand."[1530] So, what is the Kingdom of Heaven? Jesus said it's "like treasure hidden in a field, which a man found and hid, and for joy over it he goes and sells all that he has and buys that field."[1531] The Kingdom of Heaven is priceless.

When we have invested our life's talents into that Kingdom, after our earthly life is over, God will judge our works. We all hope we will hear Him say, "Well done, good and faithful servant; you were faithful over a few things, I will make you ruler over many things. Enter into the joy of your LORD."[1532] And when we continue to stand for Him especially through persecution, Jesus tells us to rejoice and leap for joy, because our reward is great in Heaven.[1533]

Jesus first sent seventy of His disciples to go and do what He did, to preach the Good News of the Kingdom of God and set people free from all sorts of disease. The disciples returned with joy, saying, "Lord, even the demons are subject to us in Your name."[1534]

The Bible tells us greater miracles happen that bring more joy than anything else. Whatever could that be? Jesus tells us more joy takes place in Heaven in the presence of the angels of God "over one sinner who repents than over ninety-nine just persons who need no repentance".[1535] Through these stories, we can feel the love and joy from our God, a demonstration of how important each of us are to His happiness and joy.

Jesus is the one who brings joy into the world. Through His life, we learn to live by His commandments as acts of love to God our Father, and one another. He said, "These things have I spoken unto you, that my joy might remain in you, and that your joy might be full."[1536]

As we make Him happy, we become happy. He compares the joy of salvation into His Kingdom like a woman in labor; she "has sorrow because her hour has come, but as soon as she has given birth to the child, she no longer remembers the anguish, for joy that a human being has been born into the world."[1537] The most glorious miracle after our natural birth is when we are born again into His Spirit.

After Jesus had risen from the tomb, the two Mary's went to tend to His body. The angel of the LORD appeared and told them, "He is risen from the dead."[1538] So they went quickly from the tomb with fear and great joy and ran to tell His disciples the good news.[1539] Even death couldn't hold Jesus, and He continues to spread His joy to the world to this very day. Forty days after His resurrection, Jesus ascended to heaven.[1540]

But Jesus leaving earth didn't stop the impartation of joy as we read again and again in the stories that follow the acts of the apostles. Phillip went out to preach about Jesus in Samaria and the great joy of the LORD came into that city, because demons were cast out and healing miracles happened.[1541] Of course, some people came against them, but word of the Lord Jesus kept on spreading. "And the disciples were filled with joy and with the Holy Spirit".[1542]

So there it is!!! Preaching the good news of Jesus Christ: His birth, death, resurrection, healing power, baptism of the Holy Spirit and His soon return is the gospel of sheer supernatural, overwhelmingly contagious peace and joy!

By these accounts, some church teachings have it all wrong. Often, we sit in pews trying to look pious on Sunday mornings. In reality, we should also be casting out demons, praying the lame to walk, the deaf to hear, the blind to see, all manner of illness healed, and multitudes added to God's Kingdom. We, as His people, should be ballistic in praising our Savior, overwhelmed with His goodness. As Paul said, "For the Kingdom of God is not eating and drinking, but righteousness and peace and joy in the Holy Spirit."[1543]

This is the bottom line of the Gospel of Jesus Christ: "The fruit of the Spirit is love, joy, peace, longsuffering, kindness, goodness, faithfulness, gentleness, self-control. Against such there is no law."[1544] What this means, is when we are filled with the Holy Spirit, we then intimately know God, and He alone is the source of these pure fruits manifested in good deeds towards others.

If we don't have an inner peace and joy but have anxiety and torment instead, something is wrong with our knowledge of who Jesus really is. I'm not saying that we feel happy all the time. But true inner joy comes when we accept Jesus' gift of salvation. We should understand by breaking God's holy laws, we are already sentenced to spiritual death, but Jesus took the punishment and died for us, so we can follow Him into eternal life when we accept Him and repent.[1545] Jesus said, "I am the way, the truth and the life, no one comes to the Father except through me."[1546]

If you've always believed you are saved but don't feel you have the Holy Spirit in your life, most likely it's because you don't really know Jesus intimately or you're unable to completely trust Him. Perhaps it's because of wrong teaching or unmet expectations. In any case, if you don't have joy but feel Jesus is a punisher, unable or unwilling to be the lover of your soul, you are completely wrong.

Being a born-again Christian without inner joy isn't possible because the Holy Spirit comes to live in us, and He is pure wisdom, peace, love, and joy. Ask Him to reveal Himself to you, then surrender to His love. He will only come to those who desire Him and share with us as much as we allow, even during trials.[1547]

Jesus told the Jewish priest, Nicodemus, "Except a man be born again, he cannot see the Kingdom of God."[1548] Are you "born again"? We must repent from our unbelief and trust that He is able to save us from all our wrongs. Then invite the Holy Spirit to live in your heart and guide you. Paul tells us, "Your body is the temple of the Holy Spirit who is in you … and you are not your own."[1549]

Do we believe the Bible and all the words of Jesus? Or do we believe the doctrines of earthly people we have followed? If you suffer from negative thinking, believe that Jesus came as our savior and deliverer. "For God hath not given us the spirit of fear, but of power, and of love, and of a sound mind."[1550]

Here is a final promise about the joy of the LORD from the Book of Jude, "Now unto Him (Jesus) that is able to keep you from falling, and to present you faultless before the presence of His glory (the Father) with exceeding joy".[1551] Amen!

CHAPTER SIX

His Names and Identities

Because God is known throughout the world in all languages, and His nature is so indescribably vast, this is just a very small and partial list of His names. Each name has many meanings, as our Creator has unlimited functions and each of us is created with different parts of Him. May we come to know Him more.

GOD THE FATHER

ABBA – "Abba, Father," He said, "everything is possible for you." Mark 14:36 NIV

ADONAI – "On the day when Adonai, God, made earth and heaven." Genesis 2:4 CJB

ALPHA AND OMEGA – "I am the Alpha and the Omega, the First and the Last, the Beginning and the End." Revelation 22:13 NIV

ANCIENT OF DAYS – "Until the Ancient of Days came." Daniel 7:22 NIV

ALMIGHTY – "If you return to the Almighty, you will be restored." Job 22:23 NIV

CREATOR – "Remember your Creator in the days of your youth." Ecclesiastes 12:1 NIV

EL, ELOHIM – "Now, Adonai Elohim, You alone are God; Your words are truth." 2 Samuel 7:28 CJB

EL SHADDAI – (Many Breasted One) "I am El Shaddai. Be fruitful and multiply." Genesis 35:11 CJB

FATHER – "Be perfect, therefore, as your heavenly Father is perfect." Matthew 5:48 NIV

"Our Father in heaven, hallowed be Your name." Matthew 6:9 NIV

GOD – "In the beginning God created the heavens and the earth". Genesis 1:1 NIV

GOD OF HEAVEN – "I mourned and fasted and prayed before the God of heaven." Nehemiah 1:4 NIV

HIGHEST – "The power of the Highest will overshadow you." Luke 1:35 MEV

HOLY ONE – "Holy One of Israel." Psalm 71:22 NIV

I AM – "God said to Moses, 'I AM who I AM. This is what you are to say to the Israelites: I AM has sent me to you.'" Exodus 3:14 NIV

JEHOVAH – "But by my name Jehovah was I not known to them." Exodus 6:3 KJV

JUDGE, LAWGIVER – "For the Lord is our Judge, The Lord is our Lawgiver, The Lord is our King." Isaiah 33:22 NIV

KING OF GLORY – "Who is this King of glory? The Lord strong and mighty." Psalm 24:8 NIV

LORD GOD – In the day that the LORD God made the earth and the heavens". Genesis 2:4 KJV

MOST HIGH – "Judgment in favor of the holy people of the Most High." Daniel 7:22 NIV

YAH – "For in Yah, the LORD, is everlasting strength." Isaiah 26:4 NKJV

YHVH, YAHWEH – "I did not make myself known to them by my name, Yud-Heh-Vav-Heh." Exodus 6:3 CJB

GOD THE SON

ADVOCATE – "We have an Advocate with the Father, Jesus Christ the righteous One." 1 John 2:1 NIV

BISHOP OF SOULS – "Now returned unto the Shepherd and Bishop of your souls." 1 Peter 2:25 KJV

BREAD OF LIFE – "I am the bread of life. Whoever comes to me will never go hungry." John 6:35 NIV

BRIDEGROOM – "He who has the bride is the bridegroom." John 3:29 MEV

CARPENTER – "Is not this the carpenter, the Son of Mary?" Mark 6:3 KJV

CHIEF CORNERSTONE – "Christ Jesus himself as the chief cornerstone." Ephesians 2:20 NIV

DAYSPRING – "The Dayspring from on high hath visited us." Luke 1:78 KJV

DOOR – "I am the door. If anyone enters by Me, he will be saved". John 10:9 NKJV

FRIEND – "Greater love hath no man than this, that a man lay down his life for his friends." John 15:13 KJV

GOD – "In the beginning was the Word, and the Word was with God, and the Word was God." John 1:1 KJV

HEAD OF THE CHURCH – "Christ is the head of the church." Ephesians 5:23 KJV

HIGH PRIEST – "Jesus, having become High Priest forever." Hebrews 6:20 NKJV

HOLY ONE – "I know who You are - the Holy One of God!" Mark 1:24 NIV

I AM – "I say unto you, before Abraham was, I AM." John 8:58 KJV.

IMAGE OF THE INVISIBLE GOD – "The Son is the image of the invisible God, the firstborn over all creation." Colossians 1:15 NIV

IMMANUEL – "Behold, a virgin shall conceive and bear a Son, and shall call His name Immanuel." Isaiah 7:14 KJV

JESUS CHRIST – "In His Son Jesus Christ." 1 John 5:20 KJV

JUDGE – "Appointed as judge of the living and the dead." Acts 10:42 NIV

KING OF THE JEWS – "The written notice of the charge against him read: THE KING OF THE JEWS." Mark 15:26 NIV

KING OF KINGS, LORD OF LORDS – "On his robe and on his thigh he has this name written: KING OF Kings and LORD OF Lords." Revelation 19:16 NIV

LAMB OF GOD – "Behold! The Lamb of God, which taketh away the sin of the world!" John 1:29 KJV

LIGHT OF THE WORLD – "I am the light of the world. Whoever follows Me will never walk in darkness." John 8:12 NIV

LION OF JUDAH – "The Lion of the tribe of Judah, the Root of David, has triumphed." Revelation 5:5 NIV

LIVING WATER – "You would have asked Him, and He would have given you living water." John 4:10 NIV

MAN OF SORROWS – "A Man of sorrows and acquainted with grief." Isaiah 53:3 KJV

MASTER – "A servant is not greater than his master." John 15:20 NIV

MEDIATER – "There is one God and one mediator between God and mankind, the man Christ Jesus." 1 Timothy 2:5 NIV

MESSIAH – "We have found the Messiah" (which is translated, the Christ)." John 1:41 NIV

ROCK – "For they drank of that spiritual Rock that accompanied them, and that Rock was Christ." 1 Corinthians 10:4 NIV

MORNING STAR – "I am the Root and the Offspring of David, and the bright Morning Star." Revelation 22:16 NIV

ONLY BEGOTTEN SON – "God sent His only begotten Son into the world." 1 John 4:9 KJV

PROPHET – "This is Jesus, the prophet of Nazareth of Galilee." Matthew 21:11 KJV

PRINCE OF PEACE – "His name will be called Wonderful, Counselor, Mighty God, the Everlasting Father, the Prince of Peace." Isaiah 9:6 KJV

REDEEMER – "I know that my Redeemer lives." Job 19:25 NIV

RESURRECTION AND THE LIFE – "I am the resurrection and the life. He who believeth in Me, though he were dead, yet shall he live." John 11:25 KJV

RABBI/TEACHER – "Rabbi, we know that You are a teacher who has come from God." John 3:2 NIV

ROSE OF SHARON – "I am the rose of Sharon, and the lily of the valleys." Song of Solomon 2:1 KJV

RULER OVER KINGS – "The ruler of the kings of the earth." Revelation 1:5 NIV

SAVIOR – "We have heard him ourselves, and know that this is indeed the Christ, the Savior of the world." John 4:42 KJV

SERVANT – "Behold! My Servant whom I have chosen, My Beloved in whom My soul is well pleased!" Matthew 12:18 KJV

SHEPHERD – "I am the good shepherd. The good shepherd givith His life for the sheep." John 10:11 KJV

SHILOH – "The scepter shall not depart from Judah, nor a Lawgiver from between his feet, until Shiloh come." Genesis 49:10 KJV

SON OF GOD – "And we know that the Son of God is come." 1 John 5:20 KJV

SON OF MAN – "When you have lifted up the Son of Man, then you will know that I am He, and that I do nothing of My own." John 8.28 NIV

TRUE VINE – "I am the true vine, and My Father is the husbandman." John 15:1 KJV

WAY, TRUTH, AND LIFE – "I am the way, the truth, and the life. No one comes to the Father except through Me." John 14:6 NIV

WITNESS – "These things says the Amen, the Faithful and True Witness." Revelation 3:14 NIV

WORD – "And the Word was made flesh and dwelt among us." John 1:14 KJV

YESHUA – "This is the genealogy of Yeshua the Messiah, son of David, son of Avraham." Matthew 1:1 CJB

GOD THE HOLY SPIRIT

ADVOCATE, COMFORTER, COUNSELOR – "I will ask the Father, and He will give you another Helper (Comforter, Advocate, Intercessor—Counselor, Strengthener, Standby), to be with you forever." John 14:16 AMP

DOVE – "The Holy Spirit descended in bodily form like a dove upon Him." Luke 3:22 KJV

FIRE – "He will baptize you with the Holy Spirit and fire." Matthew 3:11 NIV

HELPER – "The Helper, the Holy Spirit, whom the Father will send in My name, He will teach you all things." John 14:26 AMP

HOLY GHOST – "I indeed have baptized you with water: but he shall baptize you with the Holy Ghost." Matthew 3:11 KJV

RUACH HAKODESH – "He will immerse you in the Ruach HaKodesh and in fire." Matthew 3:11 CJB

SPIRIT OF GOD – "And the Spirit of God was hovering over the waters." Genesis 1:2 NIV

SPIRIT OF TRUTH – "When He, the Spirit of truth comes, He will guide you into all the truth." John 16:13 NIV

WATER – "The water I give them will become in them a spring of water welling up to eternal life." John 4:14 NIV

CHAPTER SEVEN

What Happens Now?

EPILOGUE

Now you know more about WHO GOD IS from the passages of the Bible! Reading the scriptures and stories about our God, who came to earth as a man through Jesus, we learned about this most compassionate wonderful Being. There is none like Him, "Who is and Who was and Who is to come, the Almighty".[1552]

Since the history of humankind, we have had countless heroes; kings and queens, emperors, presidents, generals, prophets, famous people, and thousands of supposed gods, but we have never known one like Jesus. His story just keeps going and giving through His people.

Jesus not only fulfilled all Old Testament prophecies, but He physically demonstrated that He was the Messiah, the Anointed One, the Christ, "the Savior of the World".[1553] He came to set us free from every hindrance, disease, and the final eternal death by substituting His own life to pay for all the harmful and deadly consequences of humanity's sins.

I used to struggle with understanding why God the Father, who said He loves me, would sentence me to death in the first place. Secondly, how could Jesus take my place? That was, until I understood God's universal laws of "cause and effect". In the natural and the spiritual, laws are established to keep order in all that exists from falling into chaos.

We can take the example from the basic Law of Gravity. When we drop a ceramic plate on a concrete ground from a distance, it will break. The higher the distance we drop it, the more pieces it will shatter into.

This is just like sin which carries negative consequences when we break God's universal laws of perfect order. The higher the rebellion we achieve, the more pieces we break into physically, spiritually, and eternally. Like the broken plate, sin also leaves a big mess and painful slivers in those around us. That is why God cannot ignore sin but must allow negative consequences to stop us.

Adam and Eve's rebellion increased with each generation until God found no other solution than to flood the earth and drown all air-breathing life because they had become too corrupted.[1554] But thankfully, even though human beings are mixed with the genetics of good and evil and have a fleshly desire for sin, God our Creator found another way to avoid having to flood the earth again.[1555]

God the Father sent His Son as a replacement to be broken instead of us. His blood was poured out to pay for all humanity's crimes. We can accept this free pass only by trusting in Him. When we really understand and value the cost of His payment, we won't be so quick to sin again.

Many claim to know Jesus and say they've accepted this gift but continue to throw down the plate either in mockery or addiction. If we use the excuse that Jesus has paid anyway, then we really don't love Him and don't care if we abuse His body, blood, and name, over and over again.

When we continue in our sin, we keep throwing down the life of our precious King. It's like we ourselves are spitting in His face or piercing His hands and disabling His power in us.[1556] Do we really value Him, or do we value ourselves more by considering our sin as a greater god? Again, the word is "choose".

King David asked God to show him his own secret faults.[1557] We should do the same to find out what's really in our hearts, then ask His forgiveness and help, to stop our bad behavior. The best way to judge ourselves is by the spiritual fruit we bear. Are our results sweet or bitter? This will tell us if we're for real or just giving God lip service.

If our fruit is inedible, then we're only fooling ourselves since God reads our hearts and not our words.[1558]

Is it possible for any of us to know the fullness of God and the many mysteries of His identity? Absolutely not! In our finite human state, we can only catch a glimpse of Him. He exists in dimensions we cannot see nor understand. Paul wrote, "For now we see through a glass darkly, but then face to face. Now I know in part; but then shall I know even as also I am known."[1559]

One of the greatest confusions among Bible scholars, is whether God is one person or three separate persons. Jews recite a prayer every day that the LORD God is one. But Christians see Him as three personalities of one being or as three separate beings.

I personally would attest that God is too far above humanity for us to fully grasp what all His dimensions are, since He is the great mystery. As finite beings, it's extremely hard for us to understand beyond our natural senses. Yet God lives outside of those. He is a being who can be everywhere at once, with no limitations in size and shape or time. The laws of physics that bind the material world, as little as we understand them, do not bind Him.

We would do best to stop arguing about things we don't know for sure and focus on the truths He allows us to have in His word, the Bible. So, I encourage everyone to search the scriptures for themselves for further truths.

The one we call God is all powerful, all consuming, everlasting, omnipotent, omnipresent, everywhere at once, knowing all things, the beginning and the end. He is eternally more than we have words in the human language to describe and as the Bible simply states, He exists, He is THE GREAT "I AM"![1560]

INVITATION

If you've come to the end of this book and haven't yet submitted your life and allegiance to King Yeshua, why wait any longer? Give Him your life today, right now. Every born-again soul knows God isn't some abstract conscience of the universe. He is our Creator, our Father, a living, loving sentient being, of whom we are each a part. He is Lord of all!

Do we dare to recognize Him and dare to approach Him? Draw near to God with your heart and He promises to draw near to us.[1561] Ask His forgiveness, His saving grace, cleansing and blessing. Then instead of spending a pointless life building a little kingdom of your own that won't last more than this brief physical (soon to be forgotten) time on earth, you will join God in building His eternal Kingdom.

This is your true inheritance already planned for you. Join Him now, your Father and the King of kings, Lord of lords is waiting for you to take your rightful place at His side as an heir to the throne of Christ, and all that exists.[1562] The choice is yours!

Do you know Him? If so, go deeper, offer Him your best sacrifice: your heart, your life. He will transform you into the person He created you to be. Do you really know Him, or just about Him? If this is you, don't be left out, and invite Jesus into your life.

Let Him be your all and all, your Lord, your Savior, your King, Yeshua our Messiah. Instantly you will begin to trade your dirty spiritual clothes covered in stench from the battlefield of this world's sins, in exchange for royal robes of righteousness and salvation, to be worn by the heirs of the throne of God.[1563]

The serpent told Eve she would have that royal position by eating the fruit of contaminated knowledge, a mixture of truth and lies, good and evil.[1564] Instead, both she and her husband Adam became tainted and birthed a tainted mankind. In turn, they ruined a perfect world through generational human confusion filled with the curses of rebellion and death.[1565]

But God had already planned a way of taking back those who choose eternal life with Him. The plan is to restore the earth to Paradise, by allowing us to partner with Him in setting up His Kingdom in perfect order, through His laws of life, truth, and love.[1566]

There is a warning to those who choose to do nothing. Jesus told the story of three servants as examples of what He expects from us during this very temporary earthly assignment we have been given. Each of us is born with certain talents for the jobs we are to accomplish during our lifetime.

This is what Jesus said: "The Kingdom of Heaven is like a man traveling to a far country, who called his own servants and delivered his goods to them. To one he gave five talents, to another two, and to another one, to each according to his own ability."[1567] The person who received five talents traded with them and made five more. The person who received two talents, made two more. But the person who received one talent, hid it, and made nothing.[1568]

In this story, when the man returned, his servants in turn showed him what they achieved, and he said to the first two who doubled their talents,[1569] "Well done, good and faithful servant; you were faithful over a few things, I will make you ruler over many things. Enter into the joy of your LORD."[1570] But to the third servant, the master said, "You wicked and lazy servant ... you ought to have deposited my money with the bankers, and at my coming I would have received back my own with interest. So, take the talent from him, and give it to him who has ten talents."[1571]

Not only did the lazy servant lose his one talent, but the judgement against him was even worse. Jesus ends this story with a fierce warning, "For to everyone who has, more will be given, and he will have abundance, but from him who does not have, even what he has will be taken away. And cast the unprofitable servant into the outer darkness. There will be weeping and gnashing of teeth."[1572]

According to Jesus' own words, spiritual laziness is a form of rebellion and can be another path to Hell. Are we using our talents, wealth, time, and abilities to profit His Kingdom? No matter how small or large, we each have a job to do. Will we choose to use our talents to reproduce His goodness, or bury the blessings we have been given? Everything in life is a choice.

Jesus instructs us how to use our talents in this next prophecy: "When the Son of Man comes in His glory, and all the holy Angels with Him, then He will sit on the throne of His glory. All the nations will be gathered before Him, and He will separate them one from another, as a shepherd divides his sheep from the goats. And He will set the sheep on His right hand, but the goats on the left."[1573]

"Then the King will say to those on His right hand, 'Come, you blessed of My Father, inherit the Kingdom prepared for you from the foundation of the world: for I was hungry and you gave Me food; I was thirsty and you gave Me drink; I was a stranger and you took Me in; I was naked and you clothed Me; I was sick and you visited Me; I was in prison and you came to Me.'"[1574]

"Then the righteous will answer Him, saying, 'Lord, when did we see You hungry and feed You, or thirsty and give You drink? When did we see You a stranger and take You in, or naked and clothe You? Or when did we see You sick, or in prison, and come to You?' And the King will answer and say to them, 'Assuredly, I say to you, inasmuch as you did it to one of the least of these My brethren, you did it to Me.'"[1575]

"Then He will also say to those on the left hand, 'Depart from Me, you cursed, into the everlasting fire prepared for the devil and his angels: For I was hungry and you gave Me no food; I was thirsty and you gave Me no drink; I was a stranger and you did not take

Me in, naked and you did not clothe Me, sick and in prison and you did not visit Me.'"[1576]

"Then they also will answer Him, saying, 'Lord, when did we see You hungry or thirsty or a stranger or naked or sick or in prison, and did not minister to You?' Then He will answer them, saying, 'Assuredly, I say to you, inasmuch as you did not do it to one of the least of these, you did not do it to Me.' And these will go away into everlasting punishment, but the righteous into eternal life."[1577]

Let's talk about the "End Goal". What is this all about? My visitation with God in Israel, left me with two important messages, the first was of His infinite supernatural love. The second is about Jesus final words in the book of Revelation: "Behold I am coming quickly: blessed is he that keepeth the sayings of the prophecy of this book."[1578] Even now we are seeing the signs all around us of His soon return as the Earth is groaning with birth pangs.[1579] The Bible tells us, He will come as a thief in the night, when many are not expecting Him[1580]. But this time He's not coming as a baby but as KING.

The instructions left for us are, "He that is unjust, let him be unjust still: and he which is filthy, let him be filthy still: and he that is righteous, let him be righteous still: and he that is holy, let him be holy still." "Behold, I come quickly; and my reward is with me, to give every man according as his work shall be. I am Alpha and Omega, the beginning and the end, the first and the last."[1581]

The destinies for our behaviors are also revealed, "Blessed are they that do His commandments, that they may have right to the tree of life, and may enter in through the gates into the city. For without are dogs, and sorcerers, and whoremongers, and murderers, and idolaters, and whosoever loveth and maketh a lie. I, Jesus, have sent mine angel to testify unto you these things in the churches. I am the root and the offspring of David, and the bright and morning star."[1582]

The final message I and so many others before me have been given, is that Jesus is coming, and each of us must be ready to welcome Him. "And the Spirit and the bride say, 'Come'. And let him that heareth say, 'Come'. And let him that is athirst come. And whosoever will, let him take the water of life freely."[1583] "He who testifies to these things says, 'Surely I am coming quickly.' Amen. Even so, come, Lord Jesus!"[1584]

This gives us the most important choice we have in life; will we be His disciple ready to welcome Him? One of the saddest and most terrifying stories Jesus told, was of Ten Virgins. They were all asleep waiting for the Bridegroom to come for the wedding. Five of them were prepared and had enough oil for their lamps as He finally came at midnight. But the other five didn't have enough oil and had to stop and buy more.[1585]

The first five went into the wedding and the door closed behind them. The other five showed up late and were locked out. They said, "'Lord, Lord, open to us!' But He answered and said, 'Verily I say unto you, I know you not.' Watch therefore, for ye know neither the day nor the hour wherein the Son of man cometh."[1586]

Oil is often symbolic of the anointing which comes in greater measure of surrender to the Holy Spirit. We must each ask ourselves how much we allow God to fill us with His Spirit. Good works also produce oil and are necessary as they are the fruit of our faithfulness to God, but good works alone will not produce enough oil to light the way to the wedding feast of God's Son. Becoming a Jesus follower is a serious business of obedient work and sacrifice. The usual Christian tradition of only confessing loyalty for a few seconds and attending church once a week isn't enough.

When I first made my dedication to Jesus, I said to Him, "Lord, I've been fooled all my life, how will I know those who are really Yours?" Then I was drawn to the scripture where Jesus said, "Every tree that does not bear good fruit is cut down and thrown into the fire. Therefore, by their fruits you will know them. Not everyone who says to Me, 'Lord, Lord,' shall enter the Kingdom of Heaven, but he who does the will of My Father in heaven."[1587]

So I gave Him my life, all that I am, working daily and diligently to advance His Kingdom here on Earth as it is in Heaven. He makes that challenge to each of us. But don't be too hard on yourself if you aren't instantly transformed or still make mistakes as we all do. Like a Bonsai tree, which needs strategic long-term pruning, it takes precision to cut old growth, and time to train new growth into the shape our Master gardener requires.

Invite Jesus to take over your life right now. Why wait another minute? It may be your last one. What else will you do? You were designed for greatness, as a son and daughter of God, an heir to His Kingdom. But it's a choice if you will use the talents your Creator has given you for your benefit only or use them for the greater works of His Kingdom which includes all mankind and creation.

To be a disciple of Jesus, takes discipline. You will need to do some important things to start. Surrender your life to Jesus, like a knight bowing before his King, offering your love, loyalty and works. Invite the Holy Spirit to dwell within you and allow him to direct you, this is the baptism of fire. Then be cleansed through the baptism of water.[1588] Ask forgiveness for past sins, mistakes, and crimes against God and others. Let go of bitterness and forgive everyone, including yourself, and anything you may hold against God. Jesus said, unless we forgive, we will not be forgiven.[1589]

Each of us must make that decision to be or not to be worthy of Him. We all know in our hearts the difference between right and wrong. When we wrong others or ourselves, we wrong Him, no matter what the excuse. Every day that we're alive, we must still make a decision to an age-old question, should I serve myself or serve Jesus (which usually means serving others)? The law of love always supersedes the law of the letter.

The best lesson I have learned is that when we serve others, we also serve ourselves. The joy of helping someone else and the peace that passes all understanding that comes from our Lord's pleasure, fills us completely whenever we do what's right. It's not an easy walk to trade our self-interests to His interests, but taking one step at a time for righteousness changes our hearts now and for eternity. Try it, you'll like it!

You can now also pray continuously, because you have the right to walk and talk with God all day long, since He lives in you. And read your Bible; every word brings a fresh revelation of His union with us and His instructions for your life. Then find a trusted, Spirit-filled church where you will learn to fellowship, grow, and receive blessings, as well as be a blessing to the Body of Christ which needs the unique talents our LORD has given to you.

My Beloved, grow with the Spirit of God, expand your wings, and let your spirit soar with Him becoming part of something infinite, for now and eternity. Jesus Christ, our Lord, loves you beyond anything you thought possible and so do I.

May God bless you more than you ever knew He would! Reverend Olga Hermann

REFERENCES

BIBLES

BibleGateway.com
Complete Jewish Bible – David Stern
King James Version
Living Bible
Modern English Version
New International Version
New King James Version
Scripture4all.org/OnlineInterlinear
Stones Tanach
The Jerusalem Bible
The Truth - M.L. Viets

NON-FICTION BOOKS

A More Excellent Way – Dr. Henry W. Wright
Answering Jewish Objections to Jesus I, II, III – Michael L. Brown
Christ the Healer – FF Bosworth
Divine Healing – Andrew Murray
Fashioned for Intimacy – Jane Hanson with Marie Powers
Feed My Sheep Feed My Lambs – Harold R. Dewberry
Four Blood Moons – John Hagee
Genesis and the Big Bang, Gerald L. Schroeder
God Calling – AJ Russell
God, Gold & Glory – Henry Falany

God's Abrahamic Covenant – Tom Hess
God's Dream Team – Tommy Tenney
Going Deeper with the Holy Spirit – Benny Hinn
Good Morning Holy Spirit - Benny Hinn
Hell's Best Kept Secret – Ray Comfort
Hungry for More of Jesus – David Wilkerson
Intimate Friendship with God – Joy Dawson
Intercession Thrilling and Fulfilling - Joy Dawson
John G. Lake The Complete Collection – Roberts Lairdon
Just As I Am - Billy Graham
Lord, Teach Us To Pray – Katheryn Kuhlman
Love Revolution – Gaylord Enns
Messianic Jewish Manifesto – David Stern
My Sojourn in Heaven and Stopover in Hell – John Bunyan
Needless Casualties of War – John Paul Jackson
New Hope for Divorced Catholics – Fr. Barry Brunsman
Our Father Abraham – Marvin R. Wilson
Revelation on Revelations – Douglas Ezell
Romans – Jamie Perez
Secrets to Spiritual Power – Watchman Nee
Science and Genesis 1 P404 – Bruce R. Booker
Son Build Me an Army – Morris Cerullo
Stripes Nails Thorns and the Blood – Dr. Bree Keyton
The Code of the Holy Spirit – Perry Stone
The Collected Works of Hal Lindsey
The Conscience of the Nations – Ronald Reagan
The Cross and the Switchblade – David Wilkerson
The Final Quest – Rick Joyner
The God Chasers - Tommy Tenney
The Perpetual Flame – Jamie L Perez
The Pilgrim's Progress – John Bunyan
The Prayer Life – Andrew Murray
The Purpose Driven Life – Rick Warren
The Pursuit of God – AW Tozer
The Seven Festivals of Messiah – Edward Chumney
The Song of the Bride – Jeanne Guyon

The Ten Commandments – Dr. Laura Schlessinger
Tribes of Israel – Gwen Shaw
To Pray as a Jew – Haim Halevy Donin
Torah Rediscovered – Ariel and D'vorah Berkowitz
Two Men From Eden – Morris Cerullo

OTHER RESOURCES

Biblehub.com/timeline
Biblical Hebrew: Step by Step – Menahem Mansoor
Christianity.com/wiki/christian-terms/what-is-the-meaning-of-shekinah-glory.html
Dreams and Visions 201 – John Paul Jackson
Encyclopedia.com
First Steps in Hebrew Prayer – Dr. Danny Ben-Gigi
Funk & Wagnalls, New Comprehensive International Dictionary
Gospeloutreach.net/613laws.html
Hebrew4christians.com
Merriam-webster.com
Prayer Study Guide – Dr. Lester Sumerall
Strongs Exhaustive Concordance – MacDonald Publishing Company
The Art of Hearing God 101 – John Paul Jackson
The Original Roget's Thesaurus – St. Martin's Press 1965 Edition
Understanding the Dreams You Dream – Ira Milligan
Wikipedia.com

ENDNOTES

1   Song of Solomon 4:9 NKJV
2   Romans 3:1-3; 1 Corinthians 12:28
3   Genesis 22:15-18, 26:1-4, 28:10-15
4   John 21:25 NKJV
5   Genesis 1:27
6   Genesis 1:28
7   Matthew 7:7-8 MEV; Jeremiah 29:13 MEV
8   Leviticus 23:24-25
9   Matthew 2:9 NKJV
10   Romans 10:9 NKJV
11   Matthew 3:11 NKJV
12   Revelations 19:11 KJV
13   2 Chronicles 2:6 NKJV
14   Ephesians 1:23 NKJV
15   Isaiah 6:3 NKJV
16   Revelation 5:4 NIV
17   Isaiah 6:5 NKJV
18   Malachi 3:2 NKJV
19   Song of Songs 8:7 NIV
20   The God Chasers, Tommy Tenney
21   Song of Songs 5:8 NIV
22   Song of Songs 5:6
23   2 Timothy 3:5 NIV
24   Ephesians 4:6 NIV
25   Revelation 1:8 NKJV
26   Exodus 3:14
27   Isaiah 9:6 NKJV
28   John 14:26 NIV
29   John 14:27 NIV
30   2 Corinthians 13:14 NKJV
31   Matthew 2:11
32   John 1:1, 14

33 John 3:8 NIV
34 John 6:51 NKJV
35 Song of Solomon 5:10-16 NIV
36 Exodus 3:14 KJV
37 John 4:24 KJV
38 https://www.christianity.com/wiki/christian-terms/what-is-the-meaning-of-shekinah-glory.html
39 Exodus 3:2-4 KJV
40 Exodus 3:5-6 NKJV
41 Exodus 16:10 NKJV
42 Exodus 16:11-14
43 Exodus 20:18-19
44 Deuteronomy 5:24 NKJV
45 Exodus 24:16-17; 29:43
46 Exodus 40:34-37
47 Exodus 40:38
48 Leviticus 9:23-24
49 Numbers 13
50 Numbers 14:10-12
51 Numbers 14:13-20
52 Numbers 16:1-35
53 1 Samuel 2:8
54 1 Kings 8:1-9, 2 Chronicles 5:1-10
55 1 Kings 8:10-11 NKJV
56 1 Kings 8:27-30 NKJV
57 2 Chronicles 7:1-3 NIV
58 1 Kings 9:3 NIV
59 1 Kings 9:8 NIV
60 2 Chronicles 7:14 KJV
61 Ezekiel 1:28 MEV
62 Ezekiel 3:12,23
63 Ezekiel 10:4 MEV
64 Ezekiel 10:18-19 MEV
65 Ezekiel 11:23 MEV
66 Ezekiel 39:21 MEV
67 Ezekiel 43:2 MEV
68 Ezekiel 40 to 45
69 2 Corinthians 4:4, Ephesians 6:12
70 Psalms 19:1 MEV
71 Psalm 24:9-10 MEV
72 Psalm 72:19 MEV
73 Psalm 84:11 MEV
74 Psalm 96:3 MEV

75   Psalm 97:6 MEV
76   Psalm 102:15 MEV
77   Psalm 102:16 MEV
78   Psalm 104:31 MEV
79   Psalm 108:5 MEV
80   Psalm 113:4 MEV
81   Isaiah 28:5 MEV
82   Isaiah 42:8 MEV
83   Isaiah 43:7 MEV
84   Isaiah 59:19 MEV
85   Isaiah 60:1 MEV
86   Isaiah 60:19 MEV
87   Isaiah 66:18 MEV
88   Isaiah 66:19 MEV
89   Habakkuk 2:14 MEV
90   Habakkuk 3:3 MEV
91   Zechariah 2:5 MEV
92   John 1:14 MEV
93   John 2:11 MEV
94   Matthew 6:13 MEV
95   Mark 8:38 MEV
96   Luke 2:9 MEV
97   Luke 9:32 MEV
98   John 17:5 MEV
99   John 17:24 MEV
100 Matthew 24:30 MEV
101 Matthew 25:31 MEV
102 Acts 7:55 MEV
103 Revelation 21:11 MEV
104 Revelation 21:23 MEV
105 Genesis 1:27 NIV
106 Genesis 4:14
107 Genesis 32:30 NIV
108 Daniel 10:6 KJV
109 Revelation 1:16 NIV
110 Matthew 17:2 NIV
111 Exodus 33:11 NKJV
112 Exodus 33:9
113 Exodus 33:20 NKJV
114 Exodus 33:18-20
115 Exodus 33:22
116 Matthew 17:1-3 NIV
117 Numbers 14:14

118   Deuteronomy 5:4
119   2 Chronicles 7:14
120   2 Chronicles 30:9
121   Psalm 13:1 NKJV
122   Psalm 17:15 NIV
123   Psalm 27:8 NKJV
124   Psalm 30:5
125   Isaiah 59:2
126   Genesis 19:13 NKJV
127   Ezekiel 20:35 NIV
128   Revelation 6:15-16 NIV
129   Ezekiel 39:29 NIV
130   Revelation 22:4 NIV
131   Isaiah 52:14 NIV
132   Isaiah 53:2 NIV
133   Genesis 3:8
134   Philippians 1:21
135   Exodus 33:22; 1 Corinthians 10:4
136   Song of Solomon 5:11 NIV
137   Revelation 14:14 NIV
138   Isaiah 59:17 NIV
139   Matthew 26:7 NKJV
140   John 19:2 NIV
141   John 20:7 NIV
142   Revelation 19:12 NIV
143   Revelation 19:16 KJV
144   Revelation 10:1 NKJV
145   Genesis 9:15-17
146   Hebrews 10:31 NKJV
147   Song of Solomon 5:11 NIV
148   Revelation 1:14 NIV
149   Daniel 7:9 KJV
150   Revelation 1:8 KJV
151   Genesis 1:18 KJV
152   Daniel 7:13 NKJV
153   1 Kings 17:6
154   Song of Songs 5:12 NIV
155   Daniel 10:6 NIV
156   Revelation 2:18 NIV
157   Matthew 3:16 NKJV
158   Psalm 17:8 NKJV
159   Deuteronomy 32:10; Psalm 32:8
160   Psalm 34:15, Psalm 66:7

161   Deuteronomy 11:12; Ephesians 1:5
162   Song of Solomon 5:12; Psalm 79:5
163   Amos 9:8 KJV
164   Habakkuk 1:13 NIV
165   Habakkuk 2:3
166   Job 34:21-22 NIV
167   Zechariah 3:9, 4:10
168   Revelation 5:6
169   Revelation 1:20
170   Revelation 19:11-12 NIV
171   Revelation 19:15 NKJV
172   Joel 2:31 KJV
173   Revelation 6:16
174   2 Peter 3:13
175   Psalm 34:15
176   Deuteronomy 1:42-44
177   Deuteronomy 1:45 NKJV
178   2 Kings 19:15-16
179   2 Kings 19:35
180   Daniel 1:3-4
181   Daniel 9:18-19
182   Ezekiel 34:30
183   Nehemiah 1:6 NKJV
184   Nehemiah 5-14
185   Psalm 10:17-18
186   Psalm 31:2
187   Exodus 22:22-24
188   Proverbs 14:31
189   Numbers 12:1-15
190   1 Samuel 8:10-18
191   2 Chronicles 6:21-31
192   Isaiah 1:15 NKJV
193   John 1:1-4
194   Matthew 9:35
195   Isaiah 65:5 NKJV
196   2 Samuel 22:8-9 NIV
197   Exodus 15:8 NIV
198   Song of Solomon 5:13 NIV
199   Micah 5:1-2 NIV
200   Isaiah 50:6 NIV
201   Luke 6:29
202   Genesis 49:12 NKJV
203   1 Corinthians 2:7

204   Song of Solomon 1:2 NIV
205   Song of Solomon 5:16 NIV
206   Song of Solomon 5:13 NIV
207   Psalm 17:4 NKJV
208   Matthew 4:4 NKJV
209   Psalm119:72 NIV
210   Proverbs 2:6 NKJV
211   Revelation 1:16 NIV
212   Lamentations 3:38 NIV
213   2 Samuel 22:9 NIV
214   Isaiah 1:20 NIV
215   Isaiah 11:4 NIV
216   Revelation 2:16 NIV
217   Revelation 3:16 NKJV
218   Matthew 7:7
219   Psalm 78:2 NIV; Matthew 13:35 NIV
220   Acts 22:14 NIV
221   1Peter 2:22 NIV
222   Hebrews 13:18 NIV
223   Genesis 2:7 KJV
224   Job 33:4 NKJV
225   Job 34:14-15 NIV
226   Genesis 7:22 NKJV
227   Isaiah 11:4 NKJV
228   Job 37:10 NIV
229   Isaiah 30:33 NIV
230   Isaiah 42:5 NIV
231   Ezekiel 37:5 NIV
232   Acts 17:25 NIV
233   John 20:22 NKJV
234   Song of Solomon 5:14 NKJV
235   Exodus 33:22-23
236   Daniel 10:6 KJV
237   Genesis 18:1-10
238   Genesis 18:20-23
239   Genesis 32-24-29
240   Genesis 32:30 KJV
241   www.popularmechanics.com/science/environment/a42709141/what-the-fourth-dimension-looks-like/
242   John 8:58 KJV
243   Genesis and the Big Bang page 34
244   Matthew 26:6-12
245   Matthew 26:26 KJV

246   John 19:38-40
247   Matthew 27:60
248   John 2:19 KJV
249   1 Corinthians 11:27-28
250   1Corinthians 11:29-30
251   1 Corinthians 11:33
252   Romans 12:5 NIV
253   1 Corinthians 12:13 NIV
254   1 Corinthians 12:27
255   John 12:24
256   1 Corinthians 15:42-43 NIV
257   1 Corinthians 15:44 NIV
258   Genesis 3:19
259   1 Corinthians. 15:45-49
260   Ephesians 5:25-26
261   Ephesians 5:31-32 NIV
262   John 14:20
263   1 John 3:1
264   John 10:3, 12:32
265   John 14:15-17, 21
266   Genesis 2:21-22
267   Genesis 2:23 KJV
268   John 19:34
269   Ephesians 5:30 KJV
270   Psalms 22:14 KJV
271   John 19:36
272   Exodus 12:46
273   Luke 24:39 NIV
274   John 20:17
275   Ezekiel 37:1-2
276   Ezekiel 37:4-6
277   Ezekiel 37:10
278   Genesis 1:27
279   Genesis 3:21
280   Genesis 2:21-22 KJV
281   Strongs Exhaustive Concordance
282   Genesis 1:26 KJV
283   John 1:1-3 KJV
284   John 1:14 KJV
285   John 1:12-13 KJV
286   John 6:51 KJV
287   John 6:56 NKJV
288   John 14:13-14

289   1 Timothy 1:15
290   Matthew 1:17; John 7:42
291   Psalm 22:14-18; Acts 2:29-31
292   John 3:3-7
293   John 6:54 NKJV
294   Genesis 9:4
295   Exodus 24:5-7
296   Exodus 24:8 KJV
297   John 4:42
298   1 Corinthians 11:25 NKJV
299   Ephesians 1:7 KJV
300   Matthew 5:17
301   Hebrews 9:22
302   Leviticus 16:15-16, 22
303   Genesis 3:16
304   Genesis 3:17, 23
305   Genesis 4:8-12
306   Genesis 22:1-13
307   Genesis 21:14
308   Romans 5:12
309   Genesis 3:17, 23
310   Acts 8:32
311   Matthew 27:46 KJV
312   John 19:34
313   John 1:29 KJV
314   John 3:16 KJV
315   John 11:25 KJV
316   Matthew 16:24 KJV
317   John 14:15 NKJV
318   Genesis 3:22-23
319   Romans 6:23 KJV
320   Exodus 20:1-17
321   Hebrews 7:26-28
322   John 1:29
323   Genesis 2:17
324   Hebrews 7:24 TLB
325   Leviticus 17:11 KJV
326   Matthew 26:27-28 NKJV
327   Colossians 1:20
328   Romans 6:23 KJV
329   Luke 16:19-24
330   Luke 16:25-26 NKJV
331   1 John 4:20 NKJV

332 Hebrews 10:19-20; 2 Corinthians 6:16
333 Exodus chapters 7 to 12
334 Exodus 12:3-11
335 Exodus 12:29-30
336 Exodus 12:13 NKJV
337 1 Peter 1:18-20
338 Numbers 23:19
339 Exodus 12:1-28
340 Matthew 16:24
341 Matthew 10:38
342 Revelation 5:8
343 Revelation 5:9-10 NIV
344 Deuteronomy 6:5
345 Matthew 22:39-40 NKJV
346 1 John 3:15 NKJV
347 Matthew 6:14-15 KJV
348 Matthew 5:44 KJV
349 John 13:34, John 15:13
350 Galatians 5:22
351 Strong's Concordance
352 Exodus 6:6-7 NIV
353 Exodus 15:16 NKJV
354 Joshua 9:24
355 2 Kings 17:36 NKJV
356 Mark 12:30
357 Job 1:8-12, Job 2:3-7
358 Job 40:9 NKJV
359 Job 42:1-4, 12-16
360 Isaiah 14:12-14 MEV
361 Isaiah 14:15-19 MEV
362 Colossians 2:18
363 Proverbs 16:18 KJV
364 John 3:18
365 Revelation 20:12 KJV
366 Revelation 22:12 KJV
367 Psalm 44:3 NIV
368 Luke 23:39-43 NIV
369 John 9:3
370 Isaiah 40:10 NIV
371 Isaiah 40:11 NIV
372 Isaiah 52:10 NKJV
373 Exodus 3:20 KJV
374 Isaiah 53:1 KJV

375   Isaiah 9:6-7
376   Isaiah 59:16 KJV
377   John 1:1-3; John 1:14
378   Isaiah 62:8 NKJV
379   Isaiah 62:6-7
380   Deuteronomy 33:27 KJV
381   Matthew 19:14 NKJV
382   Matthew 5:48 NKJV
383   Exodus 3:20 KJV
384   Exodus 7:4-5 KJV
385   Exodus 4:21
386   Exodus 9:16 NKJV
387   Exodus 5:1
388   Genesis 37:28; Genesis 41:25-49
389   Exodus 14:5
390   Exodus 14:15-30
391   Deuteronomy 2:24-25
392   Exodus 15:6, 9, 12 NKJV
393   Exodus 16:3 NKJV
394   Exodus 16:13-16
395   Exodus 32:2-4
396   Genesis 12:2-3
397   Luke 11:2
398   Exodus 17:6
399   Matthew 25:1-44
400   Exodus 7:19-20
401   John 14:6, 15 NKJV
402   Deuteronomy 30:19 NKJV
403   Exodus 33:20-23 NKJV
404   Matthew 21:42
405   Deuteronomy. 3:24 NIV
406   Deuteronomy 4:34 NIV
407   Deuteronomy 5:15
408   Deuteronomy 7:19 NIV
409   Deuteronomy 32:39, 41 KJV
410   Deuteronomy 33:2 KJV
411   Deuteronomy 33:3 KJV
412   Matthew 5:48
413   Joshua 4:24 KJV
414   Galatians 3:8
415   Judges 2:12-15
416   Jeremiah 31:18; Proverbs 13:24
417   1 Samuel 4:17

418   1 Samuel 5:2-6
419   1 Samuel 5:7 NKJV
420   1 Samuel 5:9 NKJV
421   1 Samuel 5:11 NKJV
422   1 Samuel 6:5 NKJV
423   1 Samuel 6:10-12
424   1 Samuel 6:19
425   Proverbs 29:15
426   2 Samuel 24:1
427   2 Samuel 24:10-14
428   2 Samuel 24:15
429   1 Chronicles 29:12 NKJV
430   1 Chronicles 29:16 NKJV
431   1 Chronicles 28:11-19
432   1 Kings 8:43 NKJV
433   1 Kings 18:42-45
434   1 Kings 18:46 KJV
435   2 Kings 3:14-20
436   2 Chronicles 18:18 KJV
437   2 Chronicles 20:6 NIV
438   2 Chronicles 20:21-23
439   2 Chronicles 30:12 NIV
440   Ezra 7:6
441   Ezra 7:10
442   Ezra 7:11-28
443   Job 1:8
444   Job 1:11 NKJV
445   Job 1:12 NKJV
446   Job 1:13-19; Job 2:7
447   Job 2:9 NKJV
448   Job 10:7 NKJV
449   Job 12:9-10 NKJV
450   Job 13:21 NKJV
451   Job 26:13-14 NKJV
452   Job 28:9 NKJV
453   Job 38, Job 39
454   Job 42:10-15
455   Psalm 10:14 NIV
456   Psalm 16:11 NIV
457   Psalm 17:7 NIV
458   Psalm 18:35 NIV
459   Psalm 21:8 NIV
460   Psalm 31:5 NIV

461   Psalm 31:15 NIV
462   Psalm 32:4 NIV
463   Psalm 37:24 NIV
464   Psalm 38:2 NIV
465   Psalm 39:10 NIV
466   Psalm 48:10 NKJV
467   Psalm 95:4 NKJV
468   Psalm 95:7 NKJV
469   Psalm 14:28 NIV
470   Psalm 118:16 NIV
471   Psalm 119:173 NIV
472   Psalm 139:10 NIV
473   Psalm 144:7 NIV
474   Psalm 145:16 NIV
475   Proverbs 21:1 NKJV
476   Exodus 7:3
477   Ecclesiastes 2:24 NKJV
478   Song of Solomon 2:6 NKJV
479   Romans 8:38-39
480   Song of Solomon 5:4 NKJV
481   Revelations 3:20 KJV
482   Psalm 42:7-8 NIV
483   Isaiah 1:25 NKJV
484   Isaiah 5:25 NIV
485   Isaiah 9:21
486   Isaiah 9:17 KJV
487   Isaiah 10:4 KJV
488   Isaiah 11:11 KJV
489   Isaiah 14:26-27 KJV
490   Isaiah 19:16
491   Isaiah 23:11
492   Isaiah 25:5-10 MEV
493   Isaiah 40:2 NKJV
494   Isaiah 41:10 NKJV
495   Isaiah 41:18-20 KJV
496   Isaiah 42:1 NKJV
497   Isaiah 42:6 NKJV
498   Isaiah 53:10
499   Isaiah 49:22 NKJV, 59:1 KJV
500   Isaiah 62:3 KJV
501   Isaiah 62:8 NKJV
502   Isaiah 64:8 NKJV
503   Isaiah 66:2 NKJV

504   Isaiah 66:14 KJV
505   Jeremiah 1:9
506   Jeremiah 15:17
507   Jeremiah 18:6 NKJV
508   Jeremiah 23:21-22 NIV
509   Jeremiah 23:23 NIV
510   Jeremiah 31:32 NKJV
511   Jeremiah 51:7 KJV
512   Jeremiah 51:25 KJV
513   Lamentations 2:4 NKJV
514   Ezekiel 1:3, 2:9 NKJV
515   Ezekiel 3:14 KJV
516   Ezekiel 6:14 KJV
517   Ezekiel 8:1-3 NKJV
518   Ezekiel 8:6-16
519   Ezekiel 13:9
520   Ezekiel 14:13
521   Ezekiel 20:6
522   Ezekiel 20:22, 36:22
523   Ezekiel 20:28
524   Ezekiel 16:27 NKJV
525   Ezekiel 20:33 NKJV
526   Ezekiel 20:36 NIV
527   Ezekiel 20:37-38 NIV
528   Psalm 19:12
529   Jeremiah 17:9 KJV
530   Ezekiel 36:26
531   Ezekiel 37:1 NKJV
532   Ezekiel 37:19 NKJV
533   Genesis 32:28
534   Genesis 32:10
535   Genesis 48:17-19
536   Isaiah 65:9
537   Romans 11:25-26 NKJV
538   Ezekiel 37:21-22 NIV
539   Ezekiel 37:24 NIV
540   Ezekiel 37:26-28 NIV
541   Genesis 49:10 KJV
542   Ezekiel 28:25
543   Ezekiel 37:21-22
544   Ezekiel Chapters 40 to 47
545   Isaiah 65.17 KJV
546   Ezekiel 40:2-3

547 Ezekiel 40:5
548 Ezekiel 47:14 NKJV
549 Daniel 4:35 NKJV
550 Daniel 5:5, 5:25-28
551 Daniel 10:10
552 Amos 9:2 NKJV
553 Habakkuk 3:4 NKJV
554 Zechariah 13:6 KJV
555 Zechariah 13:7 NKJV
556 Zechariah 13:8-9
557 James 2:19, Revelations 20:13-14
558 Malachi 3:3
559 Malachi 3:1
560 Matthew 3:11
561 Malachi 3:2
562 Matthew 3:12 NKJV
563 Matthew 4:17 NKJV
564 Matthew 8:14-15
565 Matthew 14:31 NKJV
566 Mark 1:41 NKJV
567 Mark 7:32-34
568 Mark 8:23-25
569 Mark 9:17-29
570 Matthew 9:18
571 Matthew 9:23-25
572 John 21:25
573 Matthew 20:23
574 Matthew 22:44 NKJV
575 Matthew 25:31-33 NKJV
576 Matthew 25:34, 41 NKJV
577 Matthew 26:63-64 NKJV
578 Matthew 27:29
579 Mark 16:19
580 Ephesians 1:20
581 Acts 5:31 NKJV
582 Acts 7:56 NKJV
583 Hebrews 8:1 KJV
584 Revelation 5:9, Hebrews 10:12
585 Hebrews 12:2 KJV
586 1 Peter 3:21-22 KJV
587 Revelation 4:9-10,
588 Revelation 5:1-7
589 Revelation 20:12-15

590 Matthew 25:31-46
591 Matthew 20:25-28 NIV
592 Acts 11:21 NIV
593 Acts 13:8-10
594 Acts 13:11-12 NIV
595 John 10:28-29 KJV
596 Revelation 1:16-20 KJV
597 Exodus 33:20 NKJV
598 2 Corinthians 12:1-4
599 Revelation 4:8-11 KJV
600 Exodus 33:20, Daniel 8:27, Isaiah 6:5, Revelation 1:17, Exodus 20:18-19
601 Revelation 5:1-7 KJV
602 Revelation 14:14-15 NKJV
603 Matthew 13:42
604 Revelation 20:12-15
605 Revelations 13:16-17, 14:9-11
606 Revelation 14:12
607 Revelation 14:13 NKJV
608 Exodus 8:19
609 Exodus 31:18, Deuteronomy 9:10
610 Psalm 8:3 NKJV
611 Daniel 5:1-4
612 Daniel 5:5, 24-28 NIV
613 Daniel 5:30-31
614 Mark 7:32-35
615 Mark 8:22-25, Luke 11:20
616 John 8:2-11 KJV
617 John 8:12 KJV
618 Isaiah 9:6-7 NKJV
619 Isaiah 22:22
620 1 Timothy 3:6 NKJV
621 Luke 15:4-6
622 Ruth 2:12
623 Ruth 4:9-10, Matthew 1:1-6
624 Deuteronomy 32:9-12
625 Psalm 36:7 NKJV
626 Psalm 57:1 NKJV
627 Psalm 61:4 NKJV
628 Psalm 91:4 NKJV
629 Matthew 23:37 NKJV
630 Psalm 2:1-5
631 Malachi 4:2 KJV
632 Ezekiel 16:8 NKJV

633 Titus 1:2
634 Acts 4:31, 1 Corinthians 3:16
635 John 3:5-7
636 Psalm 27:10 NKJV
637 Matthew 6:9, Song of Solomon 4:10
638 Jude 1:7 NKJV
639 Genesis 19:24
640 Psalm 91:4 NKJV
641 Isaiah 53:5 NKJV
642 2 Corinthians 5:17
643 Philippians 4:7 KJV
644 Psalm 17:8
645 Song of Solomon 5:15 KJV
646 John 19:33, Psalm 22:14-17
647 Genesis 3:8 KJV
648 Exodus 24:10 KJV
649 Daniel 10:6 KJV
650 Revelation 1:13-15 NKJV Revelation 2.18 KJV
651 Revelation 1:17 KJV
652 2 Samuel 22:10 KJV
653 Nahum 1:3 KJV
654 Habakkuk 3:5 KJV
655 Psalm 74:3 KJV
656 Ezekiel 43:7 NKJV
657 Isaiah 60:13-14 NKJV
658 Luke 8:41
659 Mark 7:25-29
660 Luke 8:27-35
661 Luke 17:11-16
662 Matthew 15:30
663 John 11:32 MEV
664 John 11:33-44
665 Deuteronomy 33:3, Luke 10:39-42
666 Genesis 18:3-4 MEV
667 Luke 7:38
668 Luke 7:47-48 KJV
669 John 13:14 KJV
670 John 8:12
671 Psalms 22:15-17 NIV
672 Matthew 28:1-10 KJV
673 Ephesians 1:22-23 KJV, Hebrews 2:8 KJV
674 Zechariah 12:10 NKJV, 14:4 NKJV
675 Isaiah 52:7 NKJV

676   Genesis 1:1-5 KJV
677   Psalm 139:16 NKJV
678   Genesis 2:16-17 NKJV
679   Genesis 2:21-22, 3:1-6
680   Genesis 3:9 NKJV
681   Genesis 3:10 NKJV
682   Genesis 3:17, 23
683   Genesis 22:18 NKJV
684   Genesis 26:1-4
685   Genesis 28:10-15
686   Acts 7:30-32 KJV; Exodus 3:6 KJV
687   Exodus 5:1 NKJV
688   Exodus 5:2 NKJV
689   Exodus 7:15 to12:42
690   Exodus 19:16-18 NIV
691   Exodus 19:19-22 NIV
692   Exodus 15:26 NKJV
693   Exodus 31:18
694   Exodus 20:2-3 NIV
695   Exodus 20:4-6 NIV
696   Exodus 20:7 NIV
697   Exodus 20:8-11 NIV
698   Exodus 20:12 NIV
699   Exodus 20:13 NIV
700   Exodus 20:14 NIV
701   Exodus 20:15 NIV
702   Exodus 20:16 NIV
703   Exodus 20:17 NKJV
704   gospeloutreach.net/613laws.html
705   Leviticus 11:2-31
706   Exodus 15:26
707   Exodus 22:16-17
708   1 Corinthians 6:9-10
709   Proverbs 6:16-17
710   2 Corinthians 7:10
711   Genesis 4:9
712   Ezekiel 33:6 NKJV
713   Matthew 4:7 NKJV
714   Exodus 19:5 NKJV
715   Hebrews 9:4
716   Numbers 7:89 NKJV
717   Numbers 14:22-23 NIV
718   Numbers 14:24

762   Deuteronomy 28:41 NIV
763   Deuteronomy 28:42 NIV
764   Deuteronomy 28:43-44 NIV
765   Deuteronomy 28:45-46 NIV
766   Deuteronomy 28:47-48 NIV
767   Deuteronomy 28:49-50 NIV
768   Deuteronomy 28:51 NIV
769   Deuteronomy 28:52 NIV
770   Deuteronomy 28:58-59 NIV
771   Deuteronomy 28:60-61 NIV
772   Deuteronomy 28:62-63 NIV
773   Deuteronomy 28:64 NIV
774   Deuteronomy 28:65-66 NIV
775   Deuteronomy 28:67 NIV
776   Deuteronomy 28:68 NIV
777   Proverbs 1:7 KJV
778   Deuteronomy 30:1-3 NIV
779   John 1:14
780   Galatians 3:10, 13 NIV
781   Galatians 3:13-14 NIV
782   Galatians 4:4-5
783   Galatians 3:24-26 MEV
784   Romans 3:1-2 MEV
785   Leviticus 3:3, 16:27
786   Deuteronomy 23:12-14; Leviticus 15:13
787   James 2:10
788   2 Corinthians 7:10
789   John 17:12
790   Matthew 27:3-5
791   Deuteronomy 30:20 NKJV
792   John 14:15
793   1 Samuel 1:9-11
794   1 Samuel 3:10-14
795   1 Samuel 3:19-20
796   1 Samuel 15:22 NKJV
797   2 Samuel 22:14 NKJV
798   2 Samuel 22:21 NKJV
799   2 Samuel 12:10 NKJV
800   1 Kings 5:5
801   1 Kings 9:3-5 NIV
802   1 Kings 9:6-9
803   John 14:21 NKJV
804   1 Kings 11:1-8

805   1 Kings 18:19-40
806   1 Kings 19:2-3
807   1 Kings 19:11-16
808   2 Kings 18:11-12 MEV
809   2 Kings 19:22 NKJV
810   2 Kings 19:35
811   2 Kings 19:36-37
812   Job 37:2-5 MEV
813   Job 1:6 to 2:7
814   Luke 14:27 NKJV
815   Job 2:8
816   Job 40:6-13 MEV
817   Jeremiah 18:6 NKJV
818   Psalm 18:13 MEV
819   Psalm 29:3-9 MEV
820   Psalm 46:6 NKJV
821   Proverbs 1:20 NIV
822   Proverbs 8:1,3-5 NIV
823   Psalm 111:10 KJV
824   Song of Solomon 2:8 NKJV
825   Song of Solomon 2:14 NKJV
826   Song of Solomon 5:2 NKJV
827   Isaiah 6:5 NKJV
828   Isaiah 6:6-7
829   Isaiah 6:8 NKJV
830   Isaiah 6:9-13
831   Isaiah 1:15 NKJV
832   Isaiah 1:18 NKJV
833   Isaiah 28:23-29
834   Isaiah 30:30 KJV
835   Isaiah 32:9-11
836   Isaiah 32:15-20 NIV
837   Isaiah 42:3-4 KJV
838   Isaiah 66:1 NKJV
839   Isaiah 66:6-8
840   Isaiah 66:9 NKJV
841   Isaiah 66:18 NKJV
842   Isaiah 66:19-21
843   Isaiah 66:22-23 KJV
844   Jeremiah 3:25 KJV
845   Jeremiah 7:23 KJV
846   Jeremiah 10:12-13 MEV
847   Jeremiah 18:6

848 Jeremiah 18:10 NKJV
849 Jeremiah 22:21 NKJV
850 Jeremiah 25:10 NKJV
851 Jeremiah 26:13 NKJV
852 Jeremiah 30:19 NKJV
853 Genesis and the Big Bang page 80
854 Jeremiah 31:15 NKJV
855 Jeremiah 38:20 NKJV
856 Jeremiah 40:3 NKJV
857 Jeremiah 38:6 NKJV
858 Isaiah 60:1 NKJV
859 Jeremiah 31:16 NKJV
860 Jeremiah 51:16 NKJV
861 Ezekiel 1:24-25 NKJV
862 Ezekiel 1:28 NKJV
863 Ezekiel 8:18 NKJV
864 Ezekiel 8:6-17
865 Jeremiah 4:18-19 NIV
866 Jeremiah 4:20 NIV
867 Deuteronomy 30:19 NKJV
868 Ezekiel 28:2 KJV
869 Matthew 18:6 NKJV
870 Isaiah 63:3-4 NIV
871 Jeremiah 7:31 NKJV
872 Ezekiel 43:6-7
873 Ezekiel 43:1-2 KJV
874 Daniel 4:28-30
875 Daniel 4:31 KJV
876 Daniel 4:32-37
877 Daniel 8:16 KJV
878 Daniel 8
879 Daniel 9:10-11
880 Daniel 10:6 KJV; Revelation 1:15 KJV
881 Joel 2:11 KJV
882 Amos 1:2 KJV
883 Micah 6:9 NIV
884 Haggai 1:9-11 NIV
885 Haggai 1:12-14
886 Zechariah 6:15 NIV
887 Isaiah 42:1-4 NIV
888 Matthew 12:18-20
889 John 1:14
890 Mark 1:10-11 NKJV

891   Deuteronomy 34:5-6; 2 Kings 2:15-17
892   Matthew 17:5 NKJV
893   2 Peter 1:17-18
894   2 Peter 1:19 NKJV
895   John 3:29 NIV
896   John 5:25 KJV
897   John 5:28 KJV
898   John 14:11 KJV
899   John 10:11 KJV
900   John 10:3-5 NKJV
901   John 10:16 KJV
902   John 10:27-28 KJV
903   John 10:12-13
904   John 11:41-42 NKJV
905   John 11:43 KJV
906   John 11:44
907   John 12:28 KJV
908   John 12:29-30
909   Matthew 26:53
910   Exodus 12:13
911   John 18:37 NKJV
912   Matthew 27:46 NKJV
913   Luke 23:46 NKJV
914   Numbers 21:4-9
915   Genesis 3:14
916   John 12:32 KJV
917   John 1:29
918   Acts 9:4-5 NKJV
919   Acts 9:7
920   Acts 10:9-12
921   Acts 10:13-15 KJV
922   Acts 10:19-23
923   Acts 10:28
924   Acts 10:34-43
925   Acts 10:44-46 NKJV
926   Leviticus 11:1-20
927   Acts 15:6-8
928   Acts 15:9
929   Acts 15:21 NKJV
930   Deuteronomy 9:10
931   Hebrews 5:13
932   Hebrews 3:7-8
933   Hebrews 4:1-3

934 Acts 9:31
935 Hebrews 12:18-21 KJV
936 Hebrews 12:22-24 NIV
937 Hebrews 12:25 NIV
938 1 Peter 2:11 KJV
939 Romans 8:38-39
940 2 Peter 2:22
941 Hebrews 12:28-29 KJV
942 Revelation 5:13 KJV
943 Revelation 1:11, 13-15 MEV
944 Revelation 3:20 KJV
945 Genesis 9:11
946 Revelation 10:1-3 KJV
947 Revelation 11:15 KJV
948 Revelation 12:7-9
949 Revelation 12:10-11 NKJV
950 Revelation 18:4 NKJV
951 Revelation 19:11-14 KJV
952 Revelation 19:15-16 NKJV
953 Revelation 21:3 KJV
954 Ephesians 6:12 KJV
955 Revelation 3:15-16 NKJV
956 Revelation 20:15
957 Genesis 6:5-6 Tree of Life Version
958 Genesis 7:1-3
959 Genesis 8:14-19
960 Genesis 1:28 KJV
961 Genesis 2:16-17
962 Genesis 3:6
963 Genesis 3:4-6 KJV
964 Genesis 24:51-53; 34:11-12; Exodus 22:16-17
965 Genesis 3:12
966 Genesis 3:16
967 Revelation 19:19
968 Genesis 3:15 KJV
969 Psalm 127:3 KJV
970 James 1:27 KJV
971 Genesis 7:1-3 NKJV
972 Genesis 7:13
973 Genesis 8:16 NKJV
974 Genesis 8:18 NKJV
975 Mark 10:8
976 Genesis 1:28

[977] Genesis 1:29
[978] Genesis 9:1-3 NKJV
[979] Genesis 49.28
[980] Genesis 8:20-21
[981] Genesis 9:11-13
[982] Genesis 9:15-16 NKJV
[983] Genesis 9:1, 8
[984] Leviticus 20:13; Romans 1:27
[985] Genesis 3:17-19
[986] Malachi 2:16
[987] Job 9:4 KJV
[988] Job 34:14-15 KJV
[989] Acts 13:22 KJV
[990] Isaiah 9:7; Matthew 1:1-6
[991] Song of Songs 3:11 NIV
[992] Song of Solomon 4:9 NKJV
[993] Jeremiah 3:14-15 NKJV
[994] 1Kings 9:3 NIV
[995] 1 Corinthians 3:16   -
[996] 1 Kings 11:2
[997] 1 Kings 11:3-5
[998] 1 Kings 11:7-8
[999] Leviticus 20:1-3, Ezekiel 16:20-21
[1000] Matthew 21:43; Jeremiah 48:7
[1001] Ezekiel 5:6-8
[1002] Proverbs 6:12-19
[1003] Esther 1:10-22
[1004] Matthew 19:3-9 NKJV; Mark 10:6-12 NKJV
[1005] Ephesians 5:25, 33
[1006] 1 Peter 3:7 NKJV
[1007] Matthew 22:30 KJV
[1008] Luke 11:2, Matthew 10:7
[1009] John 4:7-42
[1010] Isaiah 11:6 NKJV
[1011] Psalm 27:10 KJV
[1012] Proverbs 1:8 KJV
[1013] Galatians 3:28 KJV
[1014] Ephesians 5:23
[1015] Joel 2:28 KJV; Acts 2:17
[1016] Deuteronomy 4:9-10 NKJV
[1017] Revelation 5:9
[1018] Matthew 9:37-38 KJV
[1019] 2 Corinthians 10.4

1020 Genesis 22:2
1021 Malachi 2:15
1022 Malachi 4:6 KJV
1023 Joel 2:11; Luke 1:13-17
1024 John 14:9 KJV
1025 Jeremiah 32:38-39 KJV
1026 Jeremiah 32:41 KJV
1027 Numbers 23:19
1028 James 1:17
1029 Acts 2:36-41; Acts 4:32
1030 John 13:35
1031 Matthew 11:28-29 KJV
1032 Ephesians 6:4
1033 Joel 2:28 KJV
1034 Leviticus 24:11-14
1035 Romans 6:23 NKJV
1036 1 Samuel 2:29
1037 1Samuel 2:22
1038 1 Samuel 2:35 KJV
1039 1 Samuel 1:26-28, 3:19-20
1040 Psalm 8:4 NKJV
1041 Psalm 111:5 NKJV Psalm 115:12 KJV
1042 Jeremiah 15:1 KJV
1043 Jeremiah 32:35 NKJV
1044 Jeremiah 44:21 KJV
1045 Daniel 9:14 NKJV
1046 Romans 8:27 NKJV
1047 Romans 11:33-34 KJV
1048 Philippians 2:5 KJV
1049 2 Timothy 1:7 KJV
1050 Romans 8:11
1051 Hebrews 10:16 KJV
1052 Acts 1:5
1053 2 Peter 3:2 KJV
1054 Matthew 3:2, 6:15
1055 Romans 6.23
1056 James 1:14-17 NKJV
1057 Luke 16:19-23
1058 Revelation 3:17-19 NKJV
1059 Hebrews 13:2 NKJV
1060 James 5:20
1061 Ezekiel 33:1-6
1062 Proverbs 22:6

[1063] Psalm 23:1-3 KJV
[1064] Proverbs 11:30 KJV
[1065] Genesis 2.7 KJV
[1066] Exodus 1:5 KJV
[1067] Leviticus 26:9-12 KJV
[1068] Leviticus 26:30 KJV
[1069] Psalm 11:5 NKJV
[1070] Isaiah 1:14 NKJV
[1071] Jeremiah 6:8 NKJV
[1072] Jeremiah 12:7 KJV
[1073] Jeremiah 13:17 KJV
[1074] Jeremiah 14:11-14
[1075] Jeremiah 32:41 KJV
[1076] Deuteronomy 6:5 NKJV
[1077] Judges 10:16 NKJV
[1078] Psalm 139:14 NKJV; Psalm 146:1 KJV
[1079] Isaiah 42:1 KJV
[1080] Isaiah 53:10 KJV
[1081] Isaiah 53:12 NKJV
[1082] John 12:27 KJV
[1083] Matthew 26:38 NKJV
[1084] Acts 2:31 KJV
[1085] Acts 2:41 KJV
[1086] Mark 8:36-37 KJV
[1087] 2 Corinthians 12:15 NKJV
[1088] 1 Thessalonians 5:23 KJV
[1089] Hebrews 4:12 KJV; 10:38 KJV
[1090] James 5:20 NKJV
[1091] 1 Peter 1:22 NKJV
[1092] 1 Peter 2:11, 25 KJV
[1093] Mark 1:7-8 NKJV
[1094] Mark 1:10 NKJV
[1095] John 3:3-4
[1096] John 3:5-7, 1 Corinthians 6:19
[1097] Acts 19:2-6 NIV
[1098] Acts 19:11-12 NIV
[1099] Revelation 12:3-4
[1100] Exodus 20:4-5, Leviticus 20:6
[1101] Exodus 20:3
[1102] 1 Corinthians 6:18
[1103] Romans 6:23 NKJV
[1104] Exodus 34:7
[1105] Revelation 20:12-15

1106 Deuteronomy 30:19
1107 Revelation 20:15
1108 Luke 12:10
1109 Acts 12:22-23 NKJV
1110 2 Corinthians 6:16 NKJV
1111 John 14:15 NKJV
1112 2 Corinthians 7:10
1113 Psalm 139:13, 16 NKJV
1114 Funk & Wagnall, New Comprehensive International Dictionary 1980
1115 Genesis 21:32-33
1116 Genesis 22:2
1117 Genesis 21:9-10, 14
1118 Genesis 22:9-13
1119 1 John 1:7
1120 Genesis 17;4-6
1121 Luke 14:27
1122 Genesis 24:67
1123 Genesis 25:28
1124 Genesis 25:29-34
1125 Genesis 27:1-29
1126 Malachi 1:2-3 KJV
1127 Malachi 1:6-8
1128 Genesis 29:30
1129 Genesis 37:3
1130 Exodus 20:6, John 14:21
1131 Deuteronomy 6:5 NIV
1132 Leviticus 19:18,34 NIV
1133 Deuteronomy 4:37
1134 Deuteronomy 7:6-9
1135 Exodus 3:15, Matthew 1:1-17
1136 Deuteronomy 7:13 NKJV
1137 Proverbs 8:21 NKJV
1138 Deuteronomy 10:12-13 NKJV
1139 Deuteronomy 10:18-19 NIV
1140 2 Samuel 12:24; 2 Kings 23:13
1141 Exodus 20:1-17
1142 Romans 6:23
1143 Hebrews 10:31 KJV
1144 Psalm 11:7 NIV
1145 Psalm 33:5 NKJV
1146 Psalm 37:28 NKJV
1147 Psalm 78:68 KJV
1148 Psalm 87:2 KJV

1149 Psalm 91:14 KJV
1150 Proverbs 8:17 KJV
1151 Song of Solomon 1:2 KJV
1152 Song of Solomon 1:7 NIV
1153 Song of Solomon 1:9 KJV
1154 Song of Solomon 2:4 KJV
1155 Song of Solomon 2:5 NKJV
1156 Psalm 63:1 NKJV
1157 Song of Solomon 2:10 KJV
1158 Psalm 42:7
1159 Psalm 42:7 delete; Song of Solomon 2:11-13
1160 Matthew 28:19 NKJV
1161 Song of Solomon 3:2 NKJV
1162 Song of Solomon 3:4
1163 Song of Solomon 4:9 NKJV
1164 Song of Solomon 8:6-7 NKJV
1165 Isaiah 43:7
1166 Isaiah 43:3-4 NKJV
1167 Isaiah 57:3-18
1168 Jeremiah 2:2 NKJV
1169 Jeremiah 3:1 NKJV
1170 Jeremiah 5:31
1171 Jeremiah 6:2
1172 Jeremiah 30:14
1173 Ezekiel 16:35-37 NIV
1174 Ezekiel 16:38-40 NIV
1175 Lamentations 1:19-20
1176 Psalm 127:3
1177 Joel 2:11
1178 Jeremiah 31:2
1179 Ezekiel 16:62-63 NIV
1180 John 3:16 NKJV
1181 Ezekiel 16:8 NKJV
1182 Ezekiel 16:31-34
1183 James 1:15 NKJV
1184 Hosea 14:4 NKJV
1185 Zephaniah 3:17 NKJV
1186 1 John 4:14
1187 John 1:1 KJV
1188 Matthew 22:37-40, Exodus 20:1-17
1189 Matthew 5:43-44 KJV
1190 Matthew 16:24
1191 Mark 10:17-22

1192   Luke 7:37-38
1193   Luke 7:47-48 NKJV
1194   Luke 23:34 KJV
1195   Mark 11:25
1196   John 5:20 NKJV
1197   John 10:17 NKJV
1198   John 3:16 NKJV
1199   John 13:34 KJV
1200   John 13:35
1201   John 14:23 NKJV
1202   John 3:3
1203   John 15:13 KJV
1204   Romans 3:23 KJV
1205   Matthew 7:15-16
1206   John 21:15-17 NKJV
1207   Romans 8:31 MEV
1208   Romans 8:35 MEV
1209   Romans 8:37 MEV
1210   Romans 8:38-39 MEV
1211   1 Corinthians 2:9 MEV
1212   1 Corinthians 13:13 MEV
1213   2 Corinthians 13:14 MEV
1214   Galatians 5:22-23 MEV
1215   Ephesians 3:19 MEV
1216   Ephesians 5:1-2 MEV
1217   Philippians 1:9 MEV
1218   Colossians 2:2 MEV
1219   Colossians 3:14 MEV
1220   1 Thessalonians 1:3 MEV
1221   1 Thessalonians 3:12 MEV
1222   1 Thessalonians 5:8 MEV
1223   1 Timothy 1:5 MEV
1224   1 Timothy 1:14 MEV
1225   1 Timothy 6:11 MEV
1226   2 Timothy 1:7 MEV
1227   2 Timothy 1:13 MEV
1228   2 Timothy 2:22 MEV
1229   2 Timothy 4:8 MEV
1230   Titus 1:8 MEV
1231   Titus 2:2-4 MEV
1232   Hebrews 6:10 MEV
1233   Hebrews 10:24 MEV
1234   Hebrews 12:6 MEV

1235 Hebrews 13:1 MEV
1236 James 1:12 MEV
1237 James 2:5 MEV
1238 1 Peter 1:8 MEV
1239 1 Peter 4:8 MEV
1240 1 John 2:5 MEV
1241 1 John 3:17 MEV
1242 1 John 3:18 MEV
1243 1 John 4:8 MEV
1244 1 John 4:12 MEV
1245 1 John 4:16 MEV
1246 1 John 4:18 MEV
1247 1 John 4:19 MEV
1248 1 John 4:20 MEV
1249 1 John 5:1 MEV
1250 2 John 1:3 MEV
1251 Jude 1:2 MEV
1252 Revelation 1:5 MEV
1253 Revelation 3:19 MEV
1254 Revelation 12:11 KJV
1255 Genesis 2:17, 3:4-7
1256 Genesis 4:1-8
1257 Genesis 27:41 KJV
1258 Genesis 37:4 KJV
1259 Genesis 1:27
1260 Exodus 20:3-5 NKJV
1261 Deuteronomy 12:31
1262 Deuteronomy 16:22 NKJV
1263 Jeremiah 44:4 KJV
1264 Proverbs 6:16-19 NKJV
1265 Matthew 22:37-40 MEV
1266 Isaiah 61:8 NIV
1267 Zechariah 8:17 KJV
1268 John 3:18 KJV
1269 Matthew 25:10-12 KJV
1270 Hosea 9:15 NKJV
1271 Amos 5:21
1272 Amos 5:15 KJV
1273 Malachi 1:2-3 KJV, Romans 9:13 KJV
1274 Malachi 2:16 NKJV
1275 Deuteronomy 21:17
1276 Genesis 25:29-34
1277 Malachi 2:10

1278 Matthew 6:24 NKJV
1279 Ephesians 5:28-33 NIV
1280 Romans 8:38-39 NKJV
1281 Exodus 20:5 KJV
1282 FreeDictionary.com
1283 Deuteronomy 4:24 NKJV
1284 Numbers 5:11-31
1285 1 Kings 11:3
1286 Proverbs 7:6-23
1287 Proverbs 6:27-33
1288 Leviticus 20:13
1289 1 Corinthians 6:18 NKJV
1290 Ezekiel 16:38 NKJV
1291 Romans 6:23 NKJV
1292 Exodus 34:6-7
1293 2 Samuel 12:15-18
1294 2 Samuel 11:2-24
1295 2 Samuel 12:1-10
1296 1 Kings 14:22 KJV
1297 Proverbs 6.34 KJV, 27:4 NKJV
1298 Song of Solomon 8:6 KJV
1299 Exodus 34:6 KJV
1300 Ezekiel 16:42 KJV
1301 Ezekiel 39:25 NKJV
1302 Zephaniah 3:8-9 NKJV
1303 James 4:4-5 NKJV
1304 James 4:8 KJV
1305 2 Corinthians 11:2 KJV
1306 Jeremiah 31:3 NKJV
1307 Exodus 3:1-10
1308 Exodus 4:10-13
1309 Exodus 4:14-16
1310 Numbers 11:1-10
1311 Numbers 12:1-15
1312 Numbers 25:1-9
1313 Romans 6:23 KJV
1314 Numbers 32:9-13
1315 Deuteronomy 9:4-5
1316 Deuteronomy 4:25-26
1317 Deuteronomy 9:18-19
1318 Deuteronomy 6:4-5 NKJV
1319 Deuteronomy 11:13-17
1320 Ezekiel 33:11 KJV

1321   Deuteronomy 31:17-18 KJV
1322   Judges 2:14 KJV
1323   2 Samuel 6:6-7
1324   Proverbs 1:7
1325   2 Samuel 6:9-11
1326   2 Samuel 6:12-15
1327   2 Samuel 6:20-23
1328   Isaiah 64:1 KJV
1329   Isaiah 6:5-7 NKJV
1330   2 Samuel 24:1-16
1331   Daniel 9:21-22, Luke 2:4-14,
1332   Genesis 19:15-25
1333   1 Kings 14:15 NKJV
1334   1 Kings 15:30, 16:2, 13, 26, 33, 1 Kings 21:22, 1 Kings 22:53
1335   Ephesians 6:12 NKJV
1336   Revelation 1:5-7
1337   Exodus 32:2-4
1338   Genesis 2:7 NKJV
1339   Numbers 35:33 NKJV
1340   2 Chronicles 25:4 KJV
1341   Psalm 127:3 KJV
1342   Jeremiah 7:18 KJV
1343   Ezekiel 16:20-21 NKJV
1344   2 Kings 17:16-17 NKJV
1345   1 Corinthians 15:42, 1 Peter 3:21
1346   Nehemiah 8:1-6
1347   Nehemiah 9:17 NKJV
1348   Nehemiah 9:36-38
1349   Psalm 21:8-9 NKJV
1350   Acts 13:22 NKJV
1351   Psalm 27:9 KJV
1352   Psalm 30:5 KJV
1353   Mark 3:5 NKJV
1354   Luke 14.16-23
1355   Matthew 11:20
1356   Matthew 11:21 KJV
1357   Matthew 18:7 KJV
1358   Matthew 23:13 KJV
1359   Matthew 23:14 KJV
1360   Matthew 23:15 NKJV
1361   Mathew 23:16 KJV
1362   Matthew 23:23-24 NKJV
1363   Matthew 23:25 KJV

1364 Matthew 23:27-28 NKJV
1365 Matthew 23:29-30 NIV
1366 Matthew 23:31-33 NIV
1367 Matthew 23:34-36 NIV
1368 John 2:13-15
1369 John 2:16 NKJV
1370 Genesis 3:16
1371 Genesis 6:5
1372 Genesis 6:6 NKJV
1373 Genesis 6:7
1374 Genesis 42:38
1375 Exodus 3:7
1376 Nehemiah 1:3-4
1377 Nehemiah 2:2-8
1378 1 Samuel 13:14, Acts 13:22
1379 Psalm 13:2 KJV
1380 Psalm 16:4 KJV 32:10 KJV
1381 Proverbs 10:22 KJV
1382 Proverbs 22:8 NKJV
1383 Ecclesiastes 11:10 KJV
1384 Isaiah 14:3 KJV
1385 Isaiah 35:10 KJV
1386 Isaiah 53:3-5 NKJV
1387 Revelation 1:18; Genesis 3:22-23
1388 Revelation 5:9-10
1389 Daniel 10:16 KJV
1390 Jeremiah 4:19 NKJV
1391 Jeremiah 20:18 KJV
1392 Jeremiah 30:15 NKJV
1393 Jeremiah 31:12-13 KJV
1394 Jeremiah 31:25 KJV
1395 John 1:1, 14 KJV
1396 John 11:32-36
1397 Luke 19:41-44 NKJV
1398 Matthew 23:37-39 NKJV
1399 Matthew 26:36-37
1400 Matthew 26:38 NKJV
1401 Matthew 17:22-23
1402 John 16:22 KJV
1403 Luke 23:26-27
1404 Luke 23:28 KJV
1405 2 Corinthians 7:9-10 NIV
1406 Revelation 21:4 KJV

1407   Exodus 33:19 NKJV

1408   Exodus 34:5-7 NKJV

1409   Deuteronomy 30:3 KJV

1410   Deuteronomy 32:36 KJV

1411   Luke 23:34 KJV

1412   2 Kings 13:23 KJV

1413   2 Chronicles 30:9 KJV

1414   2 Chronicles 36:15

1415   2 Chronicles 36:17

1416   Psalms 78:38 KJV

1417   Psalms 86:15 KJV

1418   Psalms 111:4 KJV

1419   Psalms 112.4; 145:8 KJV

1420   Isaiah 49:15 NKJV

1421   Jeremiah 12:15 KJV

1422   Lamentations 3:22,32 KJV

1423   Micah 7:19 NKJV

1424   Psalms 103:12 NKJV

1425   Zechariah 7:9 NKJV

1426   Matthew 1:23

1427   Luke 1:33-35

1428   John 1:1-3 NKJV

1429   John 1:10 NKJV

1430   John 1:14 NKJV

1431   Exodus Chapters 20-23

1432   Proverbs 6:23 KJV

1433   John 14:15, 21 NKJV

1434   Romans 3:23

1435   Matthew 16:24

1436   Luke 23:40-43

1437   Psalm 127:3

1438   Psalm 127:4-5

1439   Genesis 1.28

1440   Genesis 3:20

1441   Luke 10:27

1442   Deuteronomy 10:12

1443   Matthew 9:35-36 NKJV

1444   Mark 6:34 NKJV

1445   Matthew 15:32 NKJV

1446   Matthew 15:33-38

1447   Matthew 18:23-32

1448   Matthew 18:33-34 NKJV

1449   Mark 11:25-26

1450   Matthew 20:29-34
1451   Mark 1:41 NKJV
1452   Mark 9:20-27
1453   Luke 10:18, Revelation 12:4
1454   Luke 7:12-16
1455   Luke 10:30-37
1456   James 2:20 KJV
1457   Luke 15:20 NKJV
1458   Romans 9:15 NKJV
1459   1 Peter 3:8 NKJV
1460   Jude 1:20-23 MEV
1461   James 1:14-15
1462   John 8:42-44 MEV
1463   John 2:14-16
1464   John 21:25 MEV
1465   Psalm 2:1-2, 4-5 MEV
1466   Psalm 37:13-14 MEV
1467   Psalm 59:7-9 NKJV
1468   Proverbs 1:25-27 NKJV
1469   Ecclesiastes 7:3 KJV
1470   Luke 6:21 MEV
1471   1 Kings 1:40 NKJV
1472   Isaiah 55:12; Luke 19:40 KJV
1473   1 Chronicles 15:16
1474   1 Chronicles 15:28 NKJV
1475   1 Chronicles 15:29
1476   1 Chronicles 29:17 MEV
1477   2 Chronicles 7:10
1478   2 Chronicles 20:27
1479   2 Chronicles 30:26
1480   2 Chronicles 30:27 MEV
1481   Esther 8:16-17
1482   Ezra 3:12-13
1483   Ezra 6:19-22
1484   Nehemiah 8:9-10 NKJV
1485   Nehemiah 12:43 MEV
1486   Job 38, Job 39
1487   Revelation 1:5
1488   Job 38:7 MEV
1489   Psalm 5:11MEV
1490   Psalm 16:11 MEV
1491   Psalm 30:5 MEV
1492   Psalm 35:9 MEV

1493 Psalm 43:4 MEV
1494 Psalm 48:2 MEV
1495 Psalm 65:13 MEV
1496 Psalm 66:1 MEV
1497 Psalm 96:12 MEV
1498 Psalm 98:8-9 MEV
1499 Psalm 67:4 MEV
1500 1 Peter 3:7; Psalm 89:15 MEV
1501 Psalm 95:1 MEV
1502 Psalm 126:5 MEV
1503 Psalm 149:2 MEV
1504 Proverbs 12:20 NKJV
1505 Proverbs 21:15 NKJV
1506 Ecclesiastes 2:26 NKJV
1507 Isaiah 9:17 KJV
1508 Isaiah 16:10 KJV
1509 Isaiah 22:13 KJV
1510 Isaiah 24:8-11
1511 Isaiah 29:19 NKJV
1512 Isaiah 32:13-14 NKJV
1513 Isaiah 35:2 KJV
1514 Isaiah 35:10 MEV
1515 Isaiah 49:13 MEV
1516 Isaiah 51:3 MEV
1517 Isaiah 56:7 MEV
1518 Isaiah 60:5 MEV
1519 Isaiah 61:3 MEV
1520 Isaiah 65:18 MEV
1521 Genesis 22:18
1522 Luke 1:5-13
1523 Luke 1:14-16 KJV
1524 Luke 1:26-34
1525 Luke 1:34-35 MEV
1526 Luke 1:43-44 MEV
1527 Luke 2:10-11 MEV
1528 Luke 2:13-14
1529 Matthew 2:10-11 NKJV
1530 Matthew 4:17 KJV
1531 Matthew 13:44 NKJV
1532 Matthew 25:21 NKJV
1533 Luke 6:22-23
1534 Luke 10:17 NKJV
1535 Luke 15:7 NKJV

1536   John 15:11 KJV
1537   John 16:21 NKJV
1538   Mathew 28:7 KJV
1539   Matthew 28:8
1540   Acts 1:9
1541   Acts 8:5-8
1542   Acts 13:52 NKJV
1543   Romans 14:17 NKJV
1544   Galatians 5:22-23 NKJV
1545   John 3:17-18
1546   John 14:6 NKJV
1547   John 14:15-18
1548   John 3:3 KJV
1549   1 Corinthians 6:19 NKJV
1550   2 Timothy 1:7 KJV
1551   Jude 1:24 KJV
1552   Revelation 1:8 NIV
1553   John 4:42 KJV
1554   Genesis 6:5
1555   Genesis 9:11
1556   Mark 14:65, Psalm 22:16
1557   Psalm 19:12-13
1558   Luke 6:43
1559   1 Corinthians 13:12 KJV
1560   Exodus 3:14 KJV
1561   James 4:8
1562   Galatians 4:7
1563   Isaiah 1:18, Zechariah 3:3-4, Isaiah 61:10, Romans 8:17
1564   Genesis 3:4-5
1565   Genesis 3:17
1566   Revelation 5:10
1567   Matthew 25:14-15 NKJV
1568   Matthew 25:16-18
1569   Matthew 25:19-22
1570   Matthew 25:23 NKJV
1571   Matthew 25:26-28 NKJV
1572   Matthew 25:29-30 NKJV
1573   Matthew 25:31-33 NKJV
1574   Matthew 25:34-36 NKJV
1575   Matthew 25:37-40 NKJV
1576   Matthew 25:41-43 NKJV
1577   Matthew 25:44-46 NKJV
1578   Revelation 22:7 KJV

[1579] Romans 8:22

[1580] 1 Thessalonians 5:2

[1581] Revelation 22:11-13 KJV

[1582] Revelation 22:14-16 KJV

[1583] Revelation 22:17 KJV

[1584] Revelation 22:20 NKJV

[1585] Matthew 25:1-10

[1586] Matthew 25:11-13 KJV

[1587] Matthew 7:19-21 NKJV

[1588] Matthew 3:11

[1589] Mark 11:25-26

ABOUT THE AUTHOR

In 1995, Olga Hermann learned about the love of Jesus Christ. In that all her sins against God could be completely erased through repentance and accepting Jesus already paid with His own life. Since then, she has served our Lord in leadership roles in her church, and in prayer and healing ministries as well as Christian media sharing the love and compassion of God. Olga is an ordained minister with The Missionary Church International and holds a bachelor's degree in Messianic Bible studies giving her a deeper understanding of the Hebrew roots of the Bible. Her goal is to share who God is and His amazing love, especially to the broken hearted and the vulnerable. Jesus came to set the captives free, and the love of God is the only answer. He wants that none of us should perish and we each fulfill our destiny's here on earth.

Printed in the United States
by Baker & Taylor Publisher Services